To Jim
Enjoy.

W9-CVO-130

Bill Berdine
November 3, 1995

The Berdine

Un-Theory of Evolution

And Other Scientific Studies

Including

Hunting, Fishing, and Sex

By William C. Berdine

1992

International Standard Book Number 0-9631802-0-7
Library of Congress Catalog Card Number 91-90760
Printed in the United States of America
Copyright © 1992 by William C. Berdine
Princeton, West Virginia 24740

Cover design by Elizabeth A. Lancaster
and R. Marlayne Nestor

Typesetting by Kristi L. Pennington

This book is dedicated to all those friends who are mentioned in the text, either by name or by inference;
And, to all those friends I was kind enough not to mention;
And, to my old and dear friend, Jim Comstock, of Richwood, West Virginia, the finest hillbilly of us all. It was his firm but gentle nudges that jiggled me a little off center.

Contents

Foreword

The foreword or introduction is usually written by someone who is a friend or an acquaintance of the author and who wants to get his (or her, as the case may be) name on a work of some importance without doing any real work to get it there. I found it necessary to write this foreword myself because I could not find a man (or woman, as the case may be) of letters such as PhD, DDS, BPOE, LOOM, WPA, NRA, or POD who was willing to affix his name to such a comprehensive and in-depth study of plant and animal behavioral patterns and how they relate to the evolutionary process. No one wanted to be connected in any way with the astonishing facts which I have uncovered nor in the way in which I have presented them.

It was the almost accidental discovery of these facts(?) after years of research, and the necessity for making them generally known which prompted me to write this book. I am surprised that such a study has not been done and the results published. Maybe no one else has seen these facts in the same light that I have.

As for all my former friends, not one of them would touch it with a ten-foot pole.

As far as I can determine, the facts presented in this book have never been made public in any form whatsoever, not even in some of those scandal sheets which have become so popular in recent years and which will print just about anything they know how to spell.

The scientific community has apparently chosen to keep ordinary people in the dark about such things as are revealed in this book. They may have been just too scared to tell. It has largely ignored the obvious conclusion that evolution is an everyday process which anyone can observe, and not something which can only be measured in millennia or eons.

Evolution is not necessarily a long, drawn-out process, but is going on under our very noses, so to speak.

All of the evidence(?) contained in this book which pertains to the evolutionary process is from my own long-time observation of the subject plants and animals in their wild and natural states. This includes humans. I didn't visit even one zoo to make these observations. Well, okay, maybe one—if you don't count the whole city of Chicago, all the states east of the Mississippi, three or four west of it (I can't seem to remember which) and half of Canada.

I hope that this book will ultimately be used as an authoritative text in our elementary and high schools as well as in our colleges, universities, barbershops, barrooms, bathrooms, honky-tonks and other places of higher learning. Someone may even one day attempt to translate it into English. If so, I feel sorry for the poor guy who has to do the rewrite.

I start a lot of my sentences with a preposition or a conjunction, split my infinitives, dangle my participles and sin in my syntax. Once in a while I even commit the cardinal sin and put "e" before "i" except after "c." There are two good reasons why I do all that. One, I don't know any better, and two, that's the way I talk.

I also like to use bowlegs "( )" now and then. There's a good reason for that, too. When you write your rough draft in wobbly longhand, they relieve writer's cramp. I like to use a lot of commas, colons, semicolons and all those other squiggly little symbols. The reason? I have only two fingers that have ever come in contact with a typewriter keyboard. One is on my right hand, the other on my left. I like to push down on one of those big keys with my left finger, and at the same time push down on one of those funny looking keys with no letter on it with the right. Whatever pops up on the paper I don't have the heart to kill. Try it sometime. It's more fun than sticking your finger into an empty light socket.

I might have a good chance of having it accepted anyway, in spite of all the errors. After all, when Darwin first came up with his theory, everybody laughed. Well, almost everybody. Some of them cried.

Now look what has happened. Almost everybody who is anybody (and even a few who aren't) is talking about it. This includes atheists, clergymen, clergywomen and clergypersons, scientists, nonscientists, film and television personalities (and would-be personalities), congressmen, and, once in a while, writers. Some of these have been even more than one of the above. I would have used the feminine gender in those places where it was omitted, but I didn't know what it was. No one else can tell the difference, anyway.

All are experts, which just goes to prove that evolution does happen. It is here to stay, even though it may have a hard time overcoming some of the obstacles. God loves them all.

Everyone has his own pet theory of evolution and goes around trying to convince himself and everyone else that his is the only one that is correct. My untheory doesn't exactly blow all those others sky-high, but it doesn't do a whole awful lot to support them either.

I have attempted to save the best until the last chapter, so don't look for a lot of sex in this book until then, unless you want to count moose and bees and people like that. I will discuss everything I know about sex in that final chapter and might throw in a little conjecture about its future. But don't peek. And if you just can't help yourself and have to peek, don't be a blabbermouth and spoil it for those with willpower.

You will notice that the subjects are in no particular order. I just wrote about something or other until I ran out of pencil and then resumed as soon as I could remember where I left my pencil sharpener. I usually could not locate my train of thought simultaneously. If you would like to arrange them alphabetically or chronologically or some other sort of order, go right ahead. But don't change the text. Nor the spelling.

I don't expect anyone to come knocking on my door to try to buy television or movie rights. There aren't enough passages that would rate a "bleep-bleep" on television. Most of this stuff would be impossible to picture, anyway, except in your mind's eye.

If you want to read a lot of four-letter expletives and vulgarities, stop right now and run out and buy another book—or a newspaper. You won't find many in here. I'm old-fashioned, and I use words like "dad-blamed," "confounded," and "thunderation." They make more sense and aren't nearly as hard on the ears. Or the face.

I used to say, "Where in Flinderation?" but I found that there is a small village by that name in West Virginia, and I had to stop. You've got to be careful these days about hurting someone's feelings.

If you want to read a dirty book, go borrow one from a friend who carried his copy in his hip pocket underground in a coal mine or in a steel mill or someplace with a similar environment. But that makes it hard to read.

Another thing you should know before you go any further: It's okay to laugh once in awhile—if you see anything funny. If God hadn't wanted us to laugh now and then, He wouldn't have given us all those little muscles that make the corners of our mouths turn up at the ends.

Any reference to a person or persons by their correct name is fully intentional. Any reference to anyone else, don't fret. I didn't mean you.

WILLIAM C. BERDINE
THE AUTHOR

Backword

The backword was written by the author and for the same reasons stated in the foreword.

A foreword is an introduction to a book that usually lets you know what to expect or not to expect to find after the first page. Sometimes they are a little vague. Maybe the author didn't want to tip his hand.

If a foreword is supposed to be an introduction, then I figured that a backword should be an extroduction. (Don't run for the dictionary. I tried to look it up already and they don't know what it means, either.) I also figured that a book like this needed one—in the worst sort of way.

You probably guessed from reading the foreword that this book was just a little bit different. It is. For one thing, it is the first book that I have ever seen that had a real honest-to-goodness backword or extroduction—at least one that was this close to the front.

Some people like to stick in a little something extra at the end of the book to let you know what you missed when you read it the first time. If you miss anything in this book on the first trip, there is no need to go back and do it over—it won't make much more sense the second time around, and even less on subsequent readings.

People who put this part at the last sometimes call it an "epilogue." I didn't want to call mine an epilogue because that sounds sort of snobbish, and I felt badly about sticking it all the way back there by itself.

Sometimes an epilogue tries to hint at something that the author thinks is going to happen in the future, usually at some unspecified date. I wanted to be more specific. I haven't the foggiest notion of what is going to happen—not even tomorrow. Your guess is as good as mine, maybe better.

xi

I had another good reason for putting it up here in front where you could get at it, the readers. I wanted to give them one more chance to back out before they got in over their heads.

You noticed that I mentioned a few of my Canadian friends —somewhere around six or eight, more or less. Writing a book makes you reminisce. That is a fancy word that means something like "look back." I'm glad writing does that. I didn't realize I had that many.

You noticed, too, that I mentioned here and there a few American friends—around six or eight, more or less. Boy! I must be better off than I thought. A man just can't have too many friends. Especially if they are self-supporting.

Some of these friends have been particularly close, and their drifting away or their passing on as a part of the continuing process of life has left some pretty big holes that people left behind cannot quite seem to fill. That's part of the plan, but Oh, Lord, how I miss them.

You probably noticed that I have not mentioned even one enemy in this book. That isn't because I haven't made any in the almost seventy years that I have been hanging around. I have made a few—one or two, maybe less. But I'll be double-doggoned if I'm going to give either one of those rascals any free space in my book.

All the bears and hares, the mooses and gooses (see, I knew there just had to be a sensible common plural hanging around somewhere), beavers, loons, groundhogs, dragonflies and all the other birds and bees and animals were my friends, too. But not those dad-blamed black flies and pesky little black mosquitoes. Somebody else can have them for friends. I don't like them.

Some of the associations with my wild friends have been of rather short duration, but they have left rather long memories. All have been rewarding.

A very few of them have put the fear of God into me, especially noticeable in the area of my feet. There must be some unexplainable quirk in the evolutionary process, because they never seemed to move as fast as I wanted. A couple of times they simply did not get the message, "Feets, get me outta here." That is when that other genetically transmitted trait took over and the evolutionary process went on.

You may have noticed a few big words. I just stuck one in now and then and here and there to fool you into thinking that I was smarter than I actually am. I don't know what half of them mean, either.

Take millennia, for example. A millennium is a thousand years as we reckon time. I'm not sure that we reckon it at anywhere near to correct. We have tried so many different ways, every one of which was absolutely correct, until we found out that it was all wrong.

The Spanish Conquistadores killed off the Aztecs before anyone had a good chance to talk to them. They had a pretty good calendar, but the soldiers were more greedy for wealth than knowledge, and Aztec gold was easy to come by—you just had to kill a few Indians and take it. We're still trying to understand what we know about their calendar. There must be some times when it is better to talk than to fight.

Not too many of us have stayed around for a full millennium to find out what it really is. My calendar doesn't say when it begins or ends. My four watches can't even agree on when noon happens. And they are all guaranteed to be accurate to within one second a month, plus or minus a few.

Some old geezer away back there about a millennium or two ago, more or less, came up with the idea that we needed a word that meant a long, long time but would be a little more definite, so he called it a millennium. He didn't know a whole lot about *esses* to make a plural, so he just droped the *um* and hung on an *a* right there behind the *i* and went around telling everybody that it meant any number more than one. They believed him.

He was a pretty smart old codger, too. Just think of how much ink he must have saved by not spelling it "millenniums" or "millenniumesses." And that was back there when ink was right scarce, too, unless you made your own out of pokeberries. A few people today don't care how much ink they waste and still spell it millenniums, but nobody pays much mind to that bunch anymore.

You probably noticed a number of equally brilliant(?) observations and conclusions as you were reading. I just stuck one in every chance I got.

You may have noticed that there were a few places where I used the vernacular to make a statement about something or another. That's because people really talked that way once. It was a fun way to say things.

You may have questioned some of the logic used in reaching my conclusions about the evolutionary process and developments. Don't question. There wasn't any logic. They just popped out.

Man is about the only animal that can alter the evolutionary process. He has had more messes than successes, but I suppose that depends on your point of view. Altering the process may be a part of the process, but you don't see monkeys monkeying around trying to make something out of something else when that something wasn't supposed to be there in the first place.

And of all the apes, gorillas, monkeys and the like that I have met, not one of them has ever called me "Son." A lot of other things, maybe, but never "Son." They may be a lot smarter than we imagine.

Sometimes men are a little short-minded and go ahead and do things that they already know are wrong. Wars are the best evidence I have of that...

And littering roadsides, public parks, campsites and boat ramps. And graffiti.

Addendum

I recently saw a picture of a horse with what looked a little like a human head—if you stretched your imagination somewhat beyond the limit. This picture was in one of those notorious journals which some people call "scandal sheets."

This picture offers absolute proof in support of my untheory which, put very briefly, states that men did not spring from apes at all. This picture indicates that a more logical source of humanity may really have been the horse.

I have been observing politicians for many years and had already reached the conclusion that a large number had sprung from a horse, but it seems that I have been concentrating all my efforts on the wrong end.

By The Author

Evolution

When you listen to the experts on evolution on television you might get the idea that all evolution is only biological. You might be led, however subtly, to believe that evolution means only that present forms of organisms, including humans, evolved through a series of changes or mutations over millions or billions of years from other organisms which were not as highly developed as today's models.

If you pursue this train of thought to the most extreme limit of which you are capable, you will find that you might recognize that all living things are related. "Living things," of course, includes plants and animals. That part is quite obvious. What is less obvious and seldom mentioned is that it also includes germs, viruses, bacteria, single cells and fetuses (which probably evolved from a single cell).

If you want to go a step further and really stretch your mind, you can make a case that some inanimate materials ordinarily classified as minerals were once living things and should fall into the category of plants and animals even though these plants and animals are long since dead and have assumed distinctly different forms. It depends upon when you want to stop calling an item alive and start calling it something else. If we do differentiate, then we are inconsistent. I just wanted to start a big argument. I'm not going to participate in it.

If you were to visit a coal mine and look carefully at the solid face or the roof of the mine, you might be able to see the fossilized remains of a primitive tree or of a crustacean-like animal called a trilobite.

Evolution does mean those things, and they are much more difficult to detect than the everyday occurrence of evolution which anyone can observe, because of the vast time period that elapsed between even minute changes.

There is another meaning for evolution which seems to me to have been neglected in all the discussion and controversy about our origins. I think that it is time that we started paying attention to that and possibly fitting it into its proper place. That place may be more important to us than where we came from—it may give us some clues as to where we are headed.

The evolutionary process that you can see daily as you just amble along through life is perhaps a little different than what you would normally consider as evolution. Perhaps not. It may be that we are seeing the everyday workings of evolution and are failing to recognize them as a part of the long-range picture.

This evolutionary process involves a lot of our everyday living. Our system of laws is the result of an evolutionary process. Laws are constantly becoming more complicated. I am not about to argue the pros and cons of the shortcomings of our system of jurisprudence. I might put some of my feelings on paper, but I'm not going to argue about it. Sometimes arguments are hard on the nose. I like to breathe through mine.

Our systems of planting, growing, harvesting and preserving food are the result of a long (but not billions of years—I can't even imagine one billion years, let alone multiple billions) evolutionary process. In fact, just about everything you do has evolved from some former system that we felt we could improve. This even includes throwing beer cans at umpires and talking back to the "boob tube." We weren't doing either of those things only a few years back. It might even include reading this book—heaven forbid. It certainly includes our language.

I read somewhere, or heard it on television (where you can hear just about anything if you'll just be patient and wait a while) that someone had called Charles Darwin the "Father of Modern Evolution." I didn't know until that very moment that evolution was modern. Darwin didn't invent evolution like Henry invented the Model T, or Tom invented the incandescent bulb. He just wrote about it. By the time he got around to writing about it, evolution was "old hat." If it hadn't been, he couldn't have. And neither could I.

The American Indians were already well-versed in evolution as it pertained to them. That was long before they ever saw a white man. At least it was long before they saw the one that we have been taught and told for years was the first. And Boy! There is sure room for a big argument there.

Some people like to call the American Indians "Amerinds," but you've got to be mighty careful what you call people these days. Evolution (and maybe a couple of other things) has made just about everybody's skin a lot thinner in the last few decades. And you had better be careful about laughing at someone, no matter how funny some situation strikes you. You could get sued, or maybe accused of some sort of slander which you never intended. If we're not careful, evolution will cause us all to have long sour faces that won't look nearly as good as the ones we are sacrificing to decorum. The funniest guy I know is me, and I laugh at myself a lot—and I'm afraid to laugh at anyone else. We need to have a sense of humor and learn to laugh with others.

The Amerinds were aware of evolution a long, long time back. It was long before Darwin's great-great-great-great-great-grandfather got the gleam in his eye that evolved into little Charley. They knew—maybe forever—that all animals were their brothers. I haven't heard or read anything that would lead me to believe that they ever called any of them "Daddy." Or "Mommie."

Most of their people practiced a sort of religious ceremony, so I have been informed, that preceded the hunt. They asked for forgiveness from an animal before they took its life to nurture their own. They ate a lot of their animal brothers.

There isn't much hard evidence pointing to any widespread rites of animal or human sacrifices among the Indian tribes which lived north of Old Mexico. When your belly begins to wonder if your throat has been cut, you have a strong tendency to eat first and say grace later, when you get the chance. You don't leave a lot of edible meat hanging on the bones, either. If some falls into the fire, you snatch it out and gnaw. If any does get burned, it is not because that was intended. The dogs ate the bones, and then the Indians ate the dogs. Waste not, want not.

They held all living things as brothers. They knew that trees, corn and cattails were living things, too. They ate the cattail shoots, the arrowroot roots, the nuts and acorns, the fruits and berries and the wild sweet potatoes. If they could

3

have found any two of those at the same time, they would have celebrated feast day on the spot by eating every bite. When they ate meat, they gorged. No refrigerators, you know. A full-sized brave could hold nearly three times as much meat as one of his white brothers in the cavalry, who was pretty much accustomed to "three squares" a day and had to have a chuck wagon follow him just about everywhere he went.

The land was the mother of all. It could not be owned. At least not in the same sense that we think that we own it today. Individuals and tribes did have certain territorial rights, but these were highly disputable.

They believed that the Great Spirit was the father of all living things. Come to think of it, that is just about what Jesus of Nazareth tried to teach us and tell us a couple of millennia ago. We appear to learn slowly.

They cared for the plants and the animals and the land and the water as though they were relatives. That may not be a good metaphor now, but it was. Once upon a time and long ago and faraway.

We could have learned a lot from the Indians, if we had not been so busy killing them off that we couldn't stop for a few minutes and listen.

Darwin wrote his theory of evolution basically because of his observation of finches while he was lost at sea. He may not actually have been lost, and he may have been on dry land, but he was still in the middle of one whale of a big puddle.

Finches are birdlike animals which are related to chipmunks (both have stripes), butterflies (both have wings) and camels (both have legs, although most camels have twice as many legs as most finches). Many finches look as though one parent or the other had been fooling around with some other birdlike creature's spouse. I suppose that is what brought them to Darwin's attention.

If you observe finches while they are at work or play, you will notice some marked resemblance to canaries, sparrows, robins, blackbirds and others. The purple finch looks like some sparrow had been playing birdhouse with a cardinal—maybe two. But then I've seen some human offspring that caused me to do more than one doubletake. The birds are our brothers, too.

4

Don't laugh. If you study evolution with any degree of objectivity at all, you will find that humans are related to all sorts of things. This includes javelina, aardvarks, birds, box turtles, camels, fish, groundhogs, iguanas, llamas, roses, snails, trees, weeds, zebras and pink lady's slippers. Everything from A to Z and all that is between and on either side.

Many anthropologists tell us that we are directly descended from the great apes through a complicated evolutionary process that is full of holes. Stop and give that some serious thought for a few minutes—not too long though, or you'll fall out of your tree.

I think that those people are somewhere out in left field. All you have to do is to walk down the streets of any large city. Be sure that you do that in groups of not less than forty. At least seventy percent of the group should consist of karate black belts, professional boxers, and green berets. Heavily armed. We didn't descend from the great apes. They descended from us.

MOOSE

My observations of moose began many years ago (as we reckon time) when I first started going to Canada to pursue my second favorite sport, fishing. Hunting was at one time right up there among the top three, but I don't hunt anymore. It has fallen to a poor thirty-ninth, or maybe even less.

I have these spells when I have a tendency to fall, and I am not able to get back on to my feet for awhile. Crawling around over logs, brush, poison ivy, snakes and the like sort of takes the edge off the sport. No, it's not the drinking—I don't. It was a broken back that did me foul.

As I rambled around the bush in Ontario, New Brunswick, Nova Scotia, and Quebec I have happened upon several different moose. Most of them not at the same time. Three adult moose at one time is enough to make anyone have some serious thoughts about where he plans to spend the hereafter. Especially when he picks them up in his highbeams while travelling a dirt and gravel road and doing a little over fifty and the moose are somewhat larger than midsize.

Most of my ramblings were because I was hunting what I consider to be much better game—a long skinny fish with over-sized glassy eyes that Canadians in Ontario call "pickerel," and which the Quebecois call "dore" and which I have called a lot of other names as well, but mostly "walleye." He doesn't look a lot like that other fish that folks in some of the eastern states call "chain pickerel" and I have never seen another fish called "dore." I suppose that the French name may have some connection with "d 'or" which means "of gold," because on a real honest-to-goodness walleye the underside is usually a golden color. He has a close relative that doesn't have that golden tinge and that fish, the sauger, can be taken over most of the natural range of the walleye.

But the walleye is fun to catch and even more fun to eat. He has cat food beat forty ways from Sunday. If I even hinted at how many I have caught, you wouldn't believe another word in this book.

The member of the opposite sex, with whom I have spent fifty years in double harness, likes to catch them, too. She learned to bait a hook before she learned to cook. I always say, "Important things first." Margy has been with me on all those trips, and she cooks pretty good, so I drag her along. I have seen her in her younger days latch onto a nice walleye and jump to her feet (in a round-bottomed boat, yet) and emit one high-pitched shriek after another. Luckily, she hasn't fallen overboard.

You will have a hard time convincing this old boy that she just goes along for the ride, or to keep a sharp and well-trained eye on me. She has calmed down a little in recent years.

Because I am committed to the pursuit of this odd-looking species, a lot of my beating around the bush in Canada has been done in boats. Metal boats, cedar strip boats, plywood chaloupes, plank boats, new boats, old boats and homemade boats that were more hope than float. But only one has capsized, and that was a canoe, and Margy was on the stream bank that time, laughing her head off. I was getting minnows in a small stream for a friend who sold them and was hard pressed for time. The water, fortunately, was just up to my chin when I waded out. I didn't get wet above that except when I went over backwards. Oh, well, I always say, "No good turn ever goes unpunished."

I have met what I suppose could be called a goodly number of moose while I was just banging around in a boat. I have met more than a goodly number while banging around in the bush. Several of those meetings were within speaking distance and some within whispering distance.

Most of the meetings were not properly planned and were probably as much of a surprise to the moose as to me, judging from some very hasty observations made while looking back over my shoulder to make sure he wasn't gaining, or even following.

This position has a distinct disadvantage in scientific research. It is hard to make any really lengthy and thorough studies while running through the bush as fast as a set of long skinny legs with knobby knees will carry you. (Mine, not the moose's.) Especially when the knobby knees are turning black and blue from knocking into each other with some regularity, and when they have turned to some liquid or other which is much thinner than water.

I think that the element of surprise had more to do with my chickening out than real fear of the moose, but I never like to trust them too far. I failed the course in Moose Mind Reading.

The moose usually demonstrated a little more composure. He normally trotted off at an easy lope with his four big feet flailing the wind on all sides. And fore and aft.

My other shortcoming is that I like to take pictures—when I can remember to take the camera. It used to be movies without the benefit of fancy lenses. But I could run faster then. And farther. Now I take any moose pictures that I get with a 35 mm SLR and a l-o-n-g telephoto lens. You can't tell me that evolution doesn't work. Nobody is going to get the opportunity to call me brave unless it is by accident. Not when it comes to moose.

My wife and I were fishing a small lake in Quebec in late summer (early fall if you put any stock in the coloring of the leaves) away back in the bush about fifty miles or so from the nearest house. We had the lake to ourselves and were picking up a nice dore now and then. One about every two minutes, which I used to consider fair-to-middlin' fishing.

We have never kept more fish than we could eat in the next day or two, so we may have been catching some of he same fish over and over. It's pretty hard to tell one walleye from another until you get to know them by their first names. You know, like Tom, Joe, Sadie or Mary. But we were sure having ourselves a time.

One of us, probably my wife since she sees a lot of stuff that I don't (but that hardly ever includes moose or girls), spotted a brown hump sticking out of the water over near the south shore among some reeds and weeds. We took off toward the hump with all the speed that I could coax out of that hull of a boat and the ten-horse Johnson. I was working with the camera and not paying a lot of attention to other things that might be considered important, such as boat, speed, distance and moose.

Suddenly, a set of antlers which were wider than the boat popped out of the water, festooned with trailing water weeds and I was eyeball to eyeball with one of the ugliest, meanest faces that I had seen in a long time. And on a moose that is some ugly. I dropped the camera, slammed the Johnson into reverse, treaded water with the boat, tried to hold the motor in the water, and said three short ones in less time than it takes to spell "moose." I swore to never run with the motor in the unlocked position again if I could just get out of that mess with a whole skin.

The moose jerked his big feet out of the mud and muck and wheeled and headed for the bush as though he had seen Old Lucifer himself. I suppose that I did look kind of mean, too. What with those stinking cigars that I always smoked to keep the black flies and mosquitoes at a distance and more than likely with a week's worth of beard.

I had just encouraged the boat to start moving ever so slowly in reverse when I saw the second moose, just as it, too, came all the way up from being submerged in the water and weeds. It had been feeding deep, almost concealed by the weeds and reeds, and in the excitement of the moment, had gone unnoticed. It took off for a quieter and more peaceful environment also.

I learned two things about evolution right then and there. First, that a moose can get into high gear faster than you can get an outboard into reverse and moving, and that he can move fairly fast for such a big awkward-looking thing even when he is standing belly-deep in water. And, second, that man's reaction to such encounters is something that has been handed down over centuries of surprise meetings between man and wild beast. I suppose you could say "from genes to jeans."

And somehow or another I missed the pictures. The only consolation that I could find was that I hadn't dumped the camera overboard and we were both still in the boat. The north end of a south-bound moose as he disappears into the bush doesn't make too good of a picture anyway. You can't see him smile.

My second observation of evolution in moose came several years and many meetings later. I don't know why it took so long for it to finally sink in, but it is probably because I am normally just a wee bit more than somewhat dense. I am so dense, in fact, that I have often been threatened by a certain member of the opposite sex, heretofore mentioned, that I had

9

better get my head on straight or else. I am still trying to figure out what she means by "or else." She has only been saying that for fifty years or so. Oh, well. Evolution takes time.

I have observed, after many years of careful study, that moose have long legs, even for such a large animal. Compared to a moose, a bison could be called "Shorty." The moose's legs seem to be disproportionately long. Not just a moose now and then like some of their more advanced(?) brothers who can range from real short to extra long, or like some of their sisters who can range from short and dumpy to long and lithe.

Even baby moose have long legs—before they learn to stand. They also have funny-looking knobby knees that look even worse as they grow older.

It finally dawned on me why a moose's legs are so all-fired long.

One would assume, without giving it a great deal of thought as I have, that those legs are long so that they can run faster. Moose can get around pretty fast sometimes, but that's not the real reason for the lengthy underpinning. Not by a long shot.

Neither is it because their long legs are as graceful and attractive as they are on some of the female members of a distinctly different moose-related animal subspecies which I hesitate to name while the aforementioned opposite sex is peering over my shoulder as I write.

She is a little short thing, but she can easily reach the top of my noggin while I'm sitting. And those heavy frying pans make nasty lumps.

If you have ever paid much attention to the legs on a female moose, you just couldn't bring yourself to vote for her for beauty queen. The legs on the males don't look any better. Unless of course, you are measuring them to see if they will fit in your skillet.

If you have ever waded around very much in that confounded brush in Canada where it grows so thick that you can't see more than five or six feet in any direction but up, you already know why. I don't understand why you didn't tell the rest of us so we could quit worrying.

It is so the moose won't scratch his belly or any other important parts on the spruce needles, alder pods, briers, thorns and sharp sticks while he is running through that brush. Could

10

any explanation be simpler?

I'll bet that if you had to hightail it through that brush with a pack of wolves nipping at your hindquarters and tender victuals (to a wolf, that is), you would want longer legs, too. But it takes a few successive generations of wanting before an evolutionary development becomes a reality. Moose have been wanting longer legs for a long, long time. They should have been asking for pretty, too. But sometimes you just can't seem to think of everything at the same time.

Another odd thing about evolution in moose is their antlers. Some people call them horns, but they aren't really. A moose horn is something entirely different. It doesn't even look like an antler. Not at all.

A moose horn is a funny-looking thing that is rolled up out of birch bark, old newspapers, rubber car mats or anything else that you might have sitting around doing nothing that can be rolled up into the shape of a megaphone.

A megaphone is a long round object, big at one end and little at the other. When you call it a moose horn, you hold the little end to your mouth and make funny noises that are supposed to sound like a cow moose in heat or a bull moose in rut when they come out of the big end. You wouldn't want to try doing that with an antler, especially one that is still attached to a bull that weighs in at just a little short of a ton. That would very likely make him nervous.

The moose horn just doesn't look like an antler. I don't understand why so many people get them confused. It doesn't look a whole lot like a moose, either, which is also big at one end and little at the other, depending on where you are standing while making your observation. You wouldn't want to mistake a moose for a moose horn either. If you were to blow on the little end of a moose, it's hard to tell what kind of a noise might come out the other.

The moose horn is supposed to sound like a moose, I think. It mostly just grunts and groans. I suppose that it all depends on who is standing nearest to the little end. But then I'm not much of a one to judge, since I am tone deaf.

Back to the antlers. Every year at some time in early winter or maybe in late winter or even in very early spring, the antlers fall off. I suppose that the time may be greatly influenced by where the moose is standing when they drop and where he

11

spends his winters.

Horns hardly ever fall off, although I have seen a few things that were called horns that I wished had fallen somewhere where the owners couldn't find them. I would even have volunteered my services to help look for them in someplace where I knew they couldn't possibly be.

Moose don't seem to pay a whole lot of attention to the calendar. One day is pretty much the same as any other when it is forty-six below zero one day and only forty-five below the next. That is in Fahrenheit. I don't know much about centigrade (also called "Celsius"), but when it is below zero outside and the temperature feels the same to a wet finger, it is a lot warmer in centigrade than in Fahrenheit. Above zero it is the other way around, but who cares when the temperature is that warm. When it is forty-five below, it is too cold for anyone with good sense to be outside, anyway. Water still freezes whether you say "Celsius" or "something elsius."

Another crazy thing about Fahrenheit and centigrade is that when one thermometer says that it is forty below, the other one does, too. That is just hearsay. I haven't really had enough good sense to stand around outside in temperatures like that to watch even one thermometer, let alone two at the same time.

And moose have to run around in weather like that all winter long stark bluejay naked. If evolution really worked properly, they would all pack up and go to Florida or Texas like everybody else. Or at least as far south as North Carolina.

Only a few (comparatively speaking) species shed antlers or even have any to shed. The moose stands out in the crowd like a sore thumb on a carpenter's left hand. He has the biggest antlers of the lot of them. Nobody else comes close. The elk (or wapiti, if you want to call him by his maiden name) tries hard, but his antlers have a lot of air holes where the moose has antlers. The elk's wind up weighing about a third as much. Air isn't nearly as heavy as that other stuff. The caribou about halfway tries for shape, but he doesn't hold a candle to a moose when it comes to big.

Evolution plays an important role in the antler shedding. Men (and a few women, I presume) have argued for many years, trying to resolve why moose shed their antlers. I want to settle the argument once and for all. The antlers fall off just to give the moose a little relief from a big pain in the neck. Carrying around upwards of eighty pounds of all that useless junk must be a real chore. Especially when it is sitting on top of that big head and stuck out there so far in front of his shoulders. Moose don't have drug stores or Walmart's where they can run in and get a bottle or two of aspirin for every little ache and pain.

Most of the time only one antler drops, leaving the other just sitting up there on the side and causing the moose to be more than just a little unbalanced. If you don't think that it would, just try tying about thirty pounds of miscellaenous junk on one side of your head and see what it does. Those of you who wear one earring would have a good place to tie it. It results in what the moose call "a crick in the neck."

Soon after the old antlers are shed, the moose gets a couple of little fuzzy knobs right where the old antlers were attached. They are the sprouts for the new antlers, and they grow so fast that you can almost hear them swish as they shoot through the air. That may be a slight exaggeration (for those of you who insist on nitpicking every little statement), but the moose has to get them big enough in about four or five months so that the hunters will want to shoot at him in the fall. He also likes nice big antlers to help him through all that foolishness that bull moose think is so much fun. Some people will do most anything for a little kick.

By all logic and reasoning the new ones should grow up to be a little bigger than the old ones that he left behind. The size of his new antlers depends on whether his grocery stores and restaurants stay open all winter so that he can get enough to eat. If they close up and go south for the winter, the moose has a lot more to worry about than antlers. If he is more than about eight or ten years old, they start growing smaller, anyway. Ten years on a moose is comparable to the upper fifties on a human. Things similar to that happen to other animals when they reach about the same comparative age. That may be a loose comparison, but it still proves that nature is pretty doggoned smart.

When the new antlers pop out, the moose trades in his pain in the neck for a pain in the head—a big one. Excedrin headache number 342.

The new antlers have a fuzzy coating of something or another which some guy who didn't know any better called "velvet" many, many years ago. No one has had enough nerve to start calling it something else that makes more sense. That includes me. It doesn't look much like the velvet or the velour on your new living room furniture. The next time that you are talking to a moose, ask him to let you stroke his velvet and see for yourself. Let me know what you think.

That fuzzy stuff covers a bunch of blood vessels that are full of the stuff that feeds the new antlers. That is the same stuff that black flies, deer flies, moose flies and mosquitoes fight over, and feast on for breakfast, lunch and supper. Supper is the same thing as dinner, for those of you who want to be uppity. The moose is a portable cafeteria, so to speak.

In case you don't know what a moose fly is, that is one of the moose's insect brothers (or other relatives) who likes to sponge a free meal now and then and visits too frequently. He is about three or four times as big as a deer fly, and I don't know how many times as big as a black fly. He can sop up blood like an old-timey Pirate's fan could sop up beer at a Fourth of July home-stand doubleheader. By "old-timey" in this case, I mean before beer was outlawed at ballgames and you could still throw empties or full ones at the umpires and the visiting outfielders when they displeased you.

If you have ever been bitten by a black fly that is so small that you have to wear your bifocals to be able to see him well enough to swat him, you know what those little buggers can do to your complexion and disposition. You have to feel sorry for the poor old moose who has to put up with all the little ones, middle-sized ones and the big ones and can't get his hooves on a little one hundred percent *deet* now and then.

Sometimes a moose will try to evade the flies and other pests by wading out into deeper water in a stream or lake and just standing there, completely submerged except for the very tip of his nose. On a moose, that is still a pretty good-sized blob sticking out of the water. This might be a trait that he inherited from his ancestors through evolution. It is far more likely that he is simply trying to get away from all those buzzing, biting, tormenting pests that swarm around his head, his back parts, his under parts and any other parts that they can reach with their sharp little beaks. He has probably figured out from experience that the little rascals can't swim underwater. At least not as well as a certain movie star of some years back that I have seen on TV a couple of times. She was prettier, too. Lots prettier.

There are more kinds of black flies than you can count on your fingers and toes. If you want to tally them, you can sneak around after dark and count your wife's fingers and toes, too. Be gentle, now. The next day you can ask three friends, if you still feel that you are up to the task, to let you count their fingers and toes. You will still be short a few digits. If they tell you that you have gone completely out of your skull, buy yourself a pocket calculator. Then after you have counted all the varieties of black flies, you can start counting mosquitoes. Let me know how it turns out. Or, you can do as I did.

Quite frankly, I have not had the time to stop and count. I was noticeably short on desire as well. I have been too busy with other things like fishing and other important stuff like that.

I did read somewhere that some guy (or girl, as the case may be) did take the time to count them one by one and came up with 110 varieties. I'm glad that he did that. It saved me ever so much time. He must not have had much of anything else to keep him busy. I'll bet that it was a little hard to tell one kind from another sometimes. They all look pretty much alike to me, but then I'm not a fly expert.

You will have to do as I did and take his word for it, if you decide not to count them for yourself because it's not worth the time and effort. I did my part in passing along that piece of useful information. And who would lie for a few pesky black flies, anyway? Not me.

Fortunately for the already unfortunate moose, not all of those varieties have tasted moose cocktails—or so we are told. I wonder if they call them "Bloody Mary's." Only a few varieties have tasted moose blood and liked it well enough to come back for seconds. Some people will drink anything they can get their hands on as long as someone else is setting them up. I hope they don't start running around and telling the other black flies about how good it is and how high you can fly on it. You know how easy it is for stuff like that to get started.

We humans say things like, "If you haven't tried it, don't knock it," and a lot of other stuff like that which we think makes us sound intelligent, if not exactly brilliant. They bolster a sagging ego.

Thousands of black flies, deer flies, moose flies, mosquitoes and who only knows what else buzzing around your head at the same time, waiting for someone to finish his meal and leave the table so that there will be landing space for another to sit down and give you a sharp nip would be enough to make you want to go soak your head. Maybe the mosquitoes and black flies and such aren't like their Eskimo brothers who have developed a liking for moose nose. Or maybe the moose doesn't mind a few nibbles on his nose if it gives him a little relief on the rest of him. At least the landing space is more limited and the holding pattern considerably longer.

Mosquitoes are a terrible nuisance to a moose. Maybe even more than black flies. In some areas of Ontario, the mosquito is called the "National Bird." They run around in huge swarms looking for a good place to eat and then split into smaller squadrons to attack.

I have heard that the biters are not those big things that look like miniature dragonflies, the ones about an inch or more long and a pretty sort of brown color. The biters are those little black rascals that set up a high-pitched whine when they buzz around your ears. They sound the same to a moose except in stereo and the sound is amplified like the sound through a boom box. He can hear them better because of those big sound-trapping ear flaps. It's enough to drive a body out of his wits.

When they buzz around your ears, you can often spot them as they line up their sights on a likely-looking dining room. They may be close relatives of truck drivers who have the reputation of knowing all the good places to eat. I'm not too sure about truck drivers. I have followed some into restaurants where the food wasn't anything to write home about. I have decided that there are a lot of cases where it may be the waitresses.

If you are careful enough and quick enough when one of those mosquitoes starts bugging you, you might manage to trap him between your palms and squash him (or her, as the case may be) to smithereens. If you average more than one out of nine over a three-day period, you have either had considerable experience or are just plain lucky.

16

A moose's palms (that's what they call those big solid areas of his antlers where the elk has air) won't come together too well, so he can't even average that many.

Most of the biters are said to be female. A moose is too much of a real gentleman to hit a lady, anyway. They don't have ERA and Women's Lib and NOW in Mooseland, so you're not supposed to hit girls there. It's okay here, though, where the females are just like males.

I have never examined a whole lot of mosquitoes that closely, and I have never actually been able to tell a male from a female. I haven't see any running around in a bikini. I understand that there are certain areas in the United States where those things are a great deal of help in trying to distinguish between the sexes in a related subspecies. I have also heard that it is almost impossible to tell without some kind of additional aid, especially since they don't put the zippers on the front and back like they used to do so that it would be easier to differentiate.

Maybe the female mosquitoes have longer noses. Most that I have examined even superficially have been a little the worse for wear, and I simply wouldn't know what to look for, anyway.

I am sure that you have heard that other old saw, "A man's best friend is his dog." (For the other old saw that I know, refer to that one a few paragraphs back.) That may be true in Tennessee, Maryland, Virginia, Pennsylvania, West Virginia, and maybe Georgia and places like that where they do a lot of coon hunting and fox chasing and where the women won't chase rabbits, but a hound dog ain't worth a hoot when it comes to catching black flies and mosquitoes. Most of them are only good at catching fleas.

In the North Country in black fly and mosquito seasons, a man's best friend(s) is a bunch of dragon flies (I know it's supposed to be all one word, but if you knew dragon flies like I know dragon flies, you'd split it too). A bevy of ten or twelve dragon flies can gobble up a swarm of black flies or those pesky little mosquitoes faster than you can gobble down a bag of potato chips. Every time a dragon fly chomps down on a black fly, it sounds just like you chomping down on a crispy chip. No need to offer to share your chips. They like flies better. His teeth crack when they come together on a black fly, and it is clearly audible if you will stop chewing long enough to listen. Aw, come

17

on now. Be imaginative. They still crack.

Dragon flies love people, but only those who are smart enough not to hit them when they aren't looking. A dead dragon fly doesn't care a whole lot about humans or anybody else. If you sit on a log at the edge of the bush for a little while, one will surely drop by and pay you a social call. He didn't come for just some pleasant conversation. He came to eat. He knows that black flies like you too, and he can get a bellyful if he just hangs around for a little while. Why do you think that some people call them "mosquito hawks?"

A moose doesn't have too many natural friends. Have you ever read any other book that even hinted at anything other than natural enemies? The dragon fly (okay, so some of them can be damsel flies. You guys who are technical make it hard on us poor writers who are not well-versed in fly sex and stuff like that), is also the moose's best friend. You hardly ever read in any of the big city newspapers about a moose murdering a dragon fly. Do you think that a moose is stupid enough to do in what may be his only true friend? In Mooseland friends are pretty hard to come by. Sometimes moose are a lot smarter than people.

A moose loves his little dragon fly friend and will let him come and sit on his antlers to pass the time of day, even if they are sore and tender. He will offer his little friend a free ride if the dragon fly just wants to goof around and isn't going to the movies or the liquor store or anywhere else in particular. A moose could teach us humans a thing or two about dragon flies and friendship and lots of stuff like that.

A moose will go into a patch of black alder bushes to hide from the bugs and to just sit and think where it is nice and quiet and there aren't so many of those little pests around. Black alder can also be gray alder, speckled alder, dwarf alder or something else. It all seems to do the trick.

Black, gray or speckled (or whatever you want to call it) alder is not at all like the box alder with which Americans, mostly those that say things like, "y'all," "cotton-pickin'," "mo-lasses," "cawn pone," and other such things, are familiar. A moose couldn't hide behind one of those skinny old things without a bunch of his parts sticking out. Box alders don't grow in bunches, and they wouldn't know a black fly from a hickory nut, so they wouldn't be much good at keeping them off.

18

Black alder is a whole lot shorter than box alder, which only loafs around on the job a couple or three days a week to get to be thirty or forty feet tall. A black alder has to work hard, even on Saturdays and Sundays, to get to be a little more than six or eight feet tall. Black alder gets little long pods on it which botanists and other such people call catkins. These dry up in the fall and get to be as rough as a cob. Black alder is one of the bushes that scratch the moose's belly and undercarriage when he tears through it in overdrive. But it repels black flies and mosquitoes.

They aren't much like elder, either. That is the bush that gets berries on it in the early summer that a lot of hillbillies use to make jelly and wine. I'm not too sure which one is consumed most. The kids cut the stems to make popguns, which they use to shoot paper wads at teachers and other friends.

Years of observation has caused me to believe that there is something about the alder that flies and mosquitoes don't like. I have just not been smart enough to figure it out yet. The next time I have a chance to talk to a moose, I'm going to ask. Maybe he can teach me a thing or two about herbal medicine. I hope that he doesn't tell me to eat something that might make me look like him.

A moose isn't like a lot of us humans. He can't lay around in a patch of bug dope all day doing nothing but enjoying life. He has a big belly. And it takes a heap of grub to keep it filled and to make him fat and tender when he sits on your table in the fall as moose roast or steak. A moose has to work hard for what he eats, even if his bedroom does come rent-free. I don't know what kind of work moose do, but they put in long hours.

Moose love water plants, the kinds that grow in a swamp or stream or lake and stick their stems and roots all the way to the bottom. Not like the filtration plants that humans call water plants and seem to like so much that they stick them around in some of the oddest places. They seem to find them essential in some localities where they have polluted the water supply and they can't find a good clear, cold spring. Nowadays that is just about everywhere.

I have never actually discussed this fondness with a moose, but I have seen them with their head completely submerged for what seemed far too long. When they do come up for air

19

they are chewing a huge mouthful of weeds. I have thought of offering one a good cigar just to see if he would stick it in his ear. He must get air from somewhere besides through that big nose. It could be his ear. Evolution has done some funny things.

I don't know for sure how long one can stay under. I've always been too busy with a fish on my line or something else that seemed more important at the time to clock him. I am also very absentminded and can never seem to remember my stopwatch or where I left it. I am so absentminded that I even forgot my fishing reels—but only once. That's another story, and I won't go into it here, if ever.

I have a friend from Ohio, by the name of George Cloeckner. He spends a lot of his time in Canada chasing fish. I have seen numerous signs in Quebec that say "Chasse-Peche." I suppose that you could say that is what George does. George is one of the old school, too. If it ain't walleye, it just ain't fish.

George and his good friend, and mine, Roy Annett, spend a lot of time together. Roy is a Canadian trapper, prospector, hunter, fisherman, guide and an otherwise fine human being from Shiningtree, Ontario.

They were going up a small tributary stream to a small lake which I shall not name, but which everybody who has ever crossed the border knows about, to do something or other that they do from a boat. The creek was in flood stage. It just about has to be to get a boat up it. They were motoring upstream when the boat hit something with a pretty good wallop and threatened to dump them, gear and all, into the swollen creek. When George grabbed for something solid to keep from getting his breeches wet, he got a handful of hair—moose hair. The moose had been standing in the bottom muck and mud and water and was completely submerged. He may have been feeding or maybe trying to get away from the flies and mosquitoes. I didn't get his reaction to being assaulted in such a manner, but his language would not likely have been fit to print in this book, no matter whether he spoke French or English or only Moose-ese.

George didn't admit it, but I'll bet that there were some wet clothes around that boat somewhere. He didn't say if they caught any fish, and I was laughing too hard to ask.

20

Another funny thing about moose that is surely a more recent evolutionary development is that they like roads—dirt roads, gravel roads, paved roads or super highways, it doesn't matter to a moose.

I have followed a moose track for miles on a backcountry bush road. It makes a lot of sense. A bull moose with a big headful of antlers can get them down an eight or ten foot roadway without whacking them into a bunch of limbs and trees. That is a simple enough reason. I didn't have much trouble figuring that one out. I'm a little taller than most people, and I am constantly banging my head into a lot of stuff like limbs and awnings that other people just walk under. I can swear to you that going around knocking your head on trees and the like will give you what is known in some circles as a splitting headache. I figure that a moose gets one once in a while, too. King-sized.

Moose like to stand in the brush at the side of the road, almost concealed, and watch the traffic go by. They often become so engrossed in the things which they see passing that they step up for a closer look. Probably the girls. Two-legged Moose have organized a club, and a lot of the members engage in this fascinating pastime. It appears to be addictive.

This preoccupation with cars, trucks and girls leads to a particularly hazardous condition known as "moose bashing." The moose call it "car bashing" or "tourist terror tantrums." Moose get a big kick out of it when they can get near enough to barely miss the car. They like to hear the tourists scream at the top of their lungs and see them turn as white as two-percent milk. If you happen to be following a car full of girls, you can hear the moose guffaw when the girls have to ride home on a wet seat. This is how the moose get their jollies in the summertime while they are waiting for the real fun to start in the fall. You know, dodging bullets and making faces at hunters.

When a one-and-a-half ton car travelling at sixty miles per hour (one hundred kilometers, give or take two or three, if you happen to be in Canada) meets a reasonably stationary moose of almost three quarters of a ton or more, you can forget about those formulae you learned in school to determine the results, because the result is always the same. Chaos. There is an immediate crunching of metal, plastic, glass, teeth, bone, meat and blood all over the place. Some of this was original equipment on the moose.

There is always a great deal of confusion, especially among the bystanders and among the paramedics who are working feverishly to try to sort out the pieces trying to determine just what belongs to which.

If you are in Canada, the Ministry of Natural Resources usually takes what is left of the moose. It is up to what is left of the humans to fend for themselves.

It hardly ever helps to tell the investigating officer that the moose had been to an all-night party and had been boozing too much.

A couple who are the other two friends we have and who sneaked out of West Virginia one dark night to go live in some foreign country (I think they called it "Arizona" or something like that), were touring the northeastern states and the southeastern end of Canada in their little MG. They were creeping along a paved backcountry road at something over forty miles per hour when their headlights revealed a huge moose standing at the edge of the road, watching for tourists to startle half out of their wits.

She is a very attractive lady, and like his two-legged brothers would do, the moose stepped up for a better look. He stepped all the way to the center of the narrow road.

Stopping was not one of the options. Divine Providence must have worked and the car was short and the moose was tall. She swears that she could have tweaked the moose's beard as they sped under his chin. Genetically transmitted reactions weren't a part of the discussion following her story.

I once had a Canadian friend who has since passed on to wherever it is that all hunters, fishermen and other good people go. Murray Summerfeldt and his wife, June, owned and operated the Country Store and Motel in Shiningtree.

I always meant to ask Murray his secret for getting June to do all the work while he and I hunted and fished, but I kept putting it off. We spent a lot of time together—hunting, fishing, working (well, everybody has to do a little of something or other now and then) and telling each other big lies about our successes—hunting, fishing and working, that is. They were our dearest friends in Shiningtree. He had served as a conservation officer for the Ministry of Natural Resources, so he knew moose.

Murray had acquired a new Ford F-250 pickup. Heavy duty. Diesel. Supercab. Four-wheel drive. XL Trim. Fancy. You would have thought that he was from Appalachia.

He was on his way to Sudbury which is around 120 miles south to pick up some supplies for the business. Just north of Sudbury, he met a deer. It made a terrible mess of the truck. The deer died. As I recall, all this took place on Thursday.

On Monday of the following week, Murray went to New Liskeard to pick up a new pickup. Bright and early on Tuesday morning, he was travelling west in his new F-250 on Route 560 about fifteen miles or so from Shiningtree, when a moose stepped out of the roadside bush and challenged the new truck to a bashing duel.

The truck won that one, but it was never quite the same afterward, what with its face all smashed in, one of its eyes all swelled shut and drooping and the hood having cauliflower ears and flying open every whipstitch without the aid of the old-time motorist's handy-dandy repair kit, baling wire. I think that the truck was always a little punch-drunk, as well. It would bob and weave, first to the right and then to the left as though trying to evade some imaginary moose by using fancy footwork.

Moose are unpredictable. They need lessons in how to flow with traffic and how to act as pedestrians.

I was coming out of Gowganda, Ontario, on my way home from guess what—another fishing trip. This was way back there in 1960, and there was no paved road then. Evolution took care of that—it is paved now and a lot straighter and a lot of the hills flattened. Sometimes evolution works pretty good. The dirt and gravel road was in pretty good shape and I was making pretty good time, all things considered.

It was about four in the morning and just about to crack dawn when I came around a slight curve and there in my high beams stood not one, but three BIG moose, hogging the whole road and me with no place to go but straight ahead. The wagon and I both slowed noticeably and hastily. The moose (I would use the plural, but I'm not sure if it is mooses or meese or something else entirely) just stood there and guffawed. One even laughed so hard that if he had been wearing pants, they would have been ready for the laundry. They were having a

23

ball and they were rude. They may have had too much Canadian moonshine. I'm not sure if it has the same effect as hillbilly moonshine or not.

I don't know yet how I got stopped in time, but I left long skid marks on the road and in my Skivvies. The opposite sex to whom I referred a couple of times earlier still reminds me to slow down and drive carefully where there might be moose. Of course that was only a little over thirty years ago. She'll probably get over it one of these days.

The ill effects on the moose were not immediately apparent. They just ambled down the road for a half-mile or so with me trailing along behind. Way behind. They looked back over their shoulders occasionally just to be sure they were achieving the desired effect. They were.

I was a little bit reluctant to get out and tell them what road hogs and inconsiderate clods they were. I might have gotten smart-alecky with only one of them, but never with three. Especially with the mood they were in.

They finally wandered off the road into the bush which back in those days was at the edge of the road. They looked at me with silly grins as I crept by. I could tell that they were scared within an inch of their lives, too.

Moose are cantankerous. And bullheaded, if you will pardon a pun. I don't know if this is from evolution or only a result of hanging around with humans too much. If it is evolution, it must be recent.

A bull moose knows his own strength—sometimes. If he wants to hog the road, let him.

I had another friend in Restoule, Ontario, who had recently purchased a cute little Renault sedan. I don't know if Renault even makes one like that today. He was quite proud of his little new car—for a while, at least.

He met a big bull moose on the road one fall evening and patiently waited for the bull to move over so that he could pass. The bull patiently waited for that little pipsqueak of a car to get out of the way so that he could pass. Canadian Standoff.

The driver became impatient and laid down on his horn. The bull became impatient and lowered his horn. (I know that I said they were antlers, but I liked that play on words, so I just stuck it in.) He walked up to the Renault, hooked his antlers under the driver's side and nonchalantly tipped it over the side

24

of the road and down a short embankment. There is a moral here. Don't blow your horn at a moose unless you are absolutely sure that you have him buffaloed. Not in the fall. And just to be on the safe side, never. Those big rascals can get nasty.

Moose sometimes react to train horns as well—or as badly, depending on your point of view. I don't know what it is about a diesel horn that sets their teeth on edge, but it does. I have heard of them charging a full-grown locomotive. Not to mention Budd cars.

For those of you whose formal education failed to acquaint you with Budd cars, I will try to describe one so that you will know what I am talking about.

A Budd car is a vehicle that looks like a passenger car from a train that got confused and left a part of itself along some wilderness track. That is where you usually see Budd cars. They seem to avoid populated areas. The Budd car doesn't have very much of a front end, and even less of a behind. You have to look carefully to see which way it is headed and then you can't tell whether it is going or has already been. If it doesn't happen to like the way it is going, it just takes off in the other direction without swapping ends or so much as a how-de-do. You still can't tell what it is doing, even after it has made up its mind.

I have never for the life of me been able to figure how a moose can tell which end is the front and which is the rear, but they hardly ever make a mistake. They put their heads down and barrel right into it to try to knock it off the tracks. They must think that they have as much right to those tracks as that crazy looking thing.

I talked to one guy who must have read too much Freud. He said that the reason the moose charged the Budd car was sex. He must have been a little off. Even a moose wouldn't make a mistake like that.

After a moose meets a Budd car head on, it is nearly always easier to tell the front from the back. The front end is the one with the new set of antlers that are hanging on backwards.

This tendency to attack trains proves that the moose either can't see too well or that he isn't too awfully bright. Even I know better than to butt heads with a locomotive. If the locomotive were of equal size and weight and the odds were right, I might bet on the bull. This crazy reaction to trains results in a lot of moose mincemeat.

Moose sometimes do things that defy my untheory and everyone else's theory. You would think that after years of facing off against hunters armed with high-powered rifles that they would realize that the combination could be hazardous to their health. Especially when the hunter is not likely to be prone to genetic pants-wetting.

A moose will charge a person carrying a gun, a stick, an axe or anything else that is portable. He will even charge a person who isn't carrying anything. Most of the time he will either trot or stalk off in the other direction. And by the way, sometimes they don't care at all for what is know as modern music. It also sets their teeth on edge.

A moose may think that a hunter or a hiker is after his girl friend, since moose season sometimes overlaps rutting season. Rutting—that is another name for what must be "Oh, Joy!" to a moose. Maybe moose aren't as crazy as I thought, but they ought to better recognize the competition.

Moose are funny-looking mixed up animals. They must have been assembled from a lot of leftover parts. A moose has a head that looks like a blue-nosed Missouri mule gone awry; a beard that could have come off of a deceased billygoat; ears like a brindle cow, only bigger; hair the color of week-old coffee that gets even blacker when it is wet; a rear end that reminds you of an enlarged running-away hyena with hip problems; an oversized nose that looks like nothing else in this world and probably not in the next; forequarters that should have been on a small bison; legs that would make a camel think seriously about entering a beauty contest, and hooves that can get to be almost as big as pie plates. On a bull moose, you can top off all that pretty with a set of funny-looking antlers that some people call a "rack."

I don't know why they call a set of antlers a "rack" unless it is because some people like to shoot a moose and then hang the antlers on their wall, often with more or less of the moose still attached, and then hang guns, bows, hats, old smelly clothing and a bunch of other junk on them. Whew!

I said in the foreword that I was saving the best part for the last chapter, but I feel that I must tell you a little something about the sex life of a moose, as much as I hate to break a promise. Maybe moose sex shouldn't count—except to a moose. I

26

mention it here only casually because it seems essential to the proof that evolution is an ongoing process and not just some hit or miss proposition.

Every fall at just about the time that the leaves are turning to all their fancy colors and you can catch a gleam in the golds and scarlets, if you meet a bull moose face to face you will also notice a gleam in his eye. To him it spells l-o-v-e, but he has to go to a lot of extra work and trouble just to get worked up to the proper pitch.

He goes around stomping and pawing the ground, butting trees and saplings and grunting and groaning as though he had a bad case of heartburn. He tries to pick fights with every other bull he meets and he usually finds a few takers. Bulls that have been on the friendliest of terms all summer long suddenly quit talking to each other except to make derogatory remarks and throw insults at each other. They become bitter enemies. He goes around the woods just making a regular jackass of himself, except that jackasses apparently know better.

Jealousy! That's what it is that causes all this foolishness. He wants every female for himself and he wants every one of them to fall head-over-heels in love with him. He never heard of share and share alike and wouldn't do it if he had. Not this late in the fall.

He could avoid all this fighting and stomping and acting like he was out of his skull if he would just agree to being monogamous. But he can't even pronounce it let alone spell it so that he can look it up in the dictionary. I tried to explain it one day to a bull friend of mine but he just looked me straight in the eye and said something that sounded a lot like "B-u-u-u-l-l." Maybe he has been watching us while we thought we were watching him. I hated to tell him that it doesn't work too well for us, either.

Females are the fickle sort. They don't seem to mind too much who, just so long as he is still standing after all that fighting and folly.

Bulls also go around sniffing the ground a lot. I had an old hound dog once that did that and all he ever caught was a little old ground squirrel. I don't know what the bulls are hunting, but I am pretty sure that they don't eat ground squirrels.

27

I have never actually seen moose in the act of procreation. I suppose that they must go hide like some of the other species that I have read about. I suppose that they do something or another, though, after doing all that hard work in preparation. And there are always little moose in the spring. They must come from somewhere. Maybe they are so secretive because they don't want the other animals laughing at them. It must be a funny spectacle.

I just can't seem to muster up much respect for a hunter who would shoot a moose he might happen to catch right in the middle of what must surely be its most ardent moments, especially since it only happens once a year. If you should happen upon such activity and want to shoot a moose, just be patient. It can't last forever. And he will be too tired to run very far.

During the rutting and pre-rutting seasons, bull moose will respond to various sounds and will investigate. Any chance at all, I suppose, no matter how slim.

I have one other friend in Canada, Ben Nadeau of Timmins. Ben and his father and brother own and operate Nadeau et Fils, a logging company.

Ben cruises the timber and lays out boundaries for cutting operations to follow. He and two of his crew were running a line and were chopping down an aspen tree that stood in the way. They were carrying on an animated conversation in French as they chopped. (Any conversation carried on in French is animated.)

The sound of the axe thunking into the tree must have sounded familiar to a moose. They heard a couple of grunts and a couple of thumps that could not have been echoes. They turned and there, not fifteen feet away, stood a big old bull. He eyeballed them with that odd stare that moose have, grunted something in moose-ese and stalked off into the bush.

The moose probably figured they weren't his type or that they weren't much competition. Or maybe he was bilingual, or maybe he wasn't. Who knows about a fool moose?

Moose cows have calves just like dairy cows. Resemblance between the offspring ends right there with the name, unless you have an overactive imagination. A moose calf is only a small edition of big ugly. Only a mother could love a face like that, and some of them don't do that. They probably didn't want to bring something like that home from the hospital. Maybe they were still in a state of shock.

A few moose mamas abandon their calves. Thank heavens, that doesn't happen very often. It could upset the whole program if it became widespread.

When it does happen, the calf gets hungry and then will follow anything that makes a noise and almost anything that doesn't. They have been known to follow logging machines, farm tractors, chain saws, people, dogs and anything else that might give them a handout. You would, too, if you were starving. It is a small miracle that baby moose don't turn out to look like something else. It could easily be an improvement.

Bears and wolves like baby moose, too. To eat, that is. Sort of like veal on the hoof and easy to do in if Big Mama isn't around. If she happens to be on the scene it's a whole different ballgame. She can strike a predator with one of those big feet hard enough to cripple or kill it with one blow. Those long legs come in handy in a knock-down-and-drag-out fight. She has the reach. They also come in handy if she has to cry "uncle" and hotfoot it out of there, as sometimes happens, leaving the calf to its slaughterers.

Bears are sneaky and lazy. They like to eat well but don't like to work too hard to put on a little fat. Seems to me that I have heard of some other species with similar traits. Bears will eat almost anything that doesn't move fast enough to get out of their way. This includes mice, rabbits, snowshoe hares (also known as varying hare), other small animals, grubs, insects, roots, garbage, carrion and baby moose. A bear can finish off a baby moose with one swipe of its mighty forearms. They will finish off a square meal with a big helping of almost any fruit that is in season. They can eat more blueberries at one sitting than you can carry in your hat.

Wolves are gregarious. That means they are the family type. It also means that they hunt together in packs in a cooperative endeavor. They gang up on some hapless animal and bring it down with teamwork.

Wolves go for baby moose, too, but they don't worry much if it is bigger and they can run it to a standstill and then tear it apart a little at a time. If you have a queasy stomach, you won't want to watch too many big game wolf kills. They can get pretty gruesome. Wolves would rather pick on one that is too sick or too old and feeble to put up much of a fight or to run very far.

That is the wild version of a fast food joint. Death comes sooner or later to all and evolution must go on.

Don't you believe, though, that predators kill only the sick and infirm. That is a big lie that some people would have you believe. Bears, wolves, wolverines, minks and other predators evolved right alongside the rabbits, voles, moose and deer. They get hungry. They are not sold on veggies. When they get hungry, they want meat. And they eat whatever is available. Its state of health is not one of the considerations, although most predators will choose the easiest prey, if they have a choice.

And with all the centuries and millennia of evolution, prey animals have never really learned to unite and fight back. When they do, look out. There will be a real revolution.

Some people like to hunt moose for food and for sport. Some spend lots of good, hard-earned money just to get a chance at a moose. Once in a while somebody gets one.

I am all for hunting, for whatever animal, as long as it is done by the rules. Man is a longtime resident of the environment, and he cannot be ignored in any equation that affects it. He must work hard for its preservation. Nonuse is not necessarily synonymous with preservation.

Hunting alone has contributed more to the preservation and expansion of habitat than all the antihunters combined. That includes both game and nongame species.

Hunting is a controlled sport. It should be, and it must be. Hunting and killing of endangered animals must be stopped. Real hunters have no argument with that argument. Poaching and indiscriminate killing of both game and nongame wild animals is just as abhorrent to hunters as it is to antihunters. Control of game and nongame animal use is based on a complicated science that requires a good deal more than emotion to administer properly. Hunters must support, assist and advise the agency which controls and serves the sport.

They should insist that the real destroyers of the environment, those who destroy habitat, those who poach and peddle animals and animal parts and those who pollute the environment beyond acceptable levels be apprehended and punished.

Destruction of habitat has cost us more species than all the hunting ever done. And let's leave the American bison out of this discussion. That wasn't hunting—that was war and wanton destruction. And that isn't one bit funny.

A moose has an inherent sense of royalty. A big old bull thinks that he is king of his realm. He may be right. He is about the biggest thing around in his neck of the woods, if you don't count the monster bears of the northwest.

If you meet him face to face and you don't chicken out, he will probably look down his nose at you sort of disdainfully, give you a grunt and stalk off into the bush or woods, if he doesn't have something else on his mind. But don't bet your life on it. Not in the fall. He might have something else on his mind.

Evolution must have been responsible for the moose. How in the world did he get to look that way if it wasn't evolution? He ranks right up there with the giraffe, the camel and the hippopotamus for the grand prize for ugly.

But if evolution is truly responsible, why in Flinderation doesn't he have a tail with a big brush on the end long enough to reach up and chase those bloomin' flies off of his face? If only he had been designed so that he could make both ends meet.

But it must have been evolution. After all, you shouldn't try to blame God for every little thing that doesn't turn out exactly right.

SNOWSHOES

The fuzzy animal that many people call a "snowshoe rabbit", isn't a rabbit at all. It is a hare. But all you have to do to know why it is called "snowshoe," is to look at its hind feet. This hare has bigger hind feet for its size than one of my many cousins had for his size.

He wore size eighteens. And that was before he was full-grown. You can't hardly ever find that size on a store shelf where they sell hand-me-downs and most of the time not even in one of those dual-purpose catalogues. My cousin tipped the scales at something over three hundred pounds, so he needed a good understanding.

The snowshoe hare, on the other hand, is only a little larger than a cottontail rabbit. It took some time to determine why he needs such big underpinning, especially when they are placed so far back. They must be almost twice as big as the hind feet on a cottontail, counting the hair. That isn't a pun, even if it does look like one.

I don't know what the big difference between hares and rabbits really is, but if you are hunting rabbits in Northern Ontario (in season, of course) and you see something that is about the size of a rabbit, has long ears like a rabbit, hops like a rabbit and looks like a rabbit, shoot it. If it turns out to be a hare, it doesn't take quite as many to fill a cook pot.

When I was a boy, we wouldn't shoot a rabbit for food until after the first hard frost. Rabbits had warbles in the warmer weather. That is the correct spelling. A warble is not the same thing as a warbler, which has feathers and sings pretty. A warble is a maggot. That isn't a nickname. It is the larva of the warble fly. The fly lays its egg under the skin of a wild animal such as a rabbit, a squirrel, or a farm animal such as a cow or a horse. The egg grows into a larva which lives under the skin.

I have seen a cow which had been assaulted by a warble fly stick her tail straight out behind her and run like a hokey-pokeyed cat. She could have saved her energy. By the time she took off around the pasture field, she had already been violated, in spite of her bellows of protest.

The warble or larva grows to about an inch long and about as big as one of those old-timey lead pencils with the eraser inserted in the upper end which sold for a penny apiece. There is a small hole at the skin surface that exudes a liquid, making the warble easy to spot. There is also a lump that is usually visible at the surface to indicate where the warble is living. The warble disappears after the first frost. We considered an infested animal as unfit for food. And food was the only valid reason we had for hunting. We hunted a lot.

The hares and rabbits belong to a zoological order which scientists call lagomorphs. Some people believe that the rabbits and hares are rodents. They do chew on live grasses, trees, shrubs and briers, and I have even seen them chew on boards (probably for the salt) around a barn or smokehouse, but they are not rodents. It has something to do with the differences in the teeth. Now that is really splitting hares (I just couldn't help myself.)

I was putting you on back there a few paragraphs when I said that I didn't know the difference between hares and rabbits. There are several differences, but when an animal the size of a cottontail rabbit or a snowshoe hare is moving at about eighteen or twenty miles an hour and heading for tall cover, and there is a little round bead on top of a long tubular piece of blue steel between you and the target, you are not going to take the time to go over all those differences before the rabbit (or hare, as the case may be) reaches cover. You are going to pull the trigger and study the differences while you are enjoying a little hasenpfeffer or a brown-fried hind leg, if you are a straight shooter.

I just read a variation of a story that I heard way back there in the thirties. The story I read was about deer, the one I heard was about rabbits. The one about the rabbits was funnier and about fifty-odd years nearer the original.

33

A friend of mine had bought a twenty-gauge double from a guy who said that it was the best rabbit gun that he had ever owned. He wouldn't part with it for love nor money ordinarily, but too much love at the wrong time had resulted in fourteen little rabbit hunters who sat around the table with their mouths open waiting for something to eat that didn't have long ears and big feet. He may have been a used car salesman, too.

He said that he had killed all the rabbits in those parts except one smart old rabbit. That rabbit lived on the top of a dome-shaped knoll at the very top of the highest hill around. The knoll was covered with broom sage. That isn't real sage. It is a nuisance weed that is nothing more than a tall skinny grass that turns brown in autumn and grows thicker than Courtwrights in that part of the country. And that is some thick.

He made one last-ditch effort to put some meat, namely rabbit, on the table for the hungry younguns. He toiled his way up the mountain to the knoll. He spotted the rabbit. The rabbit spotted him.

He had only one shotgun shell left, a Remington Nitro-Express loaded with number six shot. He knew that he dare not miss. There would be no second chance. He took careful aim just as the rabbit crossed from left to right at top speed. He led what he thought would be just right and followed through with the gun just as he should have. He had made a perfect shot. He ran down to pick up the rabbit, but it wasn't there.

He knew deep down that he couldn't possibly have missed that shot, so he walked around the knoll for about a half to three-quarters of a mile and wound up at his starting point. He looked at his watch and saw that it was right at noontime, so he trudged back to the house to break the bad news.

He sat at the table and stared at the younguns and thought about the rabbit. The longer he thought, the more he was convinced that he had hit that animal, so he decided to take one more look.

He plodded back up the mountain about one-thirty to take a good look. He went to the exact spot where he had last seen the rabbit. No signs. He got down on all fours and started searching in the grass for some clue as to what had happened.

34

He was spreading the blades of grass apart when he heard a "ssst, ssst, ssst" above his head. He kept on looking, and when he heard the same noise a second time, he looked up and there went that charge of number sixes, every one of them with a bead of sweat on it as big as a green pea, still chasing that confounded rabbit. I can't remember if he got the rabbit, but he sold my friend that very same shotgun.

I think that the extreme effort must have strained the gun because my friend was never able to hit the side of a barn with it. From inside.

The Lagomorpha order has another family member that you might ought to know about. It is a small animal called a pika. I don't have any idea how he got to be a member of that family. He looks like a red-headed stepchild if you ask me.

He doesn't look anything like a rabbit or a hare that I ever saw, except that he does have fur of sorts. He looks more like a rat that backed into a rotary mower. He doesn't even live where any self-respecting hare or rabbit would want to take up permanent residence.

He hides on some of the highest hills in this country among rocks and boulders where there can't be a whole lot to eat. When he is disturbed, he runs right at one of those rocks, and you would swear that he is going to slam his head right into it. At the very last instant, he disappears. When he gets turned around, he sticks his head back out, and then you can see the hole or chink in the rock where he disappeared.

I suppose that it is a good thing that he does live out west in the Rockies. If he lived here in the East, somebody would have already figured how to cook him to make him taste almost as good as round steak, especially if he had lived in West Virginia where it is somewhat difficult to get more than a thousand or so acres of flat ground for wheat or corn and steak is dear.

If you get very much involved in the study of the lagomorph family tree, you will find that there are more branches than you can shake a stick at. The pikas look pretty much alike to me, but authorities say that there are more than thirty subspecies of that little rascal alone. There are twenty or so subspecies of hares and rabbits on this continent. I don't want to go anywhere else to try to make a tally.

I don't want to stray too far from the primary animal in this chapter, the snowshoe hare, but it might be well to tell you a

35

little about the pika and how he is similar to and how he differs from the rabbits and hares while I am telling you about the similarities and differences of those two. I might even slip in a peculiarity or two.

Pikas don't have long ears. Their ears are about the shape of a single lobe of a four-leaf clover. The four-leaf clover is carried by a few superstitious people as a good luck charm. Pikas carry rabbit feet. Rabbits carry rabbit feet for good luck, too, like some people. They usually carry four, but the charm doesn't work for rabbits like it does for people.

Practically every rabbit alive today will wind up in the belly of some predator (including man) or be the victim of parasites or disease before the year is out. That is a fiscal year, not the calendar year. And it doesn't make any allowance for road kills. It is estimated that only about a fourth of them will survive to reproduce the next year.

The hare and rabbit families make up the largest group of prey animals on this continent. I don't know about the other continents. I haven't had enough time to explore this one thoroughly. The only reason that they can survive such depredation is their ability to reproduce in unbelievable numbers. They believe in quickie courtships, quickie marriages, quickie kids and quickie divorces. Two rabbits can multiply so fast that you need a pocket calculator to keep track of the bunnies. There is one small factor to be considered.

I once had two friends in Fairmont, West Virginia, who decided to go into the rabbit business. After I tell this true story, I may have two less.

The business of raising rabbits for market is, theoretically, a lucrative business. Tame rabbit, cleaned and dressed, sells like chicken in some areas, except that it sells for more money. They are cleaner than chickens, and the meat has a better flavor to the connoisseur, so it brings a higher price. On top of that, chickens lay only one egg at a time—the hens, mostly. It takes a hen fifteen days to lay enough eggs for a clutch, and she has to have a visit from the rooster every day. I think that is the same thing as a "consort." It may be just an escort. In the natural state, she might hatch as many as twelve chicks from the clutch if the eggs don't get wet or cold, or if the rooster is the man he thought he was. It takes twenty-one days from the time she starts to "set" to achieve her goal. It takes another five or six months before the young are fit to peddle.

Rabbits are entirely different. The male rabbit starts "feeling his oats" about a month before the breeding season, and by the time the female is ready, he has already been. And getting anxious. He has been biting and kicking his buddies around and even picks on some of the reluctant girls. He jumps straight up into the air and turns pinwheels and cartwheels. He sometimes attacks car wheels. I don't think that running into a moving car wheel has anything to do with having sex on his mind. If it does, he has made a big mistake.

It takes about five seconds for him to get a receptive female in the mood and about the same length of time for him to complete his task. As soon as the first explosion is over, he may fall over onto his back and lay there with all four feet in the air. The female (called a "doe") understands and waits patiently for him to recover from his thrill of a lifetime. In a few seconds he jumps up and goes at it again. He may repeat the performance a number of times at one meeting. His efforts are good for a whole bundle of eggs, and he rarely has to be called back because he failed the first time.

When he fertilizes the doe, she drops her eggs, or ovulates, after the fun session. She may drop more than fifteen at one time, but some of them that are not fertile will be absorbed by her body, along with any dead fetuses that might be present. This is called "resorption."

She can give birth to as many as ten bunnies or leverets. That number may be less than the chicks, but the rabbits don't have to wait so long to reproduce. She is ready again the next day, and the new females are ready within three months. And they don't worry about incest. By the end of eight months, there are still only twelve chicks, but there can be as many as two or three hundred rabbits, assuming no fatalities. Actual counts are around thirty leverets from each female for a full season. In warmer climates where the breeding cycle can produce six litters instead of three, the numbers get out of hand.

Now you can see why we need hawks, bobcats, lynx, minks, weasels, men and cars. The cars get their share along the roadways.

Looking only at the figures, what they had was a gold mine.

My two friends purchased a couple of large domestic rabbits for breeding stock and placed them together in a cage. They then worked furiously to construct additional sophisticated cages to take care of the anticipated large family. Then they waited for their fortunes to begin to multiply literally as fast as rabbits. And they waited. And waited. And waited.

They learned two things about evolution during the period when they were expectant fathers. Rabbit daddies, that is. After about five or six months of waiting for the rabbits to decide to start up the production line, they finally discovered that both of the rabbits were males (also called "bucks"). If you want evolution to work properly, you have to provide the proper environment. The idea of unmixed marriages is unacceptable to rabbits. You have to have a male and a female or it will fail miserably.

Then they made their second mistake. They told their wives. That's how the rest of the world found out about it.

One of the friends left the country and moved to Florida. The other stayed in Fairmont and tried to live it down. I am not going to give you their names. They have been through enough.

Hares and rabbits belong to the family Leporidae or leporids. The pikas belong to another family in the order Lagomorpha. We are told that they all descended from an ancestor who was common to the deer and elk as well as the lagomorphs. Now you can see what I meant back there in the beginning when I told you that we were all brothers.

Hares rarely build a nest. They dig a shallow depression in the sand or dirt and deposit the young there. They are born ready to run. Their eyes are open, and they are fully clothed. Hares rarely care for the young beyond two days, maybe less.

Rabbits build nests, usually at the end of some burrow they have borrowed from some other animal that has abandoned it. But not always. They sometimes build nests in a patch of briers or dense brush. The nests are lined with fur from the doe's underbody and sides. I have seen some with bits of string and soft manmade materials in areas where there is human habitation. I have seen females whose undersides were almost as bald as the heads on some men. I said almost.

The young are born stark naked and with their eyes closed. They may be afraid to face the world that awaits them. They are ready to leave the nest in about two weeks. When they do, they can eat clover and broad-leaf plantain and other tender plants. After about five or six weeks, they can start killing your fruit trees like their parents.

Cottontail rabbits are now thriving in the East. They have accepted the presence of man and have learned to live with him. I have a few rabbits that feed in my lawn and under my bird feeder. They like the grain that the birds kick out. I can walk outside, and they normally pay me no never mind, unless I walk toward them and get within about fifteen feet. About the only predators that they have to worry about are free-roaming dogs, and house cats, some of which accept the rabbits as part of the neighborhood. I don't own either. Once in a while some dummy will come in and start shooting within a few yards of some of the houses on the periphery of the development, but not many do that. I can't see the fun in hunting tame animals, even if they don't have Christian names.

Rabbit hunting in the eastern states is big-time stuff. Time spent in hunting, breeding and raising rabbit dogs, and training them runs into millions of hours annually. The expenditures for guns, shotgun shells, clothing, boots and other paraphernalia runs into the millions of dollars. The rabbit is probably the most hunted of any game animal, and the annual kill is estimated at something around thirty million, depending on whose figures you accept. It is a delightful sport, and the eating is fine.

Most of the cottontails in the East are descendants of some Eastern cottontails imported into the eastern states from a few midwestern states around the early part of the twentieth century. The New England cottontail which was here couldn't stand the gaff when the area became overpopulated beyond his liking. He could not successfully adapt to the changing tides of civilization and urbanization. The new rabbits could.

We have a few snowshoes here in West Virginia. Comparatively speaking. They live in the higher elevations. Northern Ontario has a pretty heavy population, but that isn't what it used to be. Back in the fifties, we have counted them along a dirt road at dusk and would average as many as twenty or more to the mile. That is one whale of a bunch of hares. We haven't seen numbers like that for several years. Ontario is getting a lot more traffic from both Canadians and foreigners (that's us).

There is another hare that should be mentioned in this space. It is the Artic Hare. I'm not sure that he should be considered eastern, since his range is far north and spans both east and west. He is a whopper as rabbits and hares go. He can reach ten to twelve pounds and more than two feet in length. That is a lot of hare. This hare also changes from brown to white—or vice versa, if you want to raise a question, since winter is a good deal longer than summer in his homeland. It eats mosses and lichens and has been known to sneak in a bite or two of meat once in a while when it is available. It usually produces one litter of a half dozen or so in early or midsummer. Up there it only takes about two quick blinks to completely miss that season.

There is one more eastern rabbit that deserves some mention. There are really two, if you want to call it that way. One is the swamp rabbit, which lives along the Mississippi from Alabama to Texas. It is the largest of our rabbits. The other is the marsh rabbit, which lives along the Atlantic coast from Alabama to Virginia. Both are cousins of the Eastern cottontail. Both seem to like water and will take to water to avoid predators quite readily. The Eastern cottontail will do that too, but not with the same frequency.

Cottontails are relatively gentle creatures and make good pets. A young cottontail is easy to tame, but I would not advise trying to make a pet of one. They harbor ticks, fleas and other parasites. They can also have tularemia or "rabbit fever" which can be transferred to humans.

The western hares and rabbits are not such important game species as their eastern cousins. They are considered as pests and are subject to extensive efforts to exterminate or drastically reduce their populations. The rabbits include the Desert Cottontail, Nuttall's Cottontail and the Pygmy Rabbit. The hares include the Blacktailed Jackrabbit, his northern cousin, the Whitetailed Jackrabbit and the rare Antelope Jackrabbit. Jackrabbits are fast. They can hit thirty miles an hour and as much as thirty-five with the throttle open. An Antelope Jack can cruise at more than forty.

The jacks are considered as pests. They eat valuable forage grasses which are needed by livestock. They girdle fruit trees and shrubs just like their eastern cousins.

Evolution (or something) made the jackrabbits as fast as greased lighting. It was also responsible for the big feet on the snowshoe hare. I have often wondered why; I finally figured it out.

Sometimes a dedicated researcher will become obsessed with a single subject. When that happens, he may ignore the obvious. That is exactly what happened to me with the feet on a snowshoe.

Then one day as I watched a huge Siberian wolf trot along a dirt road in Northern Ontario, it hit me like a flash. Hares like to sit at the side of a dirt road and throw dirt and sand all over themselves. I have seen them almost buried in soft sand and they will still be digging until the sand is piled up on their back.

Those big hind feet are the most sophisticated defense system that the hare has against the wolves that like a little hare in their soup now and then. The hare waits until the wolf is just about ready to make his leap to grab supper with both jaws, and then he uses those big feet to throw almost a bucketful of sand in the wolf's face.

Have you ever tried to run with a handful of sand in your eyes? You run into fences, trees, rocks and everything else that pops up in your way. If it works on you, it ought to work on a wolf.

One thing that I haven't figured out about rabbits, hares and pikas and evolution is why they eat their own excrement. I told you earlier that I might mention a peculiarity.

If evolution is so cotton-pickin' smart, why didn't it provide the lagomorphs with a digestive system designed to get all the good out of the food on the first time around? Why does it have to make the second trip?

If you ever find the answer, let me know. I've quit looking. It turns my stomach.

BASS

Once upon a time many years ago when I was still young and foolish, I fished for several species of fish other than walleye. Almost any kind that I could possibly catch, and even some that I thought that I couldn't.

Don't let that opening sentence fool you. I may not be quite so young as then, but I'm still just as foolish, and I still like to fish for other species.

I like to fish for striped bass (which we always called "rock"), bluefish, flounder, drum, spotted weakfish (which we call "sea trout"), perch (both sand and brown), brook trout (also called "speckled trout" in Ontario and "truite mouchette" in Quebec), brown trout, rainbow trout, lake trout, Quebec red trout, crappie, carp, catfish and bass. That list isn't anywhere near complete, but it was getting too long.

When I am on the arctic watershed, I fish for walleye because I like to eat as many as my two hundred and twenty five pounds of solid empty will hold. I no longer go after any other species unless I have near my limit. But I often catch others accidentally. I hate to think about how many years that I have already spent up there and realize that there cannot be that many more.

But I smile when I think about how many fish I have caught over the years and have turned loose for someone else to enjoy. I suppose that I am like the old fellow who was on his deathbed and was regretting the time that he had not spent with his kids as they were growing up, graduating and getting married. He had missed all that association because he was off somewhere fishing. But he had caught one whale of a bunch of fish. That could have been me.

I didn't always fish for only walleye while in Canada. Back there in the early fifties and sixties, I fished for speckled trout in Ontario and truite mouchette in Quebec. I have caught a boatload of both. I have kept somewhere around fifteen to twenty to eat—total. I have fished for lake trout (called "truite gris" in Quebec) and I have caught more than a boatload of them. I have kept less than ten to eat. I have fished for bass in Canada, and I couldn't begin to guess how many of them I have caught. I have never kept a one. My better half has caught hundreds of them, too, and she has kept only two. The rest were returned unharmed to furnish pleasure for someone down the stream a piece.

I was sorely tempted to keep one smallmouth bass one time. My wife and I were fishing a tiny lake in Quebec and how we happened to fish it is a story in itself.

We saw it on an area map and asked several natives who had already steered us to some excellent fishing holes if it was productive. Everyone told us that there were no fish in it. We bypassed it for a few years, but one day when we were just out exploring, as we frequently do, I slipped the boat into the water to do a little looking. We were interested only in the flowers, trees and animals that we might see along the shoreline. We weren't looking for fish. The lake was so clear that you could see every pebble in sixty feet of water, and there was no sign of bottom growth or structure. But I always carry a rod or two and some gear.

When you are in a small boat it is sometimes necessary to go to shore, especially when you have a member of the opposite sex with you. She sees flowers growing on the shore that she needs to look at a little more closely and pine cones that she wants to pick up and any of at least a dozen other things that will serve as an excuse to get her feet on dry ground once in a while. That day was no exception.

We docked at a fallen tree that had lodged against the shore and climbed out of the boat to forage. We had not paid a lot of attention to the lake while we were moving around it because after the first fifteen minutes or so, we had seen nothing that would lead us to believe that there might be any fish in it. We had made the circuit with our noses pointing skyward while we searched the shoreline for wildlife.

But when I returned to the boat for boarding, I stepped on the log pretty hard. When I tilted my 225 pounds forward, I stepped hard on just about everything, including logs. Out from under it shot a little bass about five inches long. I pointed him out to my wife, and we quit looking for flowers.

I told her that where there was a baby there had to be a pappy and maybe a mama or two and maybe even some other more ancient ancestors. We retraced our course, but this time we were pointing our noses toward the water and looking down instead of up. And I was wearing my Ray-Bans. We were not more than two hundred yards from the tree when we spotted a school. They were suspended over bottom that was devoid of cover in about sixty or seventy feet of water and about one third of the way down. We caught every fish in the school and some of them at least two or three times before they quit hitting. It was like the teacher had told them that school was dismissed.

We tried a few more casts and then moved on. We saw a small bay with a few deadheads sticking above the surface. A "deadhead" is a log that was a part of a raft during timbering operations many years ago. The rafts of logs were placed in a lake or stream for holding until they could be transported to the mill or sawn at the site. The log became waterlogged on one end, and that end sank to the bottom and became lodged in the mud and muck of the bottom. The upper end was still buoyant and remained at the top of the water long enough for the lower end to become fixed so that the log has remained there in either a slanting or an upright position ever since. They deteriorate very slowly. We have observed some deadheads over a period of forty years and can detect very little change in some of them. Timbering in that area had been done forty years before, and the lake had been used as a holding area for the logs.

We approached the deadheads carefully and cast to the area several times before we came to one that was completely submerged, slanting toward the surface in about fifteen feet of water. I tossed my homemade lure beyond the log so that it would pass within about six inches of the upper end when I retrieved it.

Everything broke loose at once. I had a powerful strike and a hook-up which I could see clearly. For once in my lifetime I did not get the "buck aguer" until later. The monster smallmouth took off for deeper water and away from the deadhead. Sometimes the Lord smiles on even sinners like me.

We fought and we tugged at each other for what seemed like hours. He didn't attempt to return to his hangout. If he had, it would have been "Katy, bar the door." I couldn't begin to turn him when he decided to make a run. My wife tried to get to the motor to get it out of the water, but she couldn't make it. She tried to paddle to follow him. That helped some. I couldn't let loose long enough to do anything.

My mother had finally given up on me and capitulated by buying me an Airex Larchmont spinning reel and fiberglass rod for my birthday. It was my first spinning outfit, and I was using it that day. It was a good thing I was.

They don't make that reel now, or at least I don't think they do. I haven't seen another one except my two for years. I have retired one of them with highest honors.

Everything worked perfectly and when I finally got him in the boat, he was the great-grandpappy of those that we had caught earlier. I did not have a tape nor a scale to determine his actual size, but I laid him on my arm with his tail even with my fingertips and his snout about an inch or so from my shoulder while my wife took movies of us. He was the biggest smallmouth I had ever seen. His broad tail sent a wigwag signal of thanks when he swam lazily away.

I took my wife's cousin, Earl, with me to Canada about six years later and took him to that lake for bass. I sent him into the little bay. The lake was still as clear as before, and he found the bass. We could see from our boat that he was after something, but he wasn't successful. He was using jigs and said that the bass would come up and bump the jig with his nose but wouldn't hit. He also said that he didn't know how long he was, but his tail was more than ten inches wide. I didn't see him that time nor since.

We did see evidence of some traffic that time. A bush road had been built along the east shore to reach some small timber. It didn't come nearer than a couple of hundred yards, but I'll guarantee you that evolution has taken care of that bass, either in the form of some fisherman or through pollution. All acid rain and runoff doesn't come from coal-fired plants. He was a fine figure of a fish and deserved the best.

I seem to find all the small lakes to fish, either by accident or by design. We were fortunate enough to need some shore time near an almost vertical cliff on one of our walleye trips. There was a good-sized stream tumbling off the top, and I decided to investigate the source. We clambered up the cliff and followed the stream a few yards through the bush and spotted a small lake. We skirted the lake while keeping one eye peeled for flowers and the other for fish. I spied the fish. Bass.

Fishing from shore was almost impossible. Even walking around the lake would have been difficult. But we found a way that offered a little easier access. It would not be too difficult, but it would require a portage up a steep incline with a boat, a motor, and all our gear.

When I got back to camp, I engaged one of the operator's sons to guide us on opening day. He was a full-grown boy and had experience in guiding. He could also pack a heap of gear.

My wife and I always take enough gear to hold us for a few days, just in case. We like to carry heavy loads, so we always tote enough gear to fish the Atlantic even when fishing a pothole. We have had people laugh at us for carrying extra rainsuits, extra food, extra rods, extra reels, extra lures and extra gasoline. But we catch a lot more fish. And I haven't had a one of them laugh when it poured the rain, and my extra rainsuit was the only one within miles, or when their rod broke and they asked to borrow mine, or when I offered them an extra sandwich or a cup of hot coffee from one of my three bottles so that they could warm their fingers by holding the cup while they drank, or offered to tow them to the landing when they ran out of gas. That is an example of evolutionary evidence that is immediately apparent. It is amazing how quickly evolution works in those cases and causes people to assume an entirely different outlook.

I always take at least six gallons of gas, even if the lake we are going to fish is only a mile long. We have never run out of fuel, but we have towed a lot of people who have. We were fishing on a particularly long lake in northern Ontario one time when we saw another boat. There was a man and his daughter in the boat, and they were flashing a light at us for help. The lake was nine miles long and we were within a half mile of the lower end. It was a good eight miles back to camp. When we investigated, they had run out of gas. It was dark and time to

46

quit fishing, so we towed them back to the upper end of the lake. We were the only two boats we saw, and they had only one paddle between them. That would have been a long row to hoe.

I would bet that you will ask, "Why didn't he just give them enough fuel to take them back to camp?" And I will reply, "I don't do that, not even in my own boat." I did lend my extra battery to three guys who were stranded in Chesapeake Bay about six miles from the landing. We were in a huge school of bluefish that were running up to eighteen pounds. The blues were hitting like mad, and I didn't want to quit long enough to tow them to shore.

I won't do that anymore, either. I should have taken a cue from a larger boat who had heard their plea for help on the radio and wouldn't respond.

We drug a small boat up the grade a day or so before and placed it at a convenient landing. On the morning of the opening day, we were at the portage at three thirty. We packed the motor, gas and fishing gear up the slope and loaded the little boat. We were ready to fish at about four.

The rental boat was designed for only two people. We were crowded into that little tub for several hours before I would give up long enough to go to shore to stretch my long legs. I took the camera with me when I climbed atop a big chunk of the Pre-Cambrian Shield. After I looked at the movies of my wife and the guide in the boat, I saw that there was no way that I could have been in there, too. Bumblebees can't fly, either.

But we caught bass that day. Boy, did we ever. All smallmouth bass and up to about four pounds or a little over, but most of them about two.

We didn't keep any fish. The guide said that he wouldn't have missed the experience even if we had paid him nothing. He had never seen anything like it. But he learned a thing or two about bass fishing.

My right shoulder got sore during the day, but I kept on fishing. It turned numb, and the numbness spread down my right arm, and I was more than three months getting over it. The guide had started counting about halfway through one of my winning streaks and said that he had counted twenty three straight casts on which I had caught a bass. I missed a strike on the next cast at the edge of the boat.

We were using a homemade lure and had cut the barbs from our hooks. Neither of us even injured one of those fish. The guide fished for only about thirty minutes and then just ran the motor.

We came off the lake at a little after ten that evening, which made an unusually long day for the guide. He ordinarily got ten dollars for the day. He figured eight hours was enough for that amount and he was worn to a frazzle when we got back to camp. But his eyes lit up, and a grin spread from ear to ear when I handed him his money and told him to keep the change. I don't remember if he said, "Thank you" or not, but he did say, "Do you want to go back up there in the morning?"

I had another pet bass a long time back that lived under a huge boulder on the Buckhannon River, in West Virginia. My father-in-law and I fished the river for bass several times every summer. I had caught that bass and measured him with a steel tape rule, so I know how long he was. He was just about the same size as the one that I caught in Quebec. Evolution took care of him, too.

A man and his two sons who lived in the area were poachers of the worst kind, if there is such a classification. They came down the river one night and dynamited every hole in a three mile long stretch of the river. I found the shooting wire, but I never saw the bass again. The only consolation I have is that when they killed him, he must have been lodged under the boulder. Someone would surely have mentioned a twenty-six--inch smallmouth, even if it was acquired by illegal means. That is a good-sized bass for these parts.

We used to wade the river and fish for bass with minnows, soft shells and hellgrammites in the riffles and deep holes. We always caught a backload of bass and turned them loose. After the dynamiting, we caught nothing. I haven't fished the river for several years now, but when I fished it the last time, I caught only stocked trout.

Industrial and domestic waste has polluted the river until it would be almost as hazardous to your health to eat fish from it as it would be to smoke cigarettes. Evolution takes care of everything eventually. Especially if it gets a little help from man now and then.

I want to be funny, but sometimes there are some things where it is impossible to find anything to laugh about.

48

Polluting and poaching are two of them.

My father-in-law and two of my wife's cousins and I were fishing a small creek in West Virginia for smallmouth bass. One of the cousins was the same one who saw the bass in Quebec, the other was his brother, Glenn.

The three of us younger fellows had not been back from our respective branches of the service in that other big one for very long, so this took place in the middle to late forties. Even wars have some beneficial aspects. This one gave some temporary relief to the fish populations which allowed them to expand.

Earl and Glenn were born hillbillies who had migrated to Washington, D.C., prior to the war, but their feet hadn't become accustomed to walking on that flat ground. They both still canted a little to larboard when they walked, just a few degrees off plumb. And neither of them could ever walk a straight line.

You get that way when everywhere you want to go is on the opposite hillside or a couple of ridges over. The state police in West Virginia have long since stopped trying to make native DUI suspects walk a straight line and have them instead walk the dividing line on a sharp curve in order to keep from arresting teetotalers, who are a genuine minority. I have never seen a hillbilly who could walk or drive a straight road for more than about a quarter of a mile without swerving to the other lane or the berm. I'm not sure if that is a result of evolution or environment. It may just be a result of all those ramps we eat.

The four of us were scattered along the tail of a long pool, the riffles just below that pool and the headwaters of the next pool. I, being of a generous nature, allowed the rest of them to fish the upper pool and the riffle while I fished the headwater of the lower pool where all the fish were. They needed the practice.

Dad and Glenn were busy telling dirty stories. First one and then the other would break loose with a whopper. They were roaring with laughter at every punch line of every raunchy tale. Don't let it ever be said that my father-in-law didn't appreciate a funny story. Glenn was just as bad. Earl was joining in occasionally, whenever he could get a word in edgewise.

Glenn got so busy trying to match Dad story for story that he allowed his line to drift down the riffle until it was directly in front of me. I was about twenty yards downstream.

We were all using bait casting reels and black nylon braided line. We might have heard of spinning reels at that time but we had never seen one.

When we fished with live bait, we always allowed the bass to run on a slack line for a few seconds. After he stopped to turn the minnow, we would allow him to start again before setting the hook.

I gently pulled Glenn's line toward me and then placed my boot over it so that it would reeve freely under the instep. I began to pull the line steadily, letting it drift on the surface of the pool below me. I must have pulled at least twenty yards of line from the reel before Glenn noticed that he was losing line.

Dad hadn't been paying attention to fishing any more than Glenn had, and when Glenn said, "Wait a minute. I'll finish that story after I catch this fish," Dad became alert and started telling Glenn how to do it. He advised him to give the bass more line. Glenn replied, "The S.O.B. has had enough line now to reach to China." Dad insisted that he wait until the bass stopped to turn the minnow. I kept pulling the line gently until surely the bare shaft must have been showing. I was laughing so hard that my legs were shaking enough to make ripples in the pool where I was standing but I was not making a sound, even though my ribs were aching. Earl had seen what was happening, and he was about to split. Just about the time that I was about to erupt, Dad yelled, "Jerk!" and Glenn gave a mighty heave that would have turned a nice bass inside out had there been one on the line. Earl and I both exploded. When Dad saw what had happened, he roared. It took Glenn a couple of seconds to recover from his dreams of a monster bass. Then he roared, too.

Evolution has taken care of that stream, too. The area became more heavily populated, and you know what that does. Look at Washington, D.C., or Detroit, Michigan. It is hard to remember that at one time the only substantial building in Detroit was a fort and stockade. And it was occupied by "the enemy." It is more difficult to remember that Washington was once a peaceful swamp where robins and meadowlarks gave out with their sounds. Compare that with the stuff that you hear coming out of there, now.

That is evolution at work.

BEARS

The bear which I know best is the one which is most familiar to all Easterners, and the one which is most familiar to the majority of Westerners, the black bear.

I like to keep you guessing as to what crazy thing I'm going to do next, so I decided that instead of starting in the middle and working toward both ends as I usually do that I would start this chapter at the beginning. That is when what is to me one of the most peculiar things about a bear takes place. It happens to a few other animals, too, so maybe it is not quite so peculiar as it seems to me.

Bears normally mate in the spring, but the sperm is not implanted in the egg until six months or so later, when the female ovulates. If the female (or "sow") doesn't have enough fat stored in her body to carry her through the winter nursing two or more cubs, she doesn't ovulate, and pregnancy doesn't occur. If she is in good condition, she becomes pregnant at the time of her ovulation, and the gestation period starts from that time rather than from the time of copulation. The cubs are born while the mother is in her winter den, and by the time she is ready to emerge, the cubs are more able to cope. That is in the areas where there is reason to "den up" because of cold weather.

It was believed for a long time that the bears hibernated. They may "den up," but it is not true hibernation. They do become dormant.

The cubs are very small, weighing only about a half-pound. The births are usually multiple with twins predominant. There

51

can be as many as four or even five young, but those numbers are unusual.

By the time fall hunting season rolls around, the cubs will weigh about sixty to seventy pounds or a little more. By the next year's fall season, they will weigh around 125 pounds. They will accompany their mother for as much as two years if there is no interruption of life in that period.

West Virginia prohibits the killing of bears under one hundred pounds. This protects the cubs until their second year. It is rather easy to tell that a bear is too small because of the difference in poundage between a cub and a yearling. A yearling is one that is in his second year of growth and until he reaches his second birthday.

Male black bears will reach a weight of three hundred pounds. Some get larger. I heard of one bear that was killed in Randolph or Pocahontas County, on Cheat Mountain in West Virginia, that was said to weigh 636 pounds. I didn't see it weighed.

I did see it alive, and it was big. It was engaged in fighting a pack of bear dogs, and it would knock a sixty pound dog end over end for about fifteen or twenty feet through thick rhododendron. I tried to shoot but couldn't for fear of hitting the dogs. By the time I was in position for a possible shot, he was heading northwest, and I was looking at the rapidly disappearing southeast end. The one with the stubby tail. I didn't get near enough to feel his muscles to see if he was solid so that I could guess his weight accurately.

I killed one bear that field dressed just over 240 pounds. I hunted a lot of them after that, but never shot at another, although I have had opportunities. I like bear meat. It is second only to moose in my list of favorite wild meats, but I figured that I had killed my quota. They have enough trouble from everyone else.

Six of us were hunting with a bear hunter who owned dogs and hired out as a guide to groups during bear season. He charged a reasonable daily fee that made you wonder how he managed to feed the dogs on the income that his guiding must have generated. He must have been doing it as an excuse to give his wife for his treks into the woods.

We had hiked into the backcountry for something over six miles before the dogs were turned loose. There was a fresh track in the three or four inches of snow, and the dogs hit it at a gallop. They hadn't gone more than a couple of hundred yards when the whole pack tore into a laurel thicket. Laurel is hillbilly-ese for rhododendron. I was leading a female bluetick that was a good trail dog. The guide yelled at me to turn her loose. By the time he hollered, I was already at the edge of the thicket.

When I turned her loose, she dived into the thicket and I dived in behind her. The brush was so thick that I couldn't walk, so I crawled on all fours until I could go no farther and then went to my belly and elbowed my way in to where the dogs were fighting the bear.

There was no way that I could shoot without hitting a dog. I started helping the bear by grabbing the collar of a dog as it leaped to grab the bear. As soon as I got a firm grip on one, I would pitch it into the laurel. After I had disposed of three or four, I had a chance to shoot. When I pulled the trigger, the gun muzzle was only about six or eight inches from the bear's head. He did not suffer.

It took the rest of the gang almost thirty minutes to work their way into the thicket and to reach me and the bear. They were breaking their way in and making a trail to carry the bear out. And carry is exactly what we did for the rest of that day.

We cut a stout pole and suspended the field-dressed bear from it. Then we took turns two-by-two carrying that bear up the mountain to the vehicles. There were twelve sore shoulders and an equal number of tired legs by the time we had toted it the six or seven miles back up a rugged trail to the road.

When the rest of the men got to me, one of them asked, "What would you have done if your gun had misfired?" I told him. I would have just grabbed a handful of brown stuff and thrown it into the bear's eyes and blinded him. No need to ask where I would have got it. I would have reached behind me, and it would have been there, waiting.

Bears don't normally attack human beings, but there is always the chance that one of them hasn't read the book. There are far too many conditions when they will that makes it not too smart to tempt them.

One hunter that I know told about another fellow who was hunting in the mountains above Durbin. He cornered a bear in a laurel thicket, and the bear had gone into a hole in a rock cliff. There were no tracks coming out of the huge thicket, so he went to the home of an old mountain man to get his help. He offered the old fellow fifty dollars to go down with him and cut a trail through the brush in order to reach the bear whose tracks indicated a right good size.

The mountain man had seen bear hunters before and was reluctant to go, but fifty dollars cash was more than a week's pay. The hunter finally convinced him that he wasn't afraid of bears and there would be no problem, since he was an excellent marksman. They went to the thicket.

He took his double-bitted axe and started cutting a trail while the others watched the edges. His bear hunter was behind him in the trail and ready with his brand new Remington semi-automatic 30-06.

They had made their way toward the bear and the dogs for probably fifteen or twenty feet when the bear decided that he had enough of that blamed foolishness. When he bolted, he took the easiest route, the trail that they were still cutting. Before the bear got anywhere near the mountain man and the hunter, they started backing out. The hunter threw his rifle into the laurel and took off at a dead run, leaving the old man to fend for himself. He was backing out as fast as he could when he caught a heel on a laurel stub and fell over backwards.

The bear came on, snarling and roaring, with saliva foaming out of his mouth and dripping off his lower jaw. The old man was stretched out flat on his back, still clutching the axe with his arms outstretched beyond his head. The bear slowed to finish off one of his tormentors, and the old man swung the axe with all his strength. It caught the bear in the middle of his forehead, and he collapsed on top of the old man. By that time, there were others there to help and they finished off the bear and pulled it off the old guy.

When he finally got to his feet, still carrying the axe, he lit into that hunter and called him every dirty name that he had ever heard, and then coined a few new ones on the spot. He also went back into the thicket and located the new rifle, retrieved it, brought it out to a nearby tree and proceeded to break it into as many pieces as possible. The hunter stood there with his

54

mouth wide open as he watched, but he didn't give the old man any lip. He wanted to get home in one piece and figured that his chances were a lot better if he didn't shoot off his mouth right then.

The mountain man also told him that he was taking his life in his own hands if he ever came back in those hills to hunt. He meant it.

That hunter wasn't me, just in case you are leaning in that direction. I am one of those stupid people who doesn't get scared until later when I stop to think. Then I fall to pieces.

I took a fellow with me on his first bear hunt. We went to the same general area where that happened. I had questioned him about the possibility of watery blood, but he assured me that he was not easily given to backing down. I took his word for it.

We went to an open area where there were eight or ten shallow caves that had been used by bears when they "holed up." It was a good place to jump a bear, and I had hunted there many times before. It was just after daybreak when we reached the cliff, and I started searching for signs. There was nothing that would indicate that the bears had left the area, so it was likely that there was a bear in at least one of the caves.

I stationed him in an open space where he could see and cautioned him not to shoot me when I came out leading a bear. I told him that the bear would probably be trailing me by a few feet, and we would both be moving at something faster than a leisurely walk. Bears can't run too fast on slippery terrain, and if one had been chasing me, he would have been running in *slippery*.

I worked all the caves, confident that I had competent help if I got into trouble. When I hit the back of each cave with the beam from my flashlight, there weren't any bears.

When I came out of the last one and went to pick up my buddy, there was nothing there but a candy wrapper. I trailed him away from the cliff and to an old logging road that led down to the trail. When I finally caught up to him, he was more than one-half mile away, leaning against a tree and smoking a cigarette.

I don't normally use foul language. I think that it bespeaks some gap in one's intelligence and a huge deficiency in adequate vocabulary. What I said to him might not have had any four-letter words, but it melted the snow for at least six feet around. I forgot to tell him about the candy wrapper. I didn't even mention evolution and how it had affected him, but that was only because I didn't think of it at the time. And we ended the hunt right there. I seriously considered more drastic action, but I knew somebody would be sure to miss him where we both worked.

My next-door neighbor and one of my best friends was also my assistant scoutmaster. He was also a hunter. He had never hunted bear, but he wanted to try. We took off early one Saturday morning in his vehicle for the mountains. He had heard stories about my driving with both eyes shut.

I had hunted with him before and thought that I knew him like a book. There was no way that he would let me down if I did some stupid thing and got myself between a rock and a hard place. We have hunted and fished together many times before and after this episode, and I can assure you now that my confidence was well placed. We and our families have spent some delightful days and weeks together in the outdoors. He is the kind of a friend that only happens to the lucky ones.

We left home in Fairmont in beautiful weather. It was cold, but there was no threat of rain or snow to make driving treacherous. We got all the way to the top of Cheat Mountain before we hit rain, snow, fog and sleet just under the crest. We were only about eight miles or so from our destination, so we decided to go on.

We had gone only a mile or two when I spotted fresh bear tracks crossing the road. We were driving slowly enough, about fifteen miles per hour or less, that I could see the tracks clearly. It was still another two hours until daylight, but the tracks were easily visible where they went down the road embankment and ended at a wet-weather pool that had not frozen. The water looked as black as pitch, but there were no tracks going away from it.

I hollered at June to stop the car. When he hit the brakes, we found out how slick it was. There was no stopping. After he got the car headed back down the grade, he feathered the brakes, and we finally got stopped about a quarter of a mile down the road where it levelled off. We turned and went back up the hill. This time the car stopped just past the crossing. I suppose that having it headed uphill may have helped a little.

56

I grabbed a flashlight and climbed out. I was wearing a pair of old sheepskin moccasins that flopped on my feet like a pair of oversized pillowcases. They were hard to keep on my feet, but they were warm over my wool socks. I liked to put on my hunting boots after we got to Uncle Luke's and Aunt Grace's house and had a second breakfast of homemade sausage or ham and buckwheat cakes like the ones we made back on the farm.

I held onto the car and made my way to the tracks. The roadway was covered with a coating of glare ice and about two inches of snow on top of that. It was hard to stand without sliding, let alone walk.

I went to the other side of the road while June watched from his open car window. I looked for tracks leading away from the water hole, but there were none. I hit the switch on the flashlight and aimed it at the water hole.

I still didn't see any tracks leading off. What I did see was a good-sized bear coming at me like a three hundred pound fullback with his head down. I tried to move to get out of his way, but my feet couldn't get traction. He passed over the same trail that he had used going down within three feet of me, and I took after him.

When he hit the road, he couldn't get a foothold either. His feet left streaks a yard long as he tried to escape that crazy human who was right on his tail. The feet on that idiot were leaving streaks on the road that were even longer, and my floppy moccasins were not helping. The only time that I could ever remember when the bloomin' things wouldn't fall off was right then when I wanted them off.

My feeble mind had played a terribly dirty trick on me, and all I could think of at that moment was catching that bear and clobbering him over the head with that little two-cell flashlight. And I was trying.

My traction was only slightly better than the bear's and I was gaining on him an inch or so at a time. Just as I was ready to tackle him, his front feet hit the gravel behind the car, and he went from two to sixty in two seconds flat. Probably one of the luckiest things that has ever happened to me was when that bear got his front paws where he could scratch gravel.

If I had jumped on that bear with only that flashlight, I would have already been a part of evolution, maybe fossilized,

57

instead of sitting here writing about it. I fought a much smaller tame bear one time after that, and he could hit you hard enough to make your eyeteeth rattle, and he was just playing.

June was first startled, then concerned, then amused. Not just amused really. He was laughing so hard that he had to pick little ice balls off the side of his face where the tears had frozen. He may have just been crying from relief that he didn't have to haul me back to Fairmont and hand me over to my wife in a sandwich bag. A greasy one.

We came back after breakfast and tracked that bear for more than seven miles before additional snow covered his tracks and we had to abandon our chase. The bear probably figured that he wanted no part of humans who weren't any smarter than that. All we got was a long winter hike and a hearty laugh, and a bear tale to tell our grandkids. We're still enjoying the laughter and the grandkids. My great-grandkids will soon be old enough to hear it. I'm looking forward to that.

Here in West Virginia, we usually hunt bears with dogs. I like to hear them run, even when I have absolutely no intention of killing a bear.

I got foolish one time and got a couple of bear dogs. If that were the only time that I had been foolish, it wouldn't be so bad, but with me it seems to be a habit. Bears, fish, rabbits, fish, deer, fish, turkey, fish and fish. It is a good thing that my wife has inexhaustible patience. Or at least that is the way I perceive her to be.

I got a good deal on a pair from the same litter when a friend of mine got to be what is called "doggoned poor." They were sisters and as nearly alike as day and night. They each had four legs, a tail, a nose and a couple of ears, but beyond that there was no resemblance.

They were a little like the two horses that the fellow bought and was telling his cronies about down at the country store where they gathered on winter evenings to pass the time and swap yarns. He said that his team was perfectly matched, and it was almost impossible to tell them apart. He had paid a good deal of extra money just to get a pair that was so well matched.

He went on to explain that they were exactly the same size in all directions and would work together better than any team he had ever seen. The only slight difference that anyone had ever noticed was that when he flipped the black one with the lines, the white one would flinch.

My little dog, "Blackie," weighed about fifty pounds and was as black as night. She wouldn't look at any animal except a bear and was one of the few good trail dogs that I have seen. If a deer ran in front of her while she was working, she would pay it no never mind. She might give it a casual glance to be sure that it wasn't something she wanted and go right back to sniffing for bear. She kept her mind on her business, but she couldn't fight worth a hoot.

The big one, "Mitzi," was huge. She weighed in at well over a hundred pounds and would run anything from field mice to deer, but she didn't pay any attention whatsoever to a bear track unless she went along with Blackie just for the fun. She was colored a light brindle, and when she put her paws on my shoulders, she could look at me eyeball to eyeball, and I stand six-three in my lightweight socks. She would fight anything that walked if you told her, "seek." That is the old pronunciation for that newfangled word, "sic."

My father-in-law kept the dogs at his house next door in an abandoned chicken house and pen. He had a monster of a possum that had taken up residence under an old building. He had lived there unmolested for a long time and was more like a pet than a wild animal. Dad got the idea one morning that when the possum was out he was going to see what the dogs would do if they met him. He turned them loose.

Blackie didn't pay a bit of attention to it and raced toward the back porch to say "hello" to Mom. She knew who buttered her toast. Mitzi took one look at the possum and went to join him for a little romp. Only she played rough. She opened her jaws and clamped down on the possum. Her jaws spanned his back and reached down both sides. She brought her new playmate to Dad and dropped him at his feet. He was far beyond "playing possum."

Some guy who trained bear dogs prior to hunting season took them to his home on Files Creek, above Elkins, to run them through their paces.

He reported that they had taken after an old "she" bear with cubs and had gotten between the mother and children. They were teasing the cubs when the sow came in from their rear and wiped them out with one swipe that took everything from stern to stem. It sounded a little fishy, but I was naive, I guess. I could understand one fatality, but two was unusual.

I was hunting with a new friend on Middle Ridge about three or four years after that man had died, and we talked about hunting. The conversation drifted around to bears and dogs.

When I told him about the two that I had owned, he remembered them clearly and described them to a tee. A dog of Blackie's caliber didn't come along every day or two. He said that they were not killed by a bear. The guy had sold them to a hunter from Maryland, who paid him twelve hundred dollars for Blackie and took Mitzi as a part of the deal. One of them would not work well without the other. That was back when that much money was more than three months' wages.

The black bear is scattered over a wide range in North America. It can be found today in the northeastern states, and in the mountains to Georgia. It ranges all of subarctic Canada and our northern states. Its mountain range in the west extends from Montana into Mexico, and from Washington to California. It can be found in the Ozarks, and in Louisiana. Its range once exceeded those limits.

It was once fairly plentiful over most of its range, or as plentiful as a meat-eater can be. Meat-eaters or carnivores depend on vegetarians for food and will not normally exceed the numbers that their territory will support. Bears are a little of both and maybe a little beyond.

As I said in an earlier chapter, bears will eat just about anything that can't move fast enough to get out of their way. Their diet consists of other animals, berries, fruits, roots, bark (the inner layer), grasses, carrion and garbage. You may be able to think of more that I failed to mention. Years ago, a friend and I counted eighteen bears on a garbage dump that was within a mile of the village. That is not really unusual in bear country.

I have gone with bear hunters in Ontario, where they hunt over bait for spring bears. I have seen a bear come to a bait of rotten beaver or fish and attempt to tear it down. I have seen lots of bears come to garbage or carrion on the ground. I don't have any desire to hunt that way. It is productive and it may be okay for others. I'm not knocking their method, but it isn't for me. It is illegal to shoot within a specified distance of a garbage dump.

Bear populations were seriously depleted with the westward spread of population and civilization. Settlers killed them for food. Farmers blamed them for killing sheep and other livestock. Some of the blame may have been justified, but much of it was not. The bears were killed. There was an occasional human death accredited to bears. More bears were killed. A bounty was offered for bears in some of the mountain counties of West Virginia as recently as the late fifties. There were protective laws then, but county courts effectively negated them.

We have become a little smarter in recent years, and our population is again growing in some areas. It is a slow process. It is estimated that the total black bear population in North America may be near half a million.

The black bear depends on wild or remote areas for his existence. He will live with people, but people have a tendency not to care a whole lot for living with him for any extended period. He can be rough on your assets.

We were camping in northern Ontario, in what was only a year before a wilderness area. A bush road had just been opened to the public for access to a lake, and the word had gotten out through one of our well-known sports magazines. We had forty-three other camps in the small area and we were jammed together worse than if we had vacationed in the Bronx. I'm lying, of course. It was only about half that bad.

We had gone in on Thursday and set up our tent in an area outside the campground. The campground was jammed full of tents, trailers, campers and what-have-you. The site we chose was open, and our closest neighbors other than our friends from Ontario, were almost a quarter mile away. We went fishing on Friday, and returned to find the area where we were camped crowded. I parked the wagon and the boat directly in front of the tent.

I should have stuck my boat at least ten feet away on one end of the tent and the wagon on the other.

Our friends were camping in a wall tent on one side of us. That helped. A family from Ohio came in near evening and squeezed their folding camp trailer in beside us on the other side and proceeded to unload all their food and gear on the ground under the overhang nearest our tent.

61

I tried to tell them about the bears. We had seen more than twenty different bears, all of them adults, but two were small cubs. The bears were not afraid of people.

They politely told me that they had camped before where there were bears and knew all about them. I returned to my camping area and watched.

They piled the food and gear directly under the beds and then proceeded to retire. We could hear every word of their conversation. The older couple who must have been the grandparents were sleeping on the side nearest us. They argued (in fun) about who was going to sleep toward the outside. The old man got into bed first, and his wife had to climb over him to get in or out of bed. It was a circus.

They had just gotten into bed and quieted their talk when a bear came by for a snack. He went immediately to the cache and knocked over a plastic garbage can of food. He got his back under one of the struts supporting the bed and started to scratch. He lifted the end of the trailer, the bed, and the older couple, and bounched them as if they were featherweights. I don't remember the exact sequence of events, but they screamed and yelled loud enough to wake Ulysses S. Grant in New York, and then four bare feet hit the floor simultaneously. The old woman came out of bed with both knees in the old man's belly and onto the floor. The adults in the other bed got into the act, and then the kids. The bear was by that time shaking the whole trailer. Their response was predictable. We don't use the same kind of language in our conversation, but it became hilarious. But they believed me then.

They poured out of the camper like mad bees from a hive. The bear ambled off. He probably didn't care much for the language either.

Another couple from Ohio had backed their pick-up camper in toward the bush. They left an aluminum icebox on the picnic table with a lead of lettuce and a pound of butter inside. A bear found it almost before they closed the door on their camper. He opened the icebox from the side with one swipe and found the lettuce. He downed it in two quick bites and then reached inside and found the butter. He started eating it, wrapper and all. After the main part of it had followed the lettuce, he sat there trying to lick the rest of it off his chin, face and forepaws.

We had our minor problems, too. I had a hard and fast rule that we leave the boat uncovered in bear country. It usually smelled strongly of fish and I didn't want some nosy critter tearing the cover off or a side out to get at something that wasn't there. I had seen a couple of new aluminum boats that had been visited by bears. They weren't what you could call shipshape after the bears got through with them.

I have hard and fast rules about a lot of things when I am camping. I like to sleep dry, eat well and relax comfortably. I make rules to insure that those things happen, not necessarily in that order. But there is often one person in the party who doesn't adhere to the rules. I had told her to put everything that smelled like food into the wagon and to make sure that the windows were closed. I loaded the stove, the table, the clean pots and pans and the food boxes. What I didn't load was the dishrags and towels that she had used. We finished our cleaning at dusk, and she hung the cloths to dry on the outside frame of the tent, just over her bed. She always sleeps to the outside of the tent, for two reasons. One, I'm pretty good-sized, and she can't move me once I get in before she does; and two, I want to be nearest the door when a bear comes snooping around.

I always sleep with a poleaxe and a fire extinguisher at my head and a six-volt lantern at each side of the bed so that we can both have one. Just in case. When I'm in the states, I add a gun, a big one.

We had just settled in when we heard a loud "whoosh" just outside the window and over my wife's head. The tent vibrated. Nobody had to tell me what it was. I grabbed the gear and headed outside with my wife at my heels.

The bear had heard the commotion and moved on. He went to the next tent where our friends were already in bed and asleep. There was no floor in their tent, and one of the young boys had slid out of his bedroll, and his bare feet were sticking out from under the tent. The bear strolled over and stuck his nose against the bare tootsie and swiped it with his tongue. That got results. There was a squall from inside the tent, and everyone hit the ground at once. The bear acted like it was nothing new to him.

The next evening after supper, we were sitting around a big bonfire that a couple of fellows had built near their tent. Some of the men were playing cards at a picnic table while the rest of us sat around and chewed the fat. The same young lad was sitting on the end of the bench watching the card game. One of the men nudged him and whispered to him to go around and shake the fifty-five gallon drum that was the garbage can.

Just as he rattled the can, which was only about twenty feet away from the semicircle of people sitting around the fire and talking, the agitator yelled "bear," and everyone jumped. He got the results he was after.

The boy had just returned and taken his seat on the bench when the can rattled again. Nobody yelled "bear" that time. A huge bear stood beside the can on all fours. His shoulders were at least eight inches higher than the rim of the drum. For you who don't know bears, that adds up to a big black bear.

He tipped the can over and investigated. When he found nothing inside worth eating, he walked casually away as though the humans presented no threat to him. He was right, we didn't.

He knew we were there. The fire blazed at least four or five feet high. He didn't care. He just walked in and made himself at home. The area had only been open for less than four months, but he must have established a working relationship with humans in that short period of his association with them.

Another episode that took place in that campground happened in broad daylight. A woman from Ohio who was camped in the regular campground had two small children. They were both preschoolers, and she was standing in the doorway of her trailer watching the two toddlers chasing a pair of bear cubs. I told her about the bears. She immediately yelled for the kids.

This is one problem that I have with the "Disney Syndrome." Many people know only what they see on television. All bears and deer and other wild animals are not tame. If you treat them as though they were, it can get you dead. Quick.

The only thing that saved those youngsters was the fact that their daddy and one of his buddies were chasing the sow with their motorcycles. I tried to get a conservation officer to interfere before someone got hurt, but he said that he was not allowed to say one word to them unless something happened. If that sow had turned, there would have been at least one stripped Harley. The conservation officer agreed that either or both could be mauled or killed. If that happened, he could offer assistance. He thanked me for telling the woman, and I stood by to give first aid to any survivors.

Wild bears are wild bears. They will kill to eat, if necessary. They will also kill for other reasons. A sow will defend her cubs from any threat, including a man with a gun. She may sacrifice herself for her young. Many wild animals are equally protective of their offspring. A mother moose, a mother grouse, a mother turkey or a mother deer will do most anything to defend the young.

While we were on that trip which spanned a time period of five weeks and a distance of a little over three thousand miles, we camped out every night but three. Two of the nights we stayed in a motel were back-to-back. That was when we went to Quebec City to try to trace my ancestry. One of my ancestors was killed in the Battle of Quebec, which took place there before there was a United States.

One of the places we camped in Ontario was a short distance from where two girls were killed in their sleeping bags by a bear. We didn't know about it until we read it in the paper a day or two later. There was a lot of guessing as to why they were victims.

Bear populations are beginning to recover from their lows in the first half of the century and the latter part of the last. There are still some problems with depredation. Bears are often blamed when some other animal is the culprit. Once one does start killing sheep, there is usually nothing to do but destroy it. Relocation sometimes helps, if the bear can be released in an area where there are no sheep, and other food is available. They would rather eat smaller animals, but when they find that sheep have little or no defense, they go for them.

Reduction of habitat is probably the biggest factor in bear declines. The bears must compete for food where there is none or very little. When that happens, the females fail to become pregnant, and the males kill and eat the cubs. I know of no other animal that has both these built-in controls on numbers. Other animals may have one of them.

The growth in bear populations is primarily due to those awful hunters who shoot them and other wild animals for sport and to other outdoorsmen who are bent on destroying all wildlife. These "bloodthirsty" people have contributed more

65

time and money to the preservation of game and nongame animals than all of the antihunters put together. (Uh-oh! I just lost my chances of this ever becoming a textbook right there.) Uneducated schoolteachers have fallen for the falsehoods or just plain lies of the antihunting groups. Some of them have even started teaching these lies to our kids. The hunters and outdoorsmen who practice sound principles of conservation have contributed to the acquisition of lands for public use and for habitat for both game and nongame animals to a greater extent than all of the rip-off artists and do-gooders in the antihunting and antigun movements put together.

The crazies who want to take away their guns don't want to acknowledge the facts. The only real objective of the antigunners is the destruction of the United States. They may want to keep the name, but they don't want the system. Your guess is as good as mine as to what they want to replace it with. Think about it, and listen with both ears when one of them opens his mouth. Don't be misled by flattery and lies. That is known as "soft-soap." If you don't believe me, read the Communist Manifesto of 1917 to see what it says about us.

The legislators in both the federal and state governments and in the local bodies who oppose private ownership of guns obviously have just that in mind. They deny it vehemently, but their actions speak so loudly that I can't understand what they are saying. If someone can prove to me that gun controls prevent crime, I would like to see that proof. Washington, D.C. has a terribly restrictive law against handguns. It hasn't helped them. It hasn't helped New York. It made crime more prevalent in that little hole-in-the-wall town out in Illinois. Look at the record.

Hunters are strongly opposed to poaching. Poaching isn't hunting, it is stealing. Legitimate hunters don't shoot game wardens or conservation officers, only poachers do that. Hunters know that the officers and the department which they represent are their best friends. If you have a friend who is a game warden, ask him about the truth of those statements.

Our system of jurisprudence is against hunters and hunting. It generally treats poachers with leniency. One judge said that one poacher only wanted some food for his family. Baloney! If he can afford to buy a thousand dollar rifle, a three hundred dollar telescope sight, and possibly a backup night sight that runs more than four thousand dollars, all topped off

66

with a twenty-two thousand dollar four-wheel-drive pick-up, he can afford to eat the best Porterhouse steak and feed it to his dog.

Poachers don't hunt for food. They hunt for money. A poacher is very likely a member of an organized crime group which peddles animal parts to the highest bidder. Who would want to eat an eagle?

There might be the rare case where some old farm boy shoots a deer for the food. It is far more likely that he would shoot it for destroying his food crops. That isn't really poaching, but he should get a permit.

Poachers have made a big hole in black bear populations in some of the western states and to some extent in some of the eastern states. They are killing the bears for the gall, which can bring as much as three thousand dollars for each bladder. The dollars are United States dollars and are tax-free because they are not reported. If you think that a poacher is going to report that much income which might affect his welfare check, you need to see a shrink.

Guess what happens to the carcass. It is left to rot. That is how much these crooks need the animal for food.

The belief in the gall is similar to the belief in ginseng, which is a really endangered species in the wild. Neither one actually works, except psychologically. If you have been studying populations in Asia, you know that they don't need much artificial inspiration. What they need is some artificial decimation. You must realize that they are doing a pretty good job of complicating the manmade environmental and ecological problems which are all a result of overpopulation. They don't need any help from bear gall and ginseng.

That may be difficult to face. Sometimes it is hard to see the forest when you have your nose pressed tightly against the largest tree.

If humans had the same built-in safeguards that bears have, I'll bet that you would see a lot more skinny women. The men would insist on it. I like the fat ones better, myself. Up to a point.

Humans do have a number of artificial systems to take care of a part of the problem. Abortion takes care of a few unwanted pregnancies. Spermicides, devices, abstinence and surgical procedures take care of several million more. We will eventually see more of these systems used as we try to control population numbers. That is if the sun continues to shine and the rain keeps falling once in a while. Sometimes it takes a long, long time to get just a little bit smarter.

If those statements seem to be a wee bit far out, take an objective look at Haiti and Ethiopia with an eye to the ecology. If that still doesn't convince you, cast a jaundiced eye toward China and India where they are in the process of self-destruction through overpopulation. If you are still in doubt, ask yourself how long New York City or Chicago would survive without a complex support system operating from outside.

That may sound hard and cruel, but evolution is even more hard and cruel. Evolution is going to happen. We may have some control over the outcome if we get into the game soon enough. But evolution will still be around long after you and I have become a part of the downhill side of it.

HUMANS

The subspecies Homo Sapiens, which is the only surviving member of the family Homonidae (not to be confused with Homonoidea—careful, now) of the larger primate order, has evolved a complex system of life that is a far cry from the simple life that it once led only a few millennia ago—as we reckon time.

Much of this complexity has arisen in just the last few centuries as the species changed first from a totally nomadic way of life to an agrarian-based economy and then changed again from what was essentially an agricultural and rural system to an industrial and urban-centered economy. Following this transition from rural to urban life so closely that it could almost be considered simultaneous was a strong movement to return to a semicountry type of living which removed the participants from the inner city. The resulting settlements were called "suburbs," and the residents of those settlements were called "suburbanites."

The suburbanites were originally those who were somewhat more affluent and could afford the inflated property prices which tended to restrict the neighborhoods to members of society who were the social and cultural equals of the majority of the first transfers. The movement has accelerated in recent years to include just about everyone who can find the means, either through the federal government or through private sources, to make the move.

The system was further complicated by a psychological phenomenon known as "keeping up with the Joneses." History is rather vague as to when this phenomenon first appeared, but it might have surfaced at about the same time that

Cain led little Abel into the glade. As time has passed, the urge to slay has been controlled to some degree by the realization that there is some sort of retribution, or at least the prospect. Usually. The urge based on financial status or wealth display has grown stronger, probably because about the only place that hurts is in the area of the left hip pocket (for those of you who carry a purse, that is where a lot of people carry a wallet).

The nomadic life was spent primarily in an almost continual search for food consisting of wild plants, animals, fish and fruits or roots and in locating suitable shelter such as trees, caves, rock overhangs or simply patches of tall grass.

Clothing was nonexistent in the earliest part of this era and when it did appear, consisted of leaves, grasses, bark and pelts taken from those animals which had been killed for food. What little clothing was available was worn for protection and modesty, not for show. Christian Dior would have been without meaningful employment in that day and age.

The people were usually members of a small group that consisted of only the family which was expanded to include only a few generations. Large groups were impractical because they could overharvest an area quite rapidly and then be forced to move frequently in order to maintain an adequate food supply.

A reasonable comparison could be made with the deer herds today. There are areas where the deer have little or no predation, and populations grow rapidly to the point that the area cannot support them. Deer will literally eat themselves out of house and home and become weakened and eventually smaller from lack of food for extended periods. They will eventually starve if there is not some reduction in numbers from hunting by predators, including man.

Humans act exactly like deer, as witness the starvation in Ethiopia and in other countries. If you think that it couldn't happen here in the United States, you had better go back and rethink the problem. One three-year-long nationwide drought could make us dependent on Ethiopia for food. Southern California farmers were praying for water only a few months back. If they hadn't had some rain, they would have gone broke. The rain they received was only a temporary respite. Water is still scarce there. The human race has survived only because it could reason and move about in search of food and water.

The adult members of the group formed a simple council which was usually headed by a matriarch or patriarch who was chosen for the experience and wisdom brought to the leadership position. The leadership was often usurped by the biggest bully in the bunch. Whoever was chosen as leader, whether it be an old man or an old woman because of seniority and knowledge or the one with the hardest fists because he put knots on all the others' heads (primitive vote-getting tactics), apparently made the decisions as to where to hunt, fish and forage for food and where to seek suitable shelter. Decisions may have been made with the advice of the family council.

It is believed that the leader had the authority to banish wrongdoers or less desirable members. Banishment may have sometimes been the result of sibling rivalry or parental subterfuge. Judaic-Christian literature confirms this theory by the Biblical accounts of Adam and Eve and the casting out of Cain, of Abraham and Sarah and the exile of Ishmael and of Isaac and Rebekkah and the trickery which resulted in the expulsion of Esau. There are similar traditions in other cultures or societies which are matriarchal rather than patriarchal.

Leaders were sometimes chosen for their prowess in battle against wild animals or against other tribes or clans. This practice continued until late in the last century in some of the tribes of American Indians. It may still be in use to some extent in some societies. One example could conceivably be Saddam Hussein in Iraq, who strong-armed his way into the presidency and has retained that position by continuing those tactics. His successes were primarily against his own people, the war against Iran notwithstanding.

The matriarchal and patriarchal systems still exist in some areas and within some groups in some small fashion, although most have been and are still gradually being replaced by more democratic or strong-arm methods.

In the early nomadic system, the members slept in caves or trees or wherever they could find a place. They made nestlike beds of leaves, grass, reeds, straw or boughs. Nobody owned a tent until many years later when someone found that he could make a simple framework of limbs and sticks and throw two or three pelts over it, and the rain would drip onto the ground instead of onto him. This allowed him to sleep a little drier. Soon everybody had caught on. The yurts which are still used by

71

some of the nomadic Mongol tribes evolved from this humble beginning.

Some old guy woke up one morning several millennia ago with his arthritis and rheumatism hurting so badly that he could hardly coax one foot to move in front of the other and said to his younger buddies something like, "Ooga. Booga mooga, tooga yooga. Hooga looga zooga," which meant, more or less, "Oh, Boy! My back is giving me fits this morning. I don't think that I can keep up with you guys, so you fellers just go on along without me, and if you get back this way anytime soon, drop in and see me and the missus. We'll have a cookout. Be sure to fetch the meat."

He found a clear, cool spring of sweet water with a salt lick not too far off. The spring drained into a little marshy meadow and formed a small pond where the animals often came to drink.

There were several nice trees around for shade and a nice patch of ramps just up on the side of the hill where he could dig enough for a good mess every day or so. He could eat ramps to his heart's content.

He stuck some cattail and arrowroot that he had been carrying around in his ditty bag in the mud at the edge of the bog and planted a few little scrubby dandelion roots and some creasy greens (for you people up North, who are sometimes called "Yankees," often preceeded by one or more adjectives, creasy greens are the same thing as dry-land cress), and the agrarian economy was born right there on that very spot.

He caught a female wild goat and tamed it. When he noticed how the kids went after the milk so enthusiastically, he figured that maybe his kids would like it, too. He had already run out of places for the younguns to eat, since the last ones were twins, and the first one refused to eat bear meat and yams.

He tied the goat to a tree and started stealing its milk and giving it to his kids. They started getting fat.

He soon learned that the milk soured rather quickly in warm weather, so he dug a ditch from the spring and put the bowls of milk in the cold water. That helped.

As soon as the raccoons, dogs, cats, and groundhogs found out about the milk, they started knocking the lids off the crocks and lapping up a free lunch. To counteract these sneaky critters, he built a little house over the ditch and the spring. He called it a "springhouse."

You don't see many of those any more, either, but in my childhood they were common. I can remember my grandmother's springhouse (or "milk house" as it was called there) and the crocks and pans of cow's milk with the cream floating to the top. By that time in history, we had learned that cows give more milk than goats, and it tastes different. Cows are also bigger and make a lot more hamburger when they quit producing milk. And the fat isn't nearly as hard after it is cooked and reaches your stomach.

The milk house kept out the four-legged varmints, but at my grandmother's house, the milk kept disappearing anyway. Noticeably larger amounts came up missing when she had a particular visitor.

I'm not exaggerating when I tell you that I often drank more than a gallon of homemade nonpasteurized milk with all the cream in it in a day. And that was after I was old enough to have been long since weaned. I always took a pan with all the cream on it. That tasted better than the blue-John.

I don't know how Grandma figured out that I was the varmint that was getting into her milk, but she called me into the kitchen one day. We sat down in front of the woodburning cookstove while she explained carefully.

"Billy (all grandmothers call their grandsons "Billy" if they happen to be named "William" until long after they are married and have children of their own), I'm giving you a big pan of milk for your own. Just stay out of the others."

After they started pasteurizing and homogenizing milk and irradiating it with Vitamin D, it just didn't taste the same. I have a sneaking suspicion that "pasteurizing" may mean that they leave a lot of that stuff in there that should have been left in the pasture. They probably beat it up so hard that you can't find it.

You never see any cream on top, anymore, either. That is because they take out all of the good stuff (called "butterfat") and then squeeze just a little of it back in. Most of it goes somewhere else. They try to fool you into believing that less butterfat is good for you. What is really good for you is getting up off the couch where you spend all that time watching TV and going out to work around the house and lawn until you work up a good sweat. When the perspiration literally pours off you it is "sweat" and not "perspiration." Perspiration doesn't do you nearly as much good.

The milk house kept the milk, butter and homemade cottage cheese (it used to be called "smearcase") cool and palatable.

Years later, when the springs failed or when it seemed too far to walk, someone invented a box lined with cork and tin and called it an icebox. It was usually placed in the kitchen or on a shady back porch. There was even a guy called an "iceman" who delivered a piece of ice for a small fee so that you didn't have to run down to the pond in the winter and cut your own. That was hard work, and the ice was difficult to store, even when you covered it with sawdust about four or five feet deep to keep it from melting. The ice kept the milk and butter even better than the springhouse, and it was right there near the stove.

The housewife had a square card with a hole in each of the four corners. Each corner had a different number designating the size block that she wanted. This number was placed at the top of the card so that the iceman could see from the street how much ice he had to carry in.

I don't think that the job paid a lot of money, but I have heard that there were considerable side benefits. Sometimes it took so long to deliver a chunk of ice that neighborhood kids would raid the ice wagon and chip off several pieces to eat. I think I know who bore the cost of the shrinkage. It wasn't the iceman.

You hardly ever see icemen anymore, either.

Some other guy (his name may have been "Frigid") came up with another box with a big round gadget on top that looked for all the world like a huge bucket turned upside down and had rings around it. He called it a "Frigidaire." That was later shortened to "fridge" and it became the common designation for all refrigerators and even for a football player that I have read about somewhere or another.

When people started crowding together so that they could all live in one place, they didn't have enough room to keep a cow, and pasture was pretty scarce on asphalt streets. Some smart guy saw an opportunity and jumped on it with both feet. He bought a little place just outside of town and started buying cows to stock it. He did the milking and put the milk in little tin buckets and peddled them from door to door. He later

74

used bottles and jugs as milk containers, and at one point, he even put milk in the containers that the customer provided. They don't do that anymore, either.

The milkman outlasted the iceman by several years. He had free samples for the right people and for the right response to certain questions that often had little relationship to the dairy business.

There was a period of time in our history when the milkman and the iceman just about held this country together. They may have been responsible for a good deal of the population explosion that will eventually destroy us, but they held the country together with milk, cheese, butter, eggs and ice cream, even if they did tear some marriages apart.

The appearance of the iceman and the milkman on the stage of history was evolution. So was their passing. That signalled the end of an era.

The old guy back at the water hole needed a better place to sleep, so he slipped off down the "crick" a ways and stole a few aspen limbs and logs from a family of beavers who had a nice house down there below the pond. They had built their own little water hole right at the edge of the house.

He stuck the logs and poles into the ground in such a way that they formed a rough sort of cave and then he daubed a little mud on the outside to fill some of the holes and started calling it a "house." That was the beginning of the first housing development. We still build them that way today, but some people have made a few improvements.

He put the toilet inside sort of over in one corner and started calling it a "ba." He set up the eating area under a big white oak and called it the "dr." He laid a pile of flat rocks in a circle near the center and called that "the kitchen stove." He put his nest of leaves and balsam boughs over in another corner and named that the "br."

When the ba developed a strong odor that interfered with his eating, he moved the house over under the big tree and over the dr. He could now eat his food inside and egest it outside. That move proved to be a pretty smart one because it cut down on a lot of nagging from the womenfolk.

He quit calling it a ba and started calling it a "latrine," since it was now just a hole in the ground. He was a little workbrickle, so the hole was pretty shallow. The only improvement was a log to squat on.

When the cold winds began to blow in from the North and when he began to get squatter's cramp, he decided that it was time for a few changes. Evolution at work again.

He stuck a few cedar and spruce branches in the ground around the perimeter to slow down the winter breezes. That also made it a little more difficult for everyone and his brother to see what was going on inside, making it just a little more private, so he changed the name to "privy."

After several years of putting up with shedding needles and falling branches and cold wind whistling through the openings and around exposed parts and rain and snow adding to his discomfort, he came up with a much-improved version.

He hewed out some flat boards (splintery ones, I'll bet) and made a rough seat with two holes so that he could have company and just sit and talk if he wanted. At first, the holes were fairly close to round, but when the porcupines started gnawing on the board near the front edge of the holes and changed them into a roughly oval shape, he found that the "porkies" were pretty smart. The oval holes fit better, so he started making them in that shape. We still do.

He put up pole or board walls and chinked them with mud so that the wind didn't come through nearly so much. They were harder to see through, too.

He added a roof so that snow and rain wouldn't be all over the seat when he needed to sit down, and time spent there would be little more pleasant. No more frosty rings. No more wet backsides. You women who live in a house with three or more males know how miserable that can be. Every time you go, the seat is either up or wet.

He put up a hinged door for easy access. He cut a hole in the door, and to make it fancy, he shaped the hole like a little quarter moon. That may have had some significance in some of his superstitions, but it was probably for added ventilation. He needed all of the fresh air that he could get.

He kept a stack of green leaves in one corner, but these turned dry and brittle rather quickly and were then entirely useless. The first really big improvement over the leaves (and later, corncobs and then newspapers) came when a fellow by the name of Sears came out with a dual-purpose catalogue.

These catalogues are not nearly as popular as they were sixty or seventy years ago—for either purpose. Back then they were free and were just the right size and texture. With a little care, you could make two or three of them last for about four months.

The company started charging five dollars for one a few years back. The money was refundable on the first order, but who in tarnation wanted to waste a perfectly good catalogue for such foolishness as that? They also put in a lot of slick pages that weren't much good for anything unless you wanted to look at the pictures. Now, instead of using a catalogue, everybody just goes to the mall.

And if that isn't evolution, too, then I don't know from diddly-squat.

About the time he got it all nice and comfy, he found that he had to move it a little farther from the house. He kept shifting the location until it was so far back that there were a number of occasions when he had to run at top speed in order to get there in time. There were even a few times when he came up short. It was high time for another change.

He again moved it back inside the house. It has stayed there ever since. If you don't believe me, just read the real estate ads in any big city newspaper. You are likely to see ads for houses with two and one-half ba's.

He got tired of running outside in all kinds of weather to eat his meals. Rain made the cattail soup thin and watery. And when the weather got so cold that he had to break his hot coffee into chunks to drink it, he decided that he had had enough. He moved the dr back inside, too. This was a big improvement. The woman of the house could now get the roast on the table while it was still hot and juicy.

This new arrangement took up so much of the living space in the limited area due to a growing family circle and from friends and relatives dropping by unannounced for a little free grub from time to time that it meant either moving the dr back outdoors or building a bigger house.

Today we do both. We build the house bigger just to hold all the necessities of life, such as a dining table and twelve chairs and all the stuff that goes with them. We don't use them much anymore, except when company comes during a big snowstorm. We move the dr and the kt out to the pt

77

(sometimes spelled "pa") and cook and eat out there. We still call flies and bugs by the same names, some of which I refuse to print.

Back to the old homestead by the ramp patch.

The woman of the house (sometimes women) had all the really fun things to do around the farm. She cleaned the house, cooked the meals, baked the bread, cleaned the fish and game (and chewed the drying skins so they would be nice and soft and not scratch hubby's legs etc.), washed the clothes on a stone washboard, sewed the skins into garments and pouches, darned the holes, planted the crops, tended them in the summer and harvested them in the fall, preserved them for later use, bore the passel of kids and fed them and changed all their diapers and saw to it that they were ready for bed when night came. She didn't have much interest in bridge and women's clubs and stuff like that. The most of her time, she just laid around the house and slept.

I want to insert a little true story here that might reflect a little of her situation. My son-in-law was explaining the facts of life to his older son, Ricky. He went into some detail about the process and the results. When he had finished his discourse, he asked Ricky if he had any questions. Ricky didn't. Did he have any comments? Ricky thought for a few seconds and then said, "Boy, Dad, it sure does look like we have the easy part."

The man had all the really hard work to do. Hunting and fishing and getting drunk on elderberry wine and fighting with the neighbors. And lying around on his backside thinking up things for his wife to do so that she wouldn't get bored and start kicking over the traces and getting into a bunch of mischief. What with all her spare time, she needed that kind of help. At times if he couldn't find a neighbor to fight, he would come home all drunked up and whomp her a few good ones. Just to be macho. Some of us haven't evolved quite far enough from that.

As soon as she had all the crops harvested, she had to preserve them. She strung apples and beans on long cords and dried them. The beans were sometimes called "leather britches." I suppose because they were as tough as whiteleather. I'll let you look that one up in the dictionary for yourself. If you don't already know what it means, surprise.

78

Potatoes and tomatoes didn't do too well in cold weather, and meat and fish didn't hold up well in hot. Something had to evolve.

One day while he was down on the lower forty (every' farm back then had either a back forty or a lower forty) digging out a groundhog for tomorrow's lunch, he noticed that while the earth was frozen as hard as a rock at the surface, it was much warmer and softer about three feet down.

He didn't know a lot about inches or centimeters and stuff like that. A foot was one of those long flat things at the bottom of his leg. He had long since quit trying to measure vertical distances by walking up a tree or cliff heel to toe. He had a couple nasty falls doing that, so he just guessed at height. He later came up with the idea of using his hands to measure those distances by laying one hand alongside the other and repeating the process as many times as necessary. He called that distance a "hand." This was more complicated than feet. He decided he needed to be more specific, so he invented the span. Evolution has stalled in this case. We still use the terms that he passed down to us, but there are a whole bunch of people out there trying to foul things up—as usual. They talk in meters, ares, liters and a bunch of other silly things. I suppose that one of these days they will have it so fouled up that you won't be able to tell anybody how far you ran to get away from a bear.

He also measured from his elbow to his fingers and called that a "cubit," just to add to the confusion. I have also heard some people use another measurement called "an arm and a leg," but it isn't pronounced that way. I don't think that it is used to measure distance, but most of the people who use that expression seem to come from the area around the Hudson River, and it is pretty hard to tell what that bunch is talking about even when they are trying to speak English. It isn't any wonder with all these different odd measures that some people still don't know their elbow from a hole in the ground.

He figured that if he put some of his cattail roots and arrowroots in that groundhog hole and covered them with dirt, they might not be so hard to chew in the wintertime. He stuck a few turnips and some sweet potatoes in with them. He learned something else. No more broken teeth from gnawing on a frozen root. Dentists and orthodontists were few and far be-

79

tween back in those days, but their fees were a good bit cheaper.

The next thing he knew, he was lining the hole with leaves, dry grasses, straw and weeds and piling in cabbages, rutabagas, apples and all kinds of good stuff. That not only kept them from freezing, it made them taste better and much easier for his wife to dig out in the winter when she got ready to cook.

The cabbage hole, the potato hole and the apple hole have all but disappeared from the scene, and all within my lifetime. That is one evolutionary development of recent vintage which has literally left a sizeable hole in my list of favorite things. I won't, however, argue with anyone who says that modern cold storage makes apples and cabbages taste better and keep longer.

He eventually figured out that if he poured a bunch of salt on his fresh meat supply that it wasn't so likely to spoil so quickly. He also learned that it was even better if he hung it in the smoke from his cook fire for a while, as long as it didn't get too hot. The smoke seemed to repel the flies, and it improved the flavor.

We still use similar methods to preserve certain kinds and cuts of meat. Here in the United States we have one state that has long been famous for its smoked hams and bacon. I don't want to mention it by name for fear of some kind of lawsuit claiming defamation or something, but if you have never tasted a Virginia cured ham, you sure have missed some good eating.

Much of the salted and smoked ham sold in the stores today has been cured by injecting brine into the product and then using an artificial smoke to lend it the smoke flavor. These may be good to eat, but they don't hold a candle to a Smithfield dry-cured, natural smoked ham, especially when you have developed a taste for that sort of food.

He figured that if salting worked on bison and moose that it should also work on fish, so he started salting down fish in a heavy brine and packing them in stone jars and crocks. The containers were soon replaced by wooden barrels and small buckets. The salt fish was sold in these buckets in recent years and was once almost a staple on the backcountry farms as a breakfast item. The fish that we used were always lake herring.

I can't remember how they were prepared, but I do recall that it was necessary to soak them in fresh water to remove some of the salt. I tasted salt fish once, but I refused to swallow. And that was after it was fried up all nice and brown and was supposed to be good. It is a small miracle that we didn't all die at the ripe old age of fourteen or less, what with all the salt and fat that we ate.

Salt fish was also packed in kegs that held about forty-five pounds. These were usually stocked for those customers who wanted some salt fish but who had the good sense not to go overboard. I don't know if the net weight included the salt, but the way things were back then, a grocer could sell a lot of fish from one keg.

We now have a department of government that looks after weights and measures to be sure that if you say a fish is a foot long, it had better be more than eleven and a half inches. I don't think the law applies to a fisherman who just tells about the size of the one that got away, just if he tries to sell one. It's not really quite that bad in fact. Only in principle. The fact that we find it necessary to police people who should have been honest enough that they would not need someone looking over their shoulder to insure that the customers were getting a fair shake is that bad.

One of my careers was meat market manager and later, store owner. I can tell you now that someone could write a book.

We have evolved some silly laws to make sure that customers get what they pay for. We haven't made many that will keep you from being victimized by some con man or used car salesman. Not ones that could be easily enforced. The crying shame is that we feel that we need them.

Some fishermen in certain areas catch cod by the boatload, and after field dressing it, place it on a rack and cover it with salt and leave it in the sun to dry. When the huge slabs of fish are dried, they are as stiff as boards. The Spanish call this dried codfish "bacalao." The Italians call it "baccala." The English-speaking people that I have heard call it anything just call it what it is, which sounds like "peee-uuuuu." No matter how you spell it, it still smells the same—terrible. The fish is usually packed in barrels or huge wooden crates for shipment to less fortunate countries like the United States where there

81

are certain groups of people who go wild over the salt cod.

The next step in his food preservation was when he learned to can. I said "he," but it was probably his wife who came up with the idea. She did all the work, I'll bet. She was the one who had to see that his belly remained reasonably full. Whoever thought of it, the idea proved to be revolutionary as well as evolutionary.

At first, the canning was done in stone or pottery jars and crocks. We used the same method to preserve sausage when I was a boy. We would fry down the sausage balls, then place them in a five-gallon pottery jar and then cover them with grease, which was called "hog-grease," since that is where it came from. We didn't know about cholesterols, high-density lipids and low-density lipids back then. It would have made absolutely no difference anyway. We ate everything that we could find.

The canning was first done in the home and for the exclusive use of the family. Later, the families and neighbors began getting together to make the work easier. They formed a sort of cooperative for canning and preserving as well as for harvesting, milling, building, sewing and other activities that could be better done as a group.

Then along came some smart cookie who started taking some of the harder work away from the housewife by canning everything for everybody—for a small fee. Another smart boy came up with the idea of a vacuum-sealed metal can, and the industry took off like a scalded dog. The canning industry has become a huge business which cans all sorts of foodstuffs and stuff that is not food and wouldn't be fit to feed a cat. Tennis balls, for example. I even saw a canned item the other day that you wouldn't believe me even if I told you what it was.

We seem to get the government in on just about everything, and the canning industry is no exception. The Department of Agriculture (also known as "U.S.D.A.," sometimes without the periods) has a bunch of people working for it that couldn't make a living at a real job, and these people go around to the canneries and tell the canners, "You can," or "You can not."

Almost every industry now has government overseers. If you want to hear some wild stories about inspectors, talk to a small businessman who has been whacked by OSHA or to a coal operator who has had some delightful experiences with the guys and gals from MSHA. You will learn why the price of a ton of coal always seems to be just a little beyond your reach.

Our life in the industrial economy is based upon an extremely complicated system of barter in which the medium of exchange is money. In the United States this money is called "the dollar," and some joker is always fooling around with it trying to increase or decrease its value so that ordinary people who have to use it to buy food, clothing and shelter will be fooled into thinking that they are getting something for nothing. What they always get is less product or service for their dollar.

He also tries to manipulate interest rates so that he can steal from the old people who have slaved all their lives in order to put something aside for their retirement. He takes the money he steals from the poor old senior citizens and gives it to the "needy" billionaires. Sort of a dooH niboR. That is a Robin Hood in reverse. If you don't believe me, just ask any older person who has laid a little aside in a bank if his money is still earning as much interest. The excuse for this action is that it will improve the economy. If you believe that it has, go back to school and learn to add two plus two. Stocks have shot up. Prices have risen. Interest income has declined so that anyone depending on his own industry and thrift to support him in his golden years has found that the golden years may have turned to pot-metal years. If you think that it has induced people to buy more, take a look at the automotive industry—objectively.

In the United States, we call that joker the "Chairman of the Federal Reserve Board," as well as a lot of other things not nearly so complimentary. He must have a lot of people fooled, because he hangs onto his job pretty doggoned tenaciously. He should be listening to some of the people who are paying his salary, instead of some of those whom he is paying.

Until late in the last century and even until early in the present one in many localities, trading goods and services was a common practice. It was standard procedure to help a neighbor to get his hay in if it was threatened by weather. The debt was repaid when he came over to help cut (by hand, of course) the corn and shuck it for winter storage. It is still done on a very limited scale. The government sort of frowns on neighbors getting along so well that one can trade a day's work for a side of hog meat because his own hog died from becoming overheated during the dry spell back there in July and August.

The Internal Revenue Service has given us another commandment which says, "Thou shalt not barter, unless thou shalt pay taxes on thy bartering." There must be a lot of times when it is difficult to place a monetary value on the difference between a pot of dandelion and plantain greens (handpicked from the backyard and cooked on the woodstove) cooked with a chunk of fatback and a mess of creasy greens cooked with a piece of salt side. For you people who don't know the difference between fatback and salt side, fatback is the one without any lean streak. Salt side may have a little lean. But sometimes the lean streak is pretty thin. If it is fresh side meat, it may be called "streak bacon" or "streaked bacon."

The complex system which has evolved over the past several decades has been made even more complicated and confusing by a subsystem which is another product of government.

The government, back in the terrible thirties, decided that it liked the role of Robin Hood and started taking from the "rich" and giving to the "poor."

That philosophy was fine and began as a philanthropic enterprise with high ideas and ideals. The system was subjected to a great deal of abuse by unethical persons who were the worst kind of thieves, if one can say that one kind of thief is worse than another. These people stole funds designated for the truly needy by claiming disabilities when they were really able to work. Some transferred their funds to a trust over which they retained control and then claimed a lack of financial ability to maintain minimum standards of living. Many failed to declare income received from cash payments with no records of the transactions, thereby avoiding income tax and robbing the poor at the same time. They apparently thought that they were taking only from the "government." The government is *you.*

The "rich" turned out to be the coal miners, steelworkers and store clerks who were willing to work for what they got. The "poor" turned out to be those who wouldn't work in a pie factory. Some of these "poor" have been apprehended, and the incomes reported by government agents would knock you out of your easy chair. Some of the "takes" would be enough to feed a poor family for a lifetime and then some. The last one reported in the media amounted to well over twenty thousand dollars a month, and that was just what was reported. The culprit had over a million dollars in the bank.

There are those who are truly poor and who are unable for one reason or another to be employed. This diatribe is not directed toward them. It is directed toward those thieves who are robbing the poor and the disabled.

Professional people such as doctors, lawyers, accountants and consultants are much more prevalent in our society than they were only a few years ago. They probably are the most affluent group in our society—if you don't count entertainers, drug dealers, professional sports "heroes," crime lords, gamblers, real estate salesmen and a certain media mogul. And politicians (who may be any or all of the above).

Most of the adult members of our society today who do not fall within any of the listed categories work at some trade or other, such as coal mining, steel production, wholesale and retail trade and service industries just so they can get enough money to buy food and clothing and pay taxes so that those who grow food and make clothing can get enough money to buy food, clothing, cars and houses and pay taxes so that those who make cars and build houses can get enough money to buy food, clothing, cars, houses, motor homes and swimming pools and pay taxes so that those who build motor homes and sell swimming pools can get enough money to buy food, clothing, cars, houses, motor homes, swimming pools and hire lawyers, doctors and accountants and pay taxes so that the doctors, lawyers, accountants and consultants can buy food, clothing, cars, houses, motor homes, swimming pools and big insurance policies and pay taxes so that those who won't work can have free food, free clothing, free cars, free houses, free motor homes, free swimming pools, free doctors, free accountants and free lawyers who can sit back and tell them how to sue the free doctors for malpractice because he didn't tell them at least ten years before he met them that free cigarettes, free beer, free snuff, free whiskey, free marijuana, free cocaine and free crack might be injurious to their health or to the health of a fetus if the mother used any or all of that free stuff which they would have gone ahead and used anyway since the coal miners, steelworkers and store clerks were paying for it anyway and how they can continue getting all that free stuff which is so essential by unethical but still legal means and how to avoid or circumvent the law so that the lawyer can continue drawing huge fees from the county court which uses your money to pay them rates up to three hundred dollars per hour for representing these people whom they are helping to steal your money.

Now that is a long and complicated and repetitive sentence. I hope that you took time to read it carefully. You are the victim of all those crazy shenanigans since the money for all of it is coming out of your pockets. The system is just as complicated and deeply entrenched. And if we don't get off our collective duffs and insist that our legislators in congress and the senate and in our state legislatures get off their collective duffs and start doing something about it—and fast—it will swallow us alive. And it won't take a couple of millennia to do it.

The best place to start is to tell your representative that you want this blooming boondoggling stopped. If he persists, vote for someone else. That will get his attention.

He will probably pass the buck to the president. Don't buy that. The president can't spend a lousy dime unless congress tells him he may. Neither can he refuse to spend a lousy dime of any budget item.

Many of the lawyers use a part of the income derived from suing doctors, drivers and homeowners on a contingent fee basis (if you think that it doesn't pay well, just listen to their spot ads on television—they aren't doing that just to get rid of their money) and from the fees they get from you for representing a "needy" criminal through dozens of appeals and years of litigation after he has been found guilty, to run for office in the Congress, the Senate and the state legislatures so that they can enact laws that even they can't understand so that other lawyers can get enough money from advising hoodlums in skirting these laws so that the lawyers will not be tempted to run for office.

They also impose more taxes so that they can continue buying houses and the like for the "needy" who will supply the most votes at the time for elections. Sometimes the vote-buying is disguised, but only thinly.

They only talk of adding taxes to the rich. If you think that doesn't mean coal miners, steelworkers and store clerks, you had better return to school for a concentrated course in economics. No company has a single thin dime for paying extra taxes unless it first gets that dime from you. Most of the time, by the time you make your down payment on the tax, the dime has grown to at least twenty cents. All those handling charges, you know.

Taxing the so-called rich class may also mean that you can join the ranks of the unemployed. If no one is willing to buy the product you are making or selling, you are out of a job. One of the best reasons for not buying a product is an increase in net cost without a corresponding increase in net value, especially if the price increase is out of line with the cost of living increases. And if the extra tax places it beyond the reach of potential customers. Or if interest rates have dropped to the point that one of the largest segments of our market, the senior citizens, can't afford to buy it.

The best example of this that I can think of for 1991 are the depressed automobile and boat markets, which both got hit with exorbitant tax increases at the beginning of the year. Politicians (I immediately think of one from Illinois) will tell you that it had no effect. Ask someone who was paying attention (I immediatley think of another guy from Illinois who writes a syndicated column which appears in the *Tribune*. He is a top-notch columnist, and he makes a lot more sense than most. You ought to read him sometime).

If you do find yourself without a job, get the best lawyer that the rest of us can afford so that he can tell you how to sit back and draw your rockin' chair money and live high on the hog and eat Virginia Cured Ham (don't nitpick, that stuff is so good that it deserves to be capitalized) and Porterhouse steak while the rest of us eat fat sausage and "jailhouse steak." For the uninformed, that is the same thing as bologna.

This book is supposed to be funny. It pokes fun at almost everything that I could think of at the moment. I even thought of a couple of funny things that my wife wouldn't let me put in the book.

That last portion precludes humor, since it affects all of us so severely. Maybe one of these days I'll be able to look back and laugh at something or another within the whole terrible mess. But not now. Not while my eyes are still so full of tears that I can hardly see to write.

It sure isn't funny yet.

Evolution is the visible evidence of history. I don't know if anyone else ever described it that way, but that is what it amounts to. If that preceding piece doesn't describe something that is visible today and if it isn't history in the making, there isn't such a thing as a crooked politician.

Females and...

Some female members of a particular subspecies of the Homonoidea group of the primate order have developed a rather odd characteristic which seems to be unique to that particular subspecies.

Although the characteristic appears to be definitely physical, certain reactions among the female members of the subspecies who lack this characteristic or who display it in only a diminutive size lead me to believe that there must be more to it than meets even the trained eye.

I have not attempted to do any extensive research on any of the female members of any of the other related subspecies within the group (Homonoids) or even within the order (Primates). I don't like to make excuses for my shortcomings, but I have just been too busy with other studies that I have found to be more important and more interesting. Besides that, there is a considerable number of researchers out there who apparently preferred the company of those other subspecies.

These researchers were mostly university graduates who did or are presently engaged in doing postgraduate work, so they were far better qualified than me. Some of them had a string of letters after their names, like PhD etc. I didn't even get as far as the "P" and no one has offered to stick anything like that behind my name unless I was willing to work for it. I'm getting too old to start trying for something like that now.

I had absolutely no desire to get into some kind of a competitive situation with my fellow researchers who did have the advantage of all those letters, so I just threw up my hands and said, "Let 'em have it." I am going to stick with the subspecies which I have been studying all these years, albeit superficially, while they look at the apes, chimpanzees, lemurs, monkeys, ringtails and what-have-you.

I have not seen a single report from these other researchers making any comparison, but then I haven't read many of their reports anyway.

I have devoted all the time that I could spare from my more important pursuits (such as fishing) to the study of that single subspecies. Now that I am nearly seventy I have begun to realize that starting my research at about the age of eleven or twelve and conducting it almost continuously except for brief interruptive periods of hunting and fishing over the intervening fifty-eight years or so just wasn't enough, timewise. I should not have spent so much time with other research. I don't know nearly enough.

I have observed that certain specimens of these female members of the subspecies have what appear to be excessively large fleshy masses surrounding the mammary glands.

I have tried unsuccessfully to find some constant that would allow me to attribute this phenomenon to evolution without fear of contradiction. Putting it bluntly, I have failed miserably. I would suppose that almost any other man who attempts to do the extensive research that I have done will face the same difficulty which confronted me from the very beginning. A lack of ability to concentrate. My mind is occupied with so much and with such a variety of subjects that I sometimes lose sight of the primary objective, pure research.

I have reached the conclusion that the wide variation in size and shape of the available specimens of these unusual masses completely rules out evolution as the factor responsible. Some of those which I have studied were almost as big as gallon Clorox jugs while a few were only about the size of eggs—fried. Some were shaped a lot like rutabagas while any number were somewhat more the shape of the ears on a Beagle or a Basset hound. I cannot, for the life of me, explain the reason for the difference.

I have observed that size and shape normally make absolutely no difference in the performance or efficiency in fulfilling the primary function. I have also observed that the larger sizes seem to have a secondary purpose which they fulfill quite

90

efficiently. They work on males of the subspecies almost as well as a candle flame works on a moth on a dark night, or as well as a properly presented Rapala works on a walleye in late August.

I have absolutely no explanation for that. I have been completely baffled by it for years. The masses have nothing whatsoever to do with anything except the feeding of the offspring of the subspecies. That function is usually of only brief duration and takes place, for the most part, in the immediate postnatal period.

I have heard that up until relatively recent times that this function was frequently relegated to other females of the species at certain times and under certain circumstances.

Not all females today choose to use these appendages for the primary purpose, and a whole industry has sprung up just to supply devices and substances to accommodate those females who are reluctant to use them thusly.

Some females (if not most) in this subgroup seem to be fully aware of the secondary purpose heretofore mentioned. They have, through evolution perhaps, transformed this secondary purpose into the primary.

These particular females display these masses prominently, especially when there are males of the species present. This activity (displaying) could be readily compared to the displays made by such animals as male cardinals and robins in the early spring. It could also be reasonably compared to the activities of the bull moose in the early autumn, although the displays by the female Homo Sapiens tend to be considerably less violent. In themselves, that is. I have seen frequent eruptions of violence among some of the male onlookers when one of them apparently gets the idea that he has the exclusive right.

Maybe that is what causes the violence with the bull moose. I haven't seen anything on a cow moose, however, that I even halfway thought would be worth fighting over. But then I'm not a bull moose, either.

Male members of the subspecies are obviously not well-versed in female behavior. They are often called "male chauvinist pigs" by certain female members. I am led to believe that these epithets are applied only at exclusively female meetings or where the females are in the decided majority. I have never heard of their being used in a one-on-one

91

situation. This could result, in part, from the tendency of some of the uncouth males to refer to these masses by various vulgar terms which are usually based on such factors as size, shape or function, or upon their effect upon these males. I rarely use such terms, and refuse to repeat them here.

My father-in-law was a longtime and devoted researcher and observer of these masses, but he obviously was afraid to put his findings in writing. If he passed along any of his accumulated knowledge acquired from all those years of dedicated research, it was by word-of-mouth, and he never revealed them to me. He never missed even the slightest opportunity, however, to make observations. You could tell by the way his eyes would light up.

He and my mother-in-law lived in Florida during the winters, and he made frequent trips to the beach to conduct his research. He always used the pretext of going fishing.

He had spent his winters in that state for so many years that the full-time residents had quit calling him "snowbird." At least they didn't call him that within earshot. Maybe that was because he paid taxes there and bought a lot of shrimp, sand fleas, hooks, rods and reels, lures and other items essential to a good disguise which is often necessary to such research. Especially when you are married to a suspicious and jealous woman. I have spent a lot of dollars trying to fool Mrs. Berdine, so I know whereof I write.

Evolution does funny things to people, more noticeable when they have eyes that reflect little dollar signs at the drop of a greenback.

My wife and I and our younger daughter, her husband and their children went down to visit them one winter to spend an extended vacation. This was in early December and the beaches weren't exactly covered with bikinis, but they weren't completely deserted, either. I made that observation while fishing from the jetty at Fort Pierce. I didn't catch anything. It is difficult to catch fish when you can't remember to bait your hook.

My father-in-law had found a buxom (to say the very least) young lady who was willing to engage in an extended conversation with him, even if he was an octogenarian. Don't ever sell the old boys short. My father-in-law loved to talk, and you could tell that he was totally engrossed in the conversation by the gleam in his eyes and by the way he kept slurring his words and frequently talking about something entirely out of context with the conversation. I'm surprised that she didn't notice that, too. Maybe she did.

My grandson, Clifford, was about five years old at that time and had accompanied his great-grandfather to watch the fishermen. He wasn't particularly enjoying the conversation, so he slipped away unnoticed to rejoin his mother, grandmother and great-grandmother who were busily looking for "monkey-faces," the coffee-bean cowry which was plentiful along the shoreline.

Great-grandpa had managed to steer the conversation and the young lady toward some shade provided by some dense shrubbery and just out of sight of the shellpickers.

When Great-grandma asked Cliff where Great-grandpa was, he told her, "He's down there behind some bushes talking to a pretty woman with big muscles." Some kids tell everything they know.

Dad is gone, now. But he left behind some great-grandsons who have taken up where he left off, proving once again that some traits are genetically transmitted. Viva la Evolution!

One evolutionary development (if one can call it that) of recent vintage is that a number of women have attempted to improve their puny condition by means of silicone implants. I have not been able to determine any valid reason for this, either, but it must have something to do with the secondary function of impressing the males of the subspecies. Some of these implants have resulted in runaway scientific flops, so to speak, when they got out of control. Some have even brought on a rash of malpractice suits, possibly when the results of the implants left more flop than desired.

I understand that there is another evolutionary development accompanying this apparently overpowering urge for supposed physical enhancement. I have heard that there is an extensive industry devoted to the manufacture and distribution of devices which are designed to display these masses to the best advantage. I don't know what that means, either, but apparently somedody does. You see a lot of ads on television describing in graphic detail what these devices will do for the female figure. From the pictures I have seen, I would gather that these devices remotely resemble the harnesses used on

93

buggy horses a few years back. They have about the same number of straps.

I also understand that this industry is highly competitive, but it must be a big market. I would guess that research and development would necessarily be extensive and expensive just to reach some small degree of standardization. The vast range of sizes and shapes would present an almost insoluble problem. There should be a terrific aftermarket for maintenance and repair parts, but I haven't seen any ads for such items. Maybe they are designed with planned obsolescence in mind, like disposable diapers.

I have heard and read that there are some segments of this industry that specialize in the manufacture of devices that contain pieces of rubber or plastic foam. These are apparently sold to what could be called "the fried-egg market." They are used to fool the male members of the subspecies into believing that they are seeing something which they aren't. And they used to say that the hand is quicker than the eye.

There is a huge number of females in the group that refuses to be taken in by the slick advertising schemes of the manufacturers of these devices. The manufacturers have spent literally millions upon millions of dollars on advertising aimed at convincing these females that they really need these products. But all their money and efforts have gone for naught. I suppose that you could say that it has resulted in some big economic flops. I haven't noticed any marked difference between the secondary function in this group and the, shall we say, controlled group.

The very little bit of observation that I have done on the females of the other subspecies within the group (Homonoidea), I'll admit, was while I was watching the Discovery Channel on television, so you must understand that the following material is at least secondhand.

I have noticed from the pictures on TV, (where you can see almost anything if you wait long enough), which were probably taken by one of those researchers who was more interested in gorillas than in Homo Sapiens, that some apes, chimpanzees, orangs and monkeys have appendages that are only slightly similar to those on their sisters in the subspecies Homo Sapiens. I have noticed also that those animals don't seem to be obsessed with size and shape. The apparent attitude of the males of those species is that they couldn't care less. I'm glad I'm not an ape. It is also obvious that there are more differences between the females of Homo Sapiens and these other species than just the opposing thumb.

The development of these masses among the females of Homo Sapiens may roughly be compared to the concurrent development of the human nose on both males and females.

The nose is another unique feature of Homo Sapiens. No other animal has a nose quite like it, but the proboscis monkey probably comes closest, but his nose sometimes hangs down over his mouth and chin. Even with the extreme size and length of the noses on some humans, very few of them hang all the way down over the chin.

I have untold problems with trying to reconcile the shape of the human nose today with the highly questionable statement that we once had noses like all the other homonoids.

The other homonoids have pretty much kept their flat noses throughout the millennia, and Homo Sapiens has pretty much kept the long pointy version. It should have been the other way around.

Man (or woman, as the case may be) is always sticking his nose into other peoples' business. That apparently hereditary trait may have resulted in a few noses being artificially flattened, but it has not resulted in any obvious effect on the length of the protuberance over an extended period of time, such as three or four generations.

Professional boxers rarely transmit flattened noses and cauliflower ears to their children. You do see a nose now and then that looks like its ancestor may have been a prober (from proboscis?) or just plain nosy, but I can't find enough evidence to support any claim that artificially flattened noses are genetically transmitted. I have seen a great deal of evidence that "nose trouble" is, but that may result from environment rather than from evolution.

I have tried for years to figure out why or how the human nose managed to grow so long. One explanation may be (or may not be—I always like to leave you enough room to decide these serious questions for yourself) that parents over untold centuries have used as a mild form of punishment for a misbehaving child or offspring a type of chastisement that is unique to the subspecies. They tweak it's nose, mostly to get it's attention. I have never understood the connection, but a tug on the nose seems to open the ear canals so that the child can hear more clearly.

This sharp forward yank on the nose also hurts like the very blazes and, if properly administered, is hard to detect by a lawyer trying to get his hands on a parent's money by charging him with child abuse in a contingent-fee suit.

It could, I suppose, if done quite frequently, result in some elongation of the nose, but I am not at all certain that such prolonged artificial elongation would be susceptible to genetic transmission. The tendency to get the child's attention in this easy-to-administer and hard-to-detect-by-lawyers method may be.

There is one thing glaringly wrong with any reasoning that the nose jerking results in evolutionary elongation. That is the fact that at the very same time that parents were attempting to make the child's nose longer, they were also ear-twisting. Sometimes simultaneously and for the same offense.

Ear twisting was usually administered with a little more force than nose jerking. The ear flap isn't so sensitive to pain as the nose, and the parents learned this quite early in life, so they compensated. Ear twisting, as I remember from my own childhood, occurred more frequently than nose tweaking. There was probably a good reason for that, too, especially in the wintertime when a teacher was usually the one who was taking care of the punishment.

In those days, we were outside a lot in all kinds of weather. We often developed runny noses in cold and rainy weather. A slick nose didn't afford nearly as good traction as a dry ear, and when the teacher twisted an ear, she didn't have to wipe her fingers on her dress. And a twisted ear didn't leave a lot of evidence except for a redness that normally disappeared after three or four hours. If the ear stayed red longer, she could always blame the cold weather.

If evolution is really responsible for our noses being so much longer than our brothers', the apes, because of all the yanking and jerking and pulling, then why in tarnation aren't our ears shaped like corkscrews?

Human noses come in a lot of different shapes and sizes, too. And in different colors. One color is red. With blue streaks. I've heard reasons given for that variation, but I can't confirm them.

Some noses are shaped like beaks. These are called "aquiline noses." If you tell someone that he has an aquiline nose, you had better be sure that you are a lot bigger or you are wearing a friendly smile. You should also be prepared to duck fast and run faster. He might know what you mean. It is the same as calling someone "eagle-beak." He might not take kindly to that. Some people are sensitive about their noses, especially if they are a little on the large size, like mine.

If you tell him that he has a "Roman nose," you had better be able to move quickly, too. They say that about some horses that happen to have oversized and outstanding proboscises.

The nose, as you have already noted above, is often called a proboscis. I have never been able to figure out why. I even use that word once in a while, myself. An elephant's trunk is a proboscis. It is also prehensile. That means that he can twist his nose around something and lift it up to his mouth to eat. Don't try that with your nose in any fancy restaurant. It won't bend enough.

Sometimes you have to choose your words carefully to avoid offending someone who may be a little oversensitive. There are times when it might be okay to tell a pretty little girl that she has a cute little pug nose. But you are putting a lot of faith in her temperament. Don't even think about telling her that she has a cute little proboscis. That could change her temperament and cause your ears to develop a sharp ringing sound—from the concussion. She might not know what you mean.

Human noses really aren't much good for anything except to filter the air that we shouldn't have polluted in the first place. They also warm the air so that our lungs don't freeze up in the wintertime.

If we all lived in Florida, Texas, Arizona, or someplace like that where the air is already warm enough that it wouldn't have to be preheated, our noses wouldn't have to work as hard as they do in Northern Ontario or Siberia.

Noses in the warmer climates should be smaller. But they aren't. Maybe it is because so many big-nosed people from the North migrated down there and threw evolution all out of kilter, since it wasn't equipped to handle the overflow.

Human noses aren't nearly as good at detecting odors and scents as most of the other animals. This fact has had a serious effect on the evolutionary process by necessitating dog breeders who come up with all kinds of weird-looking animals to do our smelling for us. Some of these have been utter failures and couldn't smell any better than we could. They nearly always smelled worse.

The lack of an acute sense of smell is why some males (and a few of the females) of Homo Sapiens buy fox hounds, coon hounds (they are not "raccoon hounds" where I come from), rabbit dogs, bird dogs, etc. So the dogs can chase the animals, and the humans can just sit back and take it easy while the dog does all the work.

If you smoke, or if you sniff a lot of other foreign materials up your nose, you can't even pick up scents as well as someone who doesn't. Some of the stuff that people sniff up the nose will make your head swell up inside until you think it will burst. People who do that usually have a pretty thick layer of bone that helps hold everything together at such times. That thick layer of bone causes them to be called "boneheads." Nature tries to take care of everything.

I once heard of a guy who spent a lot of time hanging around beer joints, barrooms, honky-tonks and other such places of social gatherings. He would make bets with other patrons over whose nose would hold the most fifty-cent pieces. He bought a lot of beer with his moneymaking nose. That guy had moxie. He also had a whopper of a nose that would stretch like a toy balloon.

The next time you walk down the street, see how many odd, big and funny noses you can count. It's a good way to pass the time. But don't make any funny remarks. The next thing you know, someone else could be counting yours.

And if all of that isn't evolution, there ain't a hound dawg in Georgia.

Males and...

Some male members of the subspecies Homo Sapiens have developed an unusual characteristic at about the same time that the female members were developing theirs. This characteristic seems to be limited to the more intelligent males. But there are exceptions to every rule. Even that one.

I have heard and read for many years now that a person's hair continues to grow long after body growth comes to a screeching halt after reaching a certain plateau. It is said to continue even after some other body parts start to shrink.

Years of careful observation has convinced me that the experts are all wrong. I have seen any number of people, both male and female, who may not have gained another fraction of an inch in height but continue to increase their girth in certain areas by several fractions. I personally have not had that problem. My chest was fifty inches and my waist thirty-two. That makes a total of eighty-two inches, so I was told by a college professor whose forte is mathematics. Now my waist is only forty, measured around my cinch strap when it is pulled tight and my chest is forty-two. That still comes out exactly the same, so I have been told. I'm not telling what my waist measurement is about an inch or so above my belt.

Humans have little patches of hair in some of the oddest places. If evolution is responsible for the locations of these little isolated patches, I have absolutely no idea what it had in mind. The only practical use for any of these random patches is limited to that pair just over the eyes on that little sticky-out part of the forehead (formerly pronounced "ford") and the sparse patches just below them. These are called "brows" and "lashes" by the uneducated. I don't know what the intelligent-sia call them, although I must surely have heard at one time or another.

The brows once upon a time helped keep sweat from running down into the eyes, but so few people do that any more that evolution may pull another one of its sneaky little tricks and leave them off future generations. You must have heard that old saw, "If you don't use it, you'll lose it." I suppose that would apply to eyebrows, too.

The lashes were supposed to help keep dust out of the eyes, but that was long before we developed the smog grinders. Now the particles in the air are so fine that it takes special mocrofine filters to strain them out. These particles slip right on by the lashes. We have even developed a system for eliminating the particles altogether. It has been named "chemical pollution." It requires a special mask which should be worn over top the dust filter. We also now have a special gaseous material that we inject into the air supply called "noxious or toxic gasses" which requires a special system in order to filter it out. This contraption should be worn over the other two. If you wear all the filtration system that you should, you really don't need the little hairs in your nose or on your eyelids, so they will probably disappear as well. The hairs in the nostrils were supposed to filter air, but that was in the old days before we became geniuses. (The correct plural may now be "geniusi," but it used to be that other word.)

The patch of hair located on the upper skull isn't of much use any more, either. This patch of filaments is the real subject of this part of the book. Some males exhibit the unusual characteristic which is obviously some kind of indication of things to come. Or go, as the case may be.

Most people attain their maximum height in their late teens or early twenties. When they reach their middle to late fifties, they begin to lose a tiny fraction of their original height. Usually by the early to midthirties or thereabouts, they start gaining a small fraction of their original weight on top of what they already weigh. In both of these cases, we are using the early maximums as the standards. This small weight increase in avoirdupois seems to worry most people, both males and females, a great deal more than the fractional loss in overall length. This is evidenced by the huge numbers of products developed to help maintain the standard weight or to reduce any flab that may have escaped unnoticed until it got out of hand, so to speak. I haven't seen a single product on the shelves of my grocery store that says one word about increasing length.

The aberrant males have apparently continued to grow in height long after their hair growth ceased. Nearly every one of these aberrations results in at least two or three inches of a glossy skin-covered dome sticking up above the natural hairline. This condition is so common among the male members of Homo Sapiens that it has been given a name. It is called a "Saint Anthony's haircut," but I have no idea why. If you will examine one of these domes rather carefully, you will notice a few little individual hairs that have not given up the fight. They have clung tenaciously to the uppermost part of the shiniest portion of the exposed skin. If some smart scientist would try to crossbreed these stubborn little rascals, he might be able to isolate their genes and create a new species that would hang on with their toenails and refuse to leave their, shall we say, domicile.

We can do that with big things like dogs. I don't see why it wouldn't work with hairs, which surely don't have as many complicated parts.

I have heard that this unusual characteristic (I hesitate to call it a trait), is indicative of a higher degree of intelligence present in those males which is lacking in their hirsute contemporaries. I can't prove that statement, it is just hearsay.

I have also read or maybe I saw it on television, where you can see just about anything if you have a program guide and know where to look, that these individuals not only have increased mental ability and agility, but that it works on their sex life in the same way. It may be that infrared and ultraviolet rays from the sun are more beneficial than we thought.

There is no need for you to run out and buy a bunch of lamps to produce these rays artificially. I already tried that and it doesn't help. At least not as far as I could determine over a six-year study, conducted in the privacy of my own home.

Further, I have not done any considerable comparison testing over any extended period, so I can neither confirm nor deny the reports. I will, however, be willing to listen to any person who has conducted such testing if he will present proper credentials, the first of which should be documentary evidence of his sanity.

I have not observed this unusual characteristic among male members of other subspecies of the primate order, but as I told you before, I haven't looked closely. About the only male gorillas or apes that I have seen were those on television, and the bald ones (if they are) may have been too shy to have their picture taken, especially on tape where it is pretty hard to sneak by with anything. They may not have wanted the whole world to see.

Their bald human counterparts do not exhibit this aversion to having their talents(?) displayed before everybody and his sister. They have been appearing on television, sans hairpiece, since away back there before J.C. (Julius Caesar). Some have even had to shave their heads just to appear bald and perpetuate or invalidate the myth, if it is such. Maybe they have heard some of the same stories that I have heard.

Males of the subspecies, Homo Sapiens, are obviously quite vain, although to look at some of them it would be pretty hard to guess. They have places called "barbershops" where they go to have their hair (on the head and face) cut and shaped. Some barbershops offer other services, like sweet smelling water, etc. I did notice one sign in my barbershop the other day that told me that evolution had taken its toll on one more thing that was once familiar. The price list had the space that had formerly said "shave—$2.00" blacked out. The barber didn't want to give anyone a haircut on his face for less than for less hair on his head. There are still a few men around who have as much hair on their head as on their face, but the numbers seem to be dwindling every day.

Barbers came up with a get-rich-quick scheme several years back that increased the price of a haircut considerably. They would offer you a "singe" for a small additional fee. The hourly rate shot up dramatically.

They would light a match or a taper (the rich ones used tapers, the poor ones used rolled up newspaper, usurping the proper purpose of read papers and creating a shortage in other parts) and hold it near the hair to "seal the ends." Once in a while the match or taper would get a little too close. That resulted in what a fireman calls "an incipient conflagration."

If you want to know what it means, ask any fireman above the rank of lieutenant. After one experience like that, the haircut-ee just said, "No thanks." After about fifteen or twenty years, the singe disappeared along with the double-bitted axe for shaving.

Some male members of the subspecies have developed another unusual trait. (It shouldn't really be called a characteristic—not yet, anyway.)

This trait causes one to worry about their ancestry, which is certainly an unresolved question at this time since gorillas, elephants, water buffaloes, domestic bulls, bull moose, and caribou exhibit similar traits within the limits of their capabilities. You must remember, though, that human males are shaped a little different than these others. Sometimes the difference may be apparent only after long and serious obser-vation. The human males seem to be a little more sophisticated, but that may be because they have better equip-ment.

These human males buy or steal big iron or steel bars with iron wheels of various sizes attached to each end of the bar. They place one of these odd-lookng devices on the floor near the center of the room, and then bend down and grasp it with both hands. They then grunt and groan just like a bull moose in rut and pretend to strain while they tug and pull at the device. It looks to me as though they want the bystanders to think that it is heavy. Sometimes they even lift the device an inch or two off the floor.

When that happens, the "heister" or whatever you call him stands, beats his chest with both fists and makes a series of guttural noises. He sometimes breaks out in a cold sweat. I suppose it is cold. He hasn't done anything that I could see that should cause him to break out in a hot sweat. It takes work to do that.

He then stalks out of the room, leaving the device in the middle of the floor. As soon as he gets out of sight, some skin-ny little female comes in, grabs the device in one hand and totes it out the other door. I have seen this happen several times on TV, so it must be true. They surely wouldn't try to fool a person.

Male gorillas do something that is remarkably similar, but they normally use tree limbs. They beat their chest the same

103

way and make the same kind of noises. Elephants do the same thing with limbs, but they usually grab the whole tree with their nose. Bull moose exhibit the same behavior, but they try to push the trees and bushes over and don't fool around trying to pick them up. They make almost the same kinds of noises.

I have observed the other animals long enough to determine that when they do those foolish things, they really have something else on their minds. But I'll be hanged if I can see the connection between the iron wheels and anything else with which the human males might be preoccupied.

These same human males have another contraption that is made of what looks to be a bunch of metal tubing with several ropes and straps attached at intervals and a sort of small bedlike structure sticking out of that bunch of paraphernalia somewhere near the middle.

The first time I saw one of these odd males climb onto that little bed, I just knew what was going to happen, especially when there were four or five big guys standing around watching, just waiting for him to make a wrong move.

Imagine my surprise when the one on the bed started grabbing those straps and ropes and pulling and jerking on them as though he were having some kind of a fit or attack. He looked as though he were under a terrible strain. I couldn't believe it when not one of those guys watching tried to grab him and tie him down. He looked for all the world like he needed to be heading for one of those cozy little rooms with thick foam padding on the walls. I figured that he needed it on the floor and ceiling, too.

One of the things that I have noticed about most of the males with this trait is that they have big unsightly bulges and knots on their arms, legs, chest, back and neck. I have the same kind of unsightly knots, nodes, lumps and bulges all over my body, but the doctor told me that it was just a bad case of hives and that I would get over them in a few days, and not to worry. I can't quite figure why those guys work so hard to get what I'm trying to get rid of.

Some of the males (not necessarily limited to those mentioned above) are extremely homely. Downright ugly is what it is. They look as though they had fallen out of the very tip top of an ugly tree and hit every limb on the way down.

104

This appearance doesn't seem to have any adverse effect on their ability to attract females of the subspecies. Pretty ones. This observation leads me to strongly suspect that there is some factor involved that is a little more than meets the eye. I haven't had time to make an intensive study of this phenomenon, but maybe I'll get around to it one of these days. If anyone has done a study under strictly scientific conditions and standards, I'd like to know what he came up with.

Some males of the subspecies engage in what they call "sports." These activities fall into two general classifications called "participating" or "participatory" and "nonparticipating" or "spectator" sports. The active, or participating sports, include such things as football, baseball, tennis, hunting, fishing and golf. The spectator sports include watching television, especially shows about the others. The participants in this sport are sometimes called "couch potatoes" or "lounge lizards." Those are the names that the other sportsmen call them. If they happen to be married, the names that their wives call them aren't fit to print.

Some of the participants in the participating sports make bushels of money. These depend upon the nonparticipating sports, such as watching television, for their livelihood. The income of some of these "players" is often as much as two or three times that of your run-of-the-mill spectator who pays their salaries by paying a little extra for the beer he consumes while reclining on the couch and watching his hired hands working via remote control. He can even see them the second or third time running through the same mistake or brilliant maneuver, whichever it happens to be, through the miracle of instant replay.

His sport should probably be classed as "active" also. Every few minutes there is a commercial. When those appear, he has to run at top speed to get to the "john" to get rid of the excess beer and get back in time so that he won't miss a single play. Advertisers and networks are aware of this breach of loyalty and compensate for it by increasing the volume of the ads automatically so that the couch potato won't miss the most important part of the game.

These commercials are presented by the sponsor who charges the couch potato a little extra for his beer so that the brewer can convince the watcher to drink a little more beer so that the owners can increase the wages of the underpaid players. It is a vicious circle that could only be broken by cutting the wages of the players to about what the television watcher makes.

The participants in the active sports such as football, soccer and tennis sometimes move around enough during a game to work up a mild sweat. After about three or four days of this activity, they develop a distinktive (not misspelled) odor. Since these people are the heroes worshipped by the couch potato, he wants to be like them. So he buys certain commercial preparations to accomplish this, some of which are endorsed by his heroes.

Hunters buy scents to cover up their body odor. They use scents like doe deer excretions that are supposed to fake estrus, red fox pee, buck musk and I don't know what else. I don't think that I would want to walk into a woods full of eight-pointers smelling like a promising doe, but maybe the hunters only put it on after they climb a tree.

I have been waiting for some firm to come up with something that smells like a hickory nut for squirrel hunters, but that might not be such a good idea. Squirrels can climb trees. And they eat nuts.

Fishermen usually buy insect repellant. That is only to keep the mosquitoes and black flies and other pests at bay. After they catch two or three fish on a warm day, they don't need much else to make them smell badly, especially if they creel the fish.

If the participants smoke cigarettes or cigars, chew tobacco or sniff snuff, the odor is noticeably worse. They then buy preparations to try to cover up the odors, but nothing works well for any extended period. When I was at home, we often smelled worse than a three-week-old sock. The only thing that would help us was a thorough scrubbing with Mom's homemade lye soap. But that stuff is hard to come by these days.

About the only sport that doesn't cause one to have a sweaty odor is the spectator sport of watching television. That is, of course, if the spectator can tear himself away long enough to take a shower about once every two weeks. There is one small problem, however. Drinking all that beer can cause you to have gas. That is sometimes almost as bad as body odor.

For many years these activities were pretty much limited to participation by men. In recent years the females have begun to infiltrate these sports, violating another "males only" sanctuary. I am unable to explain the reason for this, but it may be that some women just enjoy looking at men in the shower as much as men enjoy looking at women.

They may do it because they want to learn some new jokes and to keep a jealous eye on the men that they claim and a wandering eye on the ones they don't. But if this infiltration by women into what has traditionally been male activities continues, it won't be long before you will have to use something else besides smell to tell one from the other.

When men hunt, they ordinarily join with one or more other males and see who can tell the biggest lies about how many animals they have killed in the past and how big those animals were. Some of these males have already established such a bad reputation among their peers that it has become necessary for them to either save or buy from others, parts of animals and have them stuffed and mounted so that they can hang them on the wall as proof.

When they fish, it is even worse.

Female hunters and fishers (I didn't know whether it should be "fisherwomen" or "fisherpersons" and I didn't want to offend anyone) are now trying to overtake the males in lying about their prowess. They have had a lot of practice in other subjects, so it won't be long until the men have to take a back seat in what may have been the last male stronghold. I suppose that evolution is inevitable.

Men have another sport which they seem to enjoy quite a bit. Women have already infiltrated it. It is called "golf." I don't know a whole lot about it, but I have watched it done.

A "golfer" walks up to a little flat piece of ground called a "tee" and goes to somewhere near the middle of the patch of grass. He puts a little ball on the ground. He looks around to see if anybody is watching, and then he pulls a little short stick out of his pocket and shoves it into the ground if he thinks nobody is looking. He places the little ball on top of that little stick to get it up off the ground. I don't know if he is supposed to do that. It may be cheating, but if you watch around for a little while, everybody does it sooner or later.

107

After he puts the little ball on top of the stick, he steps back a step or two and goes through a ritual that sort of reminds you of a bull moose. He takes a club from a bag that is absolutely chock full of them. It appears sometimes that he doesn't know for sure what club to pick, because he will pull one out and then shove it back into the bag. He may do that four or five times before he finally takes the same one that he pulled out first and walks back to the stick with the little ball on top. I don't know how he knows which club to take. They all look alike to me, except that some have big wooden ends on the top and some have what looks like metal. No matter what one he grabs, he turns it upside down and starts talking to the ball while shaking that stick at it and making other threatening gestures.

I heard someone who was standing next to me and watching the golfer say that he was addressing the ball. But I never did see anybody put any writing on one nor a stamp or return address. I figured that he was just telling it where to go.

After about a minute or so of this gesturing and talking, he seems to get worked up to a real rage. He draws back that club and swings at the ball hard enough to knock it into the next county. The golfer hardly ever knows for sure whether he put the right address on the ball or not, because just as soon as it takes off, he puts one hand up to his brow to shield his eyes and looks away off like to see where the ball is going after it took off like it was rocket-propelled. When the ball hits the ground and bounces a couple of times, the golfer always stomps his feet and hits the ground with the club and makes ugly faces. I'm not sure what that ritual means, but nearly everybody does it. Maybe he didn't get the address right.

He then slams the club back down in the bag. The bag must be pretty heavy because most golfers drive funny little cars just to haul the bags around. The cars usually carry two bags and their golfers.

The cars must be pretty versatile. They seem to go just about anywhere. The golfers take it first to one side of the field, and then to the other. They run it through brush and weeds and into the woods and turn them in circles all over the place. They even run them into the little ponds and swamps that are scattered around the field.

They must not do too well in sand, because every one that I have watched would run right up to the edge of a big hole full of sand and stop just short of falling in. One of the golfers would jump out and beat the sand as if he had seen a snake. Once in a while he must have had a job killing it, because the second golfer would jump out and run into the sand and start beating at something, too.

He spends a lot of time looking for that little ball that he hit. He may want to double check to be sure he got the address right. Sometimes he obviously can't find the ball. When that happens, he will watch around a while and then slip his hand into his pocket and take a few steps toward the middle of the mowed field and drop the ball when no one is looking. He then yells out, "I found it." That ball looks to me as though it is just like the other one. He then hits it with a club after about three or four swings and it goes sailing off and he takes off after it in that little car and then goes through the whole rigmarole again.

The golfer repeats this performance several times before giving up in disgust. He drives the little car right up to the door of the saloon that is located near the golf field and jumps out and runs inside. A few minutes later he comes out with a can of beer in his hand, jumps into the little car and takes off to try again. I don't know if that is the proper way to play golf, but that is the way men do it.

I don't know what is so hard about playing golf. Women play it, too. But they don't often have such violent reactions as the men. I have seen two or three of them sit down on one of those little benches that they have scattered around the field under almost every shade tree and put both hands over their face and cry.

I have heard any number of people say that the other animals aren't as intelligent as humans. That may be, but I haven't seen any of the others chasing a little ball all over a big field trying to hit it with a club.

I don't know yet what the effect of this will be on evolution, but whatever it is, it can't be too good for humans to become as frustrated as golfers appear to be when they play that game.

Glossary

Every book of any scientific importance needs a glossary to define some of the more complicated terms which are not in common usage. There are a few terms in this book which may not be familiar to you, especially if you are less than forty years old and have never lived in the country, let alone Appalachia. Wherever that is.

I decided to follow the format of this book and put the glossary in some unusual place where you would least expect it. I chose somewhere near the middle. I figured that by the time you had read this far, you needed all the help you could get. And besides, if I stuck it all the way in the back, you might be too tired to turn all those pages just to find the real meaning of some word you didn't understand.

Most of these words or terms have been used at one time or another in this neck of the woods, and a few of them have been used elsewhere, although I can't understand why anyone in his right mind would want to talk like us. Anyway, here goes.

avoirdupois the dictionary says that this word is derived from the Latin words "habere" which means "to have," "de" which means "of," and "pensum" which means "weight." Anyone who has a little too much avoirdupois knows what it means. I think that the dictionary went a little too far back to find something that doesn't even sound anything near to the way we spell it. I could have stopped at the French, which also takes three words to make just one. French looks a whole lot more like our word when you shove all three French words together like the dictionary did with the Latin. In French, "avoir" means "to have," "du" can mean "some" and "pois" means "green peas." Maybe if some of us had translated back to the French and had taken a few more green peas instead of so much ice cream, cake, pie, and fat hamburger, we could have wound up with a lot less avoirdupois.

beaver dam obstruction in an otherwise free-flowing stream constructed by beavers who seem to love to dam things, especially creeks and sometimes rivers. The beaver dam is built with sticks, limbs, grass, weeds, mud and stones which the beavers carry between their forepaws or between their big buck teeth. They build the dam in order to form a pond or pool of water that is just deep enough that it is over your hip boots if you are wading or shallow enough so that your prop churns mud and gook and hits submerged limbs if you are in a boat. If the animal kingdom has an Army Corps of Engineers, the beavers are it. If they see a nice stream with nothing in it to interfere with the flow, they immediately say, "Dam it."

beaver house or lodge pile of sticks, limbs, grass, weeds, mud and stones which the beaver carries to the building site between his forepaws or between his teeth and piles up in such a way that there is a space inside where the beavers live. Humans do exactly the same thing, except for the toothy part. The beaver house is roughly dome-shaped and possibly the forerunner of the geodesic dome house used by some of the beavers' human brothers. The beaver house is usually near the waterfront of the pond formed by the dam or on the shore of a nice lake. For the view, I suppose. The houses are always built in some of the most unlikely places where there is no cable TV and where porcelain facilities and fixtures would be hard to tote in.

bejabers pronounced bee-jay-bers with the accent on the "jay." Also "bejabbers." This is an Irish expression of unknown antiquity. Nobody knows for sure what it means, but as it is used in the text it means—Uh, Oh! I almost told you what it meant. Just read it and imagine your own meaning.
    An old Irishman, who used to live in the neighborhood where I was raised, used it as a catch-all expression much as

most of us use some other less sophisticated expressions.

He lived about a mile and a half from the old country store where everyone dealt except when they didn't need a little credit.

He hitched his horse to the buggy and drove to the store to get a hundredweight of horse feed. (I could have said "commodities," but we were too ignorant to know about such things back in those days.)

He liked to swap yarns, so after he got his bag of horse feed and had the storekeeper put it "on the tick" he plopped the bag down in a vacant place in the circle of loafers around the Burnside (potbellied stove) and proceeded to tell a few knee-slappers and listen to a few new ones and a lot of old ones with a new wrinkle.

After an hour or so of this jolly pastime of chit-chat, he arose, hefted the sack of feed to his shoulder and disappeared out the door.

About forty minutes or so later, he popped his head in the door and said, "Be faith and bejabers, boys, and I forgot me horse."

Evolution has just about eliminated situations like that. Hardly anybody ever forgets his horse anymore. Car, maybe, but not horse.

blue-John   when we kept our milk in the milk house, we would let the cream rise to the top so that it could be skimmed off with a cup or other implement and then stored in a special stone or pottery jar. It was allowed to just barely start to sour, and then it was churned into butter using a wood churn. The churn had a hole in the center of the lid through which passed a wooden handle that resembled a broom handle with a fixture on the lower end that consisted of two pieces of wood secured at right angles to each other. These pieces had holes drilled in them to allow the cream to pass through as the dasher was moved briskly up and down to agitate the cream and turn it into country butter. There are more sophisticated methods today, and you have a hard time finding country butter. Dairy butter isn't the same thing.

The milk that was left after the skimming was called "blue-John." I know why it was called "blue," but I'll be hanged if I know why they named it "John." The milk left after the churning was called "buttermilk," of all things. It wasn't anything like the so-called product in the stores today. I doubt that it even came from the same source.

The blue-John was fed to calves, pigs, lambs, etc. and wasn't used for human consumption except when we made smearcase (cottage cheese).

Evolution has changed the whole blooming world. We now buy blue-John in preference to whole milk, which really isn't, and buy oleomargarine instead of butter, because about the only people who can afford butter are those who get food stamps which we pay for. We use the excuse that there is too much fat in four-percent milk and in butter.

cantankerous quarrelsome, ill-natured. Sometimes used in referring to a person. Men often use this term to describe women whom they know. Women use it to describe men whether they know them or not.

cawn pone kind of flat bread made from cornmeal and a few other things. Popular in the southern United States. In the south, people don't pronounce their "r's" plainly, just exactly like Bostonians don't pronounce theirs, only in different places.

cock-of-the-north a pileated woodpecker, or so I have heard. His territorial call is an almost constant series of high-pitched shrieks that sound like a well-known female country singer when she tries to yodel—always off-key. She makes lots more money, though. He flies high overhead in an erratic flight that could be described as roughly circular. He bobs up and down during the noisy exhibition which can last for hours. After about two hours or so of this continual shrieking, your teeth begin to feel odd and your nerves begin to fray. He is almost as crazy over courting in the spring as his larger cousin, the bull moose, is in autumn. I have never heard this call in this area or anywhere else but in Northern Ontario. He surely carries on the reproductive process here, too. I may be wrong as to the cause of this raucous behavior. It may be that he is complaining because it is too cold to enjoy mating up there on the Arctic watershed.

codger usually preceded by "old." I read somewhere several years ago that the difference between an old codger and an

113

old geezer was about ten years. Now that I am old enough to be either one or both, I can tell you that there is no difference. An old codger is every bit as crotchety as an old geezer.

corn squeezin's potent alcoholic beverage, often homemade, derived from corn or cornmeal and a few other things. The mixture is allowed to ferment, preferrably in a wooden barrel, and then cooked in a huge pot called a "kettle."
The container is constructed so that the steam can escape only through a spiral tube called a "coil." When the steam condenses and the liquid drips out of the end of the coil, it ain't water. If it is for home consumption, it will not likely contain any additives. If it is to be sold or "bootlegged," it may have a few things like lye, kerosene, iodine and a couple of other things in it to give it flavor and make it age faster. I have heard that the longer it ages, the better it tastes. Some of the better stuff has been aged as much as two or three days. If it is pure corn squeezin's, it is often called "moonshine" or just "shine." If it contains addivites, it is called "rotgut." If it has additives, it can be hard on your innards. If you drink more than three big tin cupsful, it can be hard on your outards as well.
If you decide to try some, be sure it is in a fruit jar or stone jug. There are a lot of imitations out there. These are usually in bottles with fancy labels and a little stamp across the cork or cap to protect the contents. The stamp ruins the delicate flavor.
You can test corn squeezin's by pouring a little in the flat zinc jar lid which has almost become extinct and striking a match to it. It will burn with a blue flame that is hot enough to fry taters. If the flame is yellow, that is probably from the kerosene or lighter fluid.
It was once made almost exclusively in homemade factories called "stills." This was small business. We later called home-run businesses "cottage industries." There are still a few around, and if you happen upon one, you may experience a buzzing in your ears. The noise is made by bullets going by at considerable speed. The ones you hear won't hurt you, but look out for those that you don't hear. If they land between your eyes, they can make you fall over in a faint.

Revenuers don't like for mountain people to be self-supporting. They want them to go on welfare so that they will be sure to vote right in the fall elections, so the revenuers go in and break up the little factories unless the operator keeps a goodly supply of those little stamps which the revenuers sell, and which they insist on being on the jar lids. They are overpriced.

If you are visiting an operation to purchase some elixir, look at the still. If the tubing is made of aluminum, don't drink the liquor. It can make you sick. Something about the way the lye eats the metal.

cotton-pickin' formerly a strictly Southern expression, it has been adopted by Yankees. In the olden days before the big war, cotton was picked by hand and stuffed into huge bags that the pickers had to drag along behind. It was hard work. After a full day in the fields, the hands would be tired and thirsty. They were generally paid less than minimum wage. They would often sneak into the storehouse to get out of the hot sun and to snitch a snifter or two of the stores to refresh themselves. One plantation owner stumbled upon this activity one evening and caught one of the hands wet-handed, so to speak. He yelled, "Get your cotton-pickin' fingers off of my gin."

It caught on. Eli Whitney even called his invention a gin, just to make things even more confusing. Nowadays, everybody uses the expression and claims that it is original.

crick in the neck should not be confused with "pain in the neck" which usually refers to a person other than one's self who does the same things to you that you do to others. A crick in the neck is a big pain, but it is often caused by turning your head too far or too much, as in watching pretty girls who walk too fast. That also sometimes affects the eyes as well.

diddly-squat as in "I don't give a diddly-squat." This is a term that seems to defy definition. As old as I am, I have never seen a diddly. I have no idea what one looks like or what kind of a sound it makes. But I do know about "squat." I used to do a lot of that when I was much younger and just about lived in the woods and along the crick banks when I could sneak away from the tater patch without getting caught. There weren't a whole lot of ba's and privies scattered through the trees and along the streams back then. I did learn that this is a poor position to assume when in a patch of poison ivy or stinging nettles. I have also learned that as you get older, your ability to rise quickly from this position becomes impaired. The impairment usually disappears in the near presence of a large bear.

dirty end of the stick I am not going to tell you what that means. You can use your imagination. When someone hands you the dirty end of the stick, you can bet your bottom dollar that he doesn't want to get his fingers in it, and that he is holding the clean end.

doggone, double-doggone sometimes used in the past tense by adding a "d" at the tailend. A common expression among people who are trying to improve their communicative skills by avoiding excessive use of four-letter words, which will cause you to have a four-letter mind. Double-doggoned is used when one dog just doesn't have enough power.

dog-takin' rare colloquialism used to denote a large size, as in "them dog-takin' woods," meaning a forest so big and so dense that even a hound dog couldn't find his way home.

extroduction exact opposite of introduction.

Flinderation small village in West Virginia, situated just off U.S. Route 50, west of Clarksburg. I think that it is in Harrison County, but it may be somewhere else. It is before you get to that place where some famous person (I forget who) came in and slick-talked the locals into changing the name of their village just so that he could make a Mountain out of a Mole Hill. Mole Hill used to be in Ritchie County, on the exact same spot where Mountain now stands. Mountain and Flinderation are about equidistant from Pickle Street which lies well to the south, in Lewis County. The cartographers were ashamed to put Flinderation on the map. They also omitted the place called simply "O." That's how evolution gets all fouled up.

geezer usually preceded by "old" just like "codger." Any person older than me or perceived to be older than me. Usually masculine. I am not certain of the feminine, but it may be "geezeress." Surely not "geezerine." Other people sometimes refer to me using this term. I don't. I only use it to refer to someone else.

groundhog the Quebecois and a few other people call it "marmot," but it is still a groundhog. Some people even call it a woodchuck, but I have never seen a groundhog do that. When I was just a boy, a lot of farms had hedgerows as fences. These hedges were mostly Osage Orange. They made fine homesites for groundhogs which were then called "hedgehogs." A hedgehog is a different animal. If you rub one the wrong way, you can tell.

Back during the big Depression, if you wanted meat, you did one of two things, up in my neck of the woods, at least. You stole sheep or hunted groundhogs. My mother loved lamb and mutton, but she detested stealing, so we ate groundhogs. By the bunch. I was fourteen before I found out that chickens didn't have four legs nor hair. We shot groundhogs, dug them out of their dens, ran them down on foot, and killed them with a stick. We ate just about every other wild animal that was so unfortunate as to meet us in the open. Except skunks and possums. I've also eaten crow a few times, but I haven't taken a bite of it.

Groundhogs, when captured young, make fine pets. They are far cleaner than dogs or cats, and they become affectionate. They eat plants that they find in the yard and will sip a little blue-John once in a while, but they are extremely particular about what they eat. It must be clean and fresh. No meat. No carrion.

Some people think that animals don't have intelligence or good sense, but when a pet groundhog curls up on your chest and goes to sleep, you begin to suspect the intelligentsia.

They aren't much good for anything else. A crow makes a lot better watch dog and they are too slow for fox hunting and can't bark worth a dime. But they can whistle at pretty girls. Loud. Their whistling causes them to be called "whistlepigs."

hat always preceded by "old." Anything that I can remember from my boyhood or anything that someone else has told me about that happened before I did.

heterosexual-homosexual I lumped them together since they are antonyms. One engages in Vice, the other Univice. If the one that engages in Univice doesn't want anybody else to know about it, he could call himself "Univical." Neither wants advice.

hokey-pokey this reference is not the dance. A chemical compound or mixture that some ornery younguns in the old-timey days used to pour on a cat's back in order to see how fast he could run. When he took off, stuff came out of both ends. What came out of the front end was a long shrill squall. I don't know how fast a cat can run, but I heard of one that was pitched into the open window of the bedroom where a man and his wife were asleep. Some of the participants in that escapade swore later that the cat circumnavigated the room four times at a height of three to four feet off the floor, squalling and spraying as he went, and never touching the floor. I wasn't there.

You didn't waste good hokey-pokey on dogs. You rubbed a turpentine-soaked corncob on some of their tender parts, and they would outrun a cat. I never took part in any such shenanigans, so all the above is hearsay from a reliable source. You shouldn't do fun things like that anymore. The SPCA will seek the cops on you.

hornycaboogery what male and female animals do when they aren't too busy doing something else; in the olden days, human animals frequently engaged in this activity after the lights were out. Today it is even done in broad daylight, right out in front of God and everybody. This one activity has caused more ecological, environmental and evolutionary disasters than all other causes combined. If we don't find some way to control it, it may lead to overpopulation one of these days.

mo-lasses just plain old sorghum with a southern accent placed on the first syllable which sometimes overlaps the second. It is sometimes used on grits, another southern staple. I like my grits with plenty of butter and salt and covered with black pepper, which is the way God intended for them to be eaten.

nitpicking origin is obscure, but it may have come from the period in human history when children and adults were somewhat susceptible to lice; I'm not sure when the period started, but it hasn't ended yet. Picking the nits or eggs out of the hair destroyed the embryos. It was time-consuming and futile. Hence, picking at small things and ignoring the larger.

pipsqueak a very little squeak.

pokeberry ink here in Appalachia, we have a valuable plant called "poke." I don't know what the real name is or whether it even has one. In the early spring, the shoots pop through the ground, and any hillbilly who knows anything at all, grabs a knife and heads for the poke patch, which can be just about anywhere that there is dirt. Poke likes damp soil, but it will do well on dry ground, too. He cuts the shoots that are just about six or eight inches tall and don't have leaves on them yet and takes them home for the missus to make "poke sallat." Also spelled "sallet." People who are a little snooty say "salad," but that isn't correct. After the shoots get a little bigger, nobody picks them. They will make you as sick as a dog.

In late summer the poke plant is about six feet or so tall and has clusters of purple berries. When I was a young lad, we picked the berries for making ink when we didn't have a dime for a bottle of "Quink." We gathered a few clusters of berries and squeezed the juice from them by placing them in a muslin bag or cloth sugar sack while compressing them with a stick or board. The resulting ink was a nice purple color. You didn't develop the habit of sticking the nib in your mouth. The ink would turn your mouth a bright purple. It would also give you an incurable disease named "rigor mortis."

privy (*pl* privies) a small house which was usually situated somewhere behind the big house, and, once in a while, just about three long strides too far back. It usually had a rough board seat with two or more egg-shaped holes that were always just a little too big or a little too small. Some people who were not talented made the holes round, but those weren't made properly. The holes were invariably a little too far from the front or too near the front. Either defect was noticeable only after the seat was securely nailed in place, and it was made from the last available board. The multiple seating arrangement was so that more than one person could take advantage of all that comfort at one time. And it was a good place for private discussions.

Some privies even had running water. This was accomplished by locating the shanty over a stream bank so that when you sat down, you were literally hanging over the creek. If you kept ducks, they were an inconvenience. But this type of construction eliminated a lot of dirty hard work by making it unnecessary to move the building every few weeks and by eliminating the need for shovelling out the eliminations.

Most were built entirely of rough green lumber which shrunk as it dried, leaving sizeable cracks. The cracks were handy for watching the path to see that you weren't getting any unwanted company. They also served as a cross-ventilation system which was always needed. Sometimes when the temperature was close to thirty below and the wind was gusting at twenty knots, there was a little too much cross--ventilation.

President Franklin D. Roosevelt was personally responsible for a marked improvement in the outhouses of this country when he sent around a bunch of skilled technicians and engineers to upgrade the facilities. The new ones weren't nearly so drafty, but what he gained in comfort, he lost in aroma. The seats were smoother, though.

He did keep the little quarter-moon cut-out in the door, although I could never quite figure out whether it was supposed to be the first quarter looking in, or the last quarter looking out.

The privy was also called "the necessary house," "the back-house," "the outhouse," and with the advent of the new improved version of the 1930s, "the Roosevelt House" or "the WPA shack." They were also called by the number of available slots, for example, a "two holer." There were one or two other names which I have chosen to omit from this book.

prowess maybe a female prow?

ramps also called "ramson" by some; one could write an entire book on ramps, and still not convey the delicate flavor and the distinctive aroma of the plant and of those who eat it. The ramp is a small green plant with broad leaves and a slender stem that ends in a white bulb that looks like a shallot. It isn't. It is beaucoup-de-pew. It is a wild leek that is far too strong for its size. They are delicious when properly prepared, but a lot of good ramps have been ruined by amateurs. If they are eaten raw (also delicious), they help you determine who your real friends are. They can make you stink for up to three weeks—au puanteur. That means "with stench." Kids used to eat a handful on the way to school in order to be suspended for the duration of the stink. Sometimes it worked. When they are properly prepared, the odor lasts for only about a day or two unless you just can't help it and make a pig of yourself. It is only offensive to the noneaters. Ramps are good for you. They are rich in vitamins and minerals. They have been used as herbal medicine for the same things as garlic.

People will tell you that they won't grow at elevations under two or three thousand feet, depending on who is talking. Wrong. Chicago was named for them. They grow in southern Ontario and in Wisconsin. Tennessee has them by the barrelful (not the same barrels as sour mash).

Early spring brings out the ramps, the ramp diggers and the ramp eaters. Richwood, West Virginia has a "Feast of the Ramson" each spring about the first or second weekend in April. Tennessee has the grandpappy of all ramp festivals. I read somewhere or another that they have as many as thirty thousand people annually. Now that is what you could call "raising a big stink."

The ramp that we have here in the hills is not a true ramson. The true ramson grows throughout northern and central Europe and is a different breed of cat, although there is a similarity. I'm satisifed with what we have here.

revenuer also spelled "revenooer," an agent of The Department of the Treasury, Bureau of Alcohol, Tobacco and Firearms (BATF). His job was to make sure that private enterprises, where individuals made sour mash, corn squeezin's and other stuff like that, couldn't get by without buying those little high-priced stamps that the revenooers sold. There was an occasional individual who objected forcefully. We even had a full-blown rebellion back in 1794, when a bunch of Pennsylvania Ridgerunners got their heads together and decided not to ante up any tax on farm produce. It was called "The Whiskey Rebellion." We have been going downhill ever since. The government slapped enough tax on the spirits to make the taxes worth more than the goods. They are now looking for novel ways to tax "team spirit," "religious spirit," "patriotic spirit" and "esprit de corps." If congress can figure some way to determine taxable quantities, you had better look out. If some smart congressman can figure some way to get maybe twenty billion dollars from you for being happy, you can bet that all the rest of them will be staying up nights figuring how to spend a hundred billion to cut off the source. This is called "a bargain" in government.

Revenuers have recently taken on some extra work after they literally broke up their livelihood and worked themselves out of a job. We still have them, but they hide out under something called IRS. This new job isn't nearly as life-threatening as the old one, and it brings in more money. Evolution has turned Americans into a bunch of softies.

rockin' chair money   this term was popular just after that little setto we had with an odd-looking little man across the pond. His name was Hitler, and he was as smart as a whip, and as dumb as a box of rocks, and as crazy as a loon. After the allies had knocked the stuffin' out of him and his buddies, there were a lot of people left over. Uncle Sam would discharge one of our servicemen that had been left over and give him the option of going back to his little cabin in the hills and sitting in his favorite rocker on the porch and watching the squirrels and the bluejays fighting over white oak acorns. He could even doze once in a while. He could do this for fifty-two weeks—a whole year—and the government would pay him twenty dollars a week just to sit and forget. Not many wanted to remember.

The term "rocking' chair money" soon became a synonym for government doles which have grown by leaps and bounds ever since. The veterans made up about the only group which deserved some consideration for what they did for the country.

Another name for "rockin' chair money" was "fifty-two-twenty," but you don't hear that term anymore. Evolution has driven prices way up.

smithereens wee little "reens" or wee little "Smiths." I'm not sure which.

sour mash usually followed by "whiskey." A type of alcoholic beverage popular in Tennessee, and a couple of other places. I am not going to tell you how to make it, but the process is somewhat similar to that for making corn squeezin's, which see. The revenuers have some funny words, too. They call that "aiding and abetting." They take exception when someone does that.

Like the other home industries, the revenuers don't like to see poor old hillbillies selling sour mash without those expensive little stamps. The revenuers must make a good deal of profit on those little pieces of paper, because they guard their territory so jealously. Appalachia (wherever that is) used to have a little factory in just about every holler (translated "hollow"), but the revenuers didn't have much use for small businessmen, so they smashed every still they could find and confiscated the sippin' whiskey for "evidence." There was always a huge loss of evidence between the time of seizure and the trial. This was due to evaporation.

Prairie farmers usually bragged about their crops in "bushels per acre." Hill farmers bragged in gallons.

springhouse also called "milk house." A small, solidly-built house built astraddle of the spring drain and sometimes over the spring itself. The springhouse was an effective method of refrigerating milk, butter, cheese, eggs, fruits, vegetables, etc., if the spring had a good cold flow. The floor was often laid of fieldstone. The water flowed through a stone-lined ditch or trough usually located at one side. Containers of milk and other produce were placed in the trough so that water would not enter the container but would keep the contents cool. Flat rocks were placed on top

123

of the containers to hold them in place to prevent spillage.

thunderation   a powerful expletive used when you don't want to spit on the grass and turn it brown.

work brickle   there are still a very few people here in West Virginia, who know what "work" means, but they are fast becoming a minority and are all set to ask for government recognition with all the attendant benefits. I suppose that it is about the same all over. "Work" has become a four-letter word. "Brickle" is from the Elizabethan Era. We still use several words from that time here in the hills. They are a little hard to come by, however. We frequently say "cheer" for "chair," "kivver" for "cover," and "airn" for "iron." "Brickle" translates into "brittle." "Work brickle" means that you think that you might snap like "peanut brickle" if you do a little of it.

y' all   another southern colloquialism used by one hundred percent Americans who live south of an imaginary line drawn on an inaccurate map of the United States. This line was drawn by two men, a Mr. Mason and a Mr. Dixon (their trucking company is known as "Handshaker" in CB lingo), and was supposed to separate what is now Virginia, Maryland, and West Virginia, from places up north which were at one time a part of Virginia. Virginia gave a lot of her property to her poor relations and they paid her back by turning against her when the chips were down. Virginia was robbed again, that's what it was. It caused a big argument which eventually led to blows.

One way that you can tell a real American from a Yankee is to listen to his "y'all." If he uses it only to speak of more than one, he is probably an American. If he uses it when speaking of only one, he is a Yankee and is trying to fool somebody into thinking that he amounts to something. But you will know that he doesn't know grits from chittlin's. (Proper spelling is "chitterlings" but nobody who is anybody ever says it that way.)

yankee   always preceded by one or more highly descriptive adjectives. The adjectives are there even when you can't hear them. A Yankee is someone from north of the Mason-Dixon line and sometimes from the near side of it. They have also been called a couple of other things. They are mostly poorly thought of and are generally just sorry people.

addendum (*pl* addenda) this definition is an "addendum." This is another one of those words that some old geezer came up with back there when Italy was something else. He didn't know anything about "esses" either, so he hung an "a" behind all those "d's" to make it plural. The "add" means just that; the "en" means "on" and the "dum" is what the author is when he doesn't think of it soon enough to put it in its proper place. He is too lazy to go back and insert it where it belongs, so he just sticks it in somewhere that has a few blank spaces left over, like I did here.

Birds

Darwin wasn't the only person who liked to watch finches. My wife and I enjoy watching them, too, as well as all the other birds we are able to spot before they spot us.

We are not experts. I'm not even sure that I can tell a purple finch from a house finch. The house finch is supposed to have been imported from the western United States to the eastern part of the country around 1940. They have taken hold pretty well.

The story related here about one particular finch which I observed carefully is absolutely true. The truth may be a little hard to find in this book, so I am telling you ahead of time that this actually happened, just as I am telling it.

I think that the bird was a house finch, but it may have been a purple. I have a hard time telling one from the other unless they are side by side, and I'm not really sure that I can tell then. It doesn't matter to me, but it might to a finch. Maybe.

We were visiting my aunt and uncle near Prospect, Pennsylvania, this past summer. We were sitting on the back porch watching the ruby-throated hummingbirds making frequent trips to the two feeders hanging at the corners of the porch. They were feeding from both feeders which were about fifteen feet apart. They seemed to be visiting one about as frequently as the other.

I have read that the hummingbird is the only bird that can fly backward. That is not true. I saw with my own two beady little eyes a male finch come to the feeder on my left and hover. He stuck his beak in one particular outlet each time he visited, hovering as he drank. He then flew backward for a couple of feet, and then took off. He would fly to a clothesline pole about twenty feet distant and perch for a minute or so, and then fly back to the same outlet for more sweetened water. He did not try to feed while there was a hummingbird at the feeder, but would zero in on it as soon as one left.

The first time that it happened, I just about fell off my chair. I thought that my bifocals were lying to me in 3-D, so I took them off and watched him repeat his act. It was the same as before.

I was finally convinced. I don't know how or if he was getting anything from the feeder. The hummingbirds that visited may have left a drop of fluid on the artificial petals. He may have been imitating the hummingbirds, because he did exactly the same things that they did, but only at the one outlet. He even landed each time on the same pole that the hummingbirds normally used. I don't know what he was accomplishing, but he was persistent.

I'll bet Darwin didn't see a finch doing anything like that. It is hard to tell what kind of a conclusion he might have reached.

While I am on the subject of hummingbirds, I want to relate to you something else that I have heard about them. I have not been able to verify it firsthand. If you have seen it, I would like to hear about it.

Hummingbirds don't like cold feet any more than I do. They have a better solution than mine, though. They go south for the winter. Not just a short way south, but way south. Like Cancun.

I have exactly the same solution. But money is a factor for me. Lack of it influences my decisions out of all proportion to its importance.

Hummingbirds are called "hitchhikers" in some areas of Canada. The people who call them that say that the hummingbirds snuggle down under the feathers on the back of a Canada goose and ride to Canada in style.

If that is true, it is another example of symbiotic relationship. I wonder if the geese charge coach or first class and what they serve. I also wonder what movies they show.

It doesn't sound as though it could be. Geese make several stops on their way north. Hummingbirds need a good deal of food to sustain them when they fly. They beat their wings so fast that it requires a lot of energy just to hover at a flower or feeder, and their only food is nectar. Unless there is something about them that I don't know. I suppose that could be, since I don't know a whole lot about anything else. It may be that they don't require much food while they are tucked away in a nice down comforter and are breezing along without so much as a flutter.

They winter in Mexico, and are said to cross the five hundred miles or so of open water of the Gulf. If they can do that, they can fly over land and make as many stops as necessary. There is one more thing. Many hummingbirds return to the same shrub in successive years. If they take the Gooseair flight number forty, how do they know where to disembark? Maybe that is the reason for all the honks when the geese migrate.

Funny things happen in the animal world. We think that man is the only intelligent animal, but we prove every day that we aren't quite as smart as we claim.

My wife and I accidentally stumble into some things that afford us some experiences that I wouldn't trade for a farm in Georgia. We were picking some blueberries that were too stubborn to give in to the frost and a couple of snowstorms that we had in Canada one year, when we were fortunate enough to be able to spend some time up there on three different trips. The first trip was in May, the second in July, and the third in the latter part of August and early September.

This separation of time gave us an opportunity to meet some of the Canada geese that were local citizens. We watched the fluffy balls of yellow as they came off their nests and up to our camp with their parents who were by that time taking pieces of bread from our hands. We visited with them a second time when they were well-covered with feathers still trailing after their parents and were competing for our bread scraps. They recognized us and would feed from our fingers just like their parents. The third time we called, they were learning to fly in formation and do their share in taking the lead or wing position as required so that the flight would not be tiring on anyone.

They came in over the blueberry patch, and treated us to a show which was a rare treat for a couple of old hillbillies. We could hear the older geese talking to the younger ones, instructing them how to switch places in the squadron without lousing up the whole thing. They circled over our heads for more than an hour in their vee-shaped flight pattern, and told the younguns to move out or move in. They didn't show them every time, they told them. After a short time, we too were able to understand the commands given by the honks, and we could anticipate some of the next moves that the young fliers were to make.

We were at an airstrip that belonged to the Ministry of Natural Resources that had a dirt and gravel runway and quite a bit of open area on each side of the strip. We found the berries in the low brush that covered the open area, and it must have protected the berries to some degree, because they were at their peak. We had been moving around, and there is absolutely no way that the geese could have been unaware of our presence. We watched with our faces upturned with no camouflage to hide them.

The geese would fly in a straight line for perhaps two miles, then they would turn and come back right over our heads, talking to each other in low voices that we could hear plainly. If a young goose failed to execute a maneuver properly, one of the older geese would give him "what for." He would then get himself in line as though the elder had taken a willow switch to his backside.

I don't suppose that we are the first or the only people to witness this spectacle. It must be commonplace. What wasn't quite so commonplace was the fact these geese had travelled almost six miles to where we were picking to go through their training. We could recognize one particular goose that was one of the elders, so we knew it was our flock.

That, to us, was a very rare experience and it proved to us, at least, that animals do communicate with each other, and if we could only understand and speak their language, we could communicate with them with something more than sign language or body language.

We have observed similar behavior in two separate dogs that were able to tell us their thoughts in a rudimentary fashion. Not every thought, of course, but enough of them that we knew what they were saying by the tone of their barks. One of these learned to say "hello" plainly enough that even a nonbeliever could understand. The two dogs were separated in time by more than twenty years.

129

I sort of strayed from the bird theme of this chapter, but I wanted to make the point that conversations aren't limited to one animal species.

One of the funniest things that I have ever seen a bird do intentionally happened in front of The Country Store and Lodge, in Shiningtree, Ontario. This is the same country store mentioned in the chapter on moose. It is now owned and operated by two more of our Canadian friends, Al and Wendy Craigie.

There are two gas pumps in front of the store. Both are made of stainless steel. To the naked eye, one looks pretty much like the other with about the same qualities of reflectivity. There must be some difference.

Wendy is a bird watcher, too, and it was she who called my attention to a male brown-headed cowbird that she had been observing. The bird would fly in from his perch on a line about three or four hundred feet from the pumps and land on the concrete pad which supported them. He would invariably land on the east end of the slab and in almost exactly the same spot each time. He would then start displaying at his image in the side of the pump at slab level, flaring his wings and touching the pump with his beak. Not pecking hard, just touching gently. He would prance and strut for a couple of minutes, and then go to the opposite side of the pump and probe for any likely looking spot to gain entrance.

As he walked around the pump he would display before the south side of the pump. His circuits were always in a clockwise direction as far as I could tell. I never saw him walk in the other direction. He would work for as much as fifteen minutes or more, and then give up and fly to his perch on the power line or to a bush in a marshy area about two hundred yards away. Two hundred meters if you are Canadian will be close enough for government work.

He would rest for a short while, and then fly back and go through the same steps as though they had been carefully rehearsed. He would repeat the entire performance several times a day. When it was time for us to leave, he had been trying to get at the bird in the pump for at least five days. I don't know when he found time to eat. I suppose that birds are a lot like humans. There are times when it seems that there are more important things than food, even to a cowbird.

In all the time that I watched that bird, he never went to the other pump. He went to the north side of the pump only one time that I saw and that time only briefly. He went to the west side, the side opposite the hose, only to try to gain entry. He did not display on that side as he had on the other.

And I thought bull moose were crazy.

We always see several ducks while we are fishing in Canada. I'm not sure of the origin of the word "duck." I have heard a Cajun from Louisiana pronounce it as almost a cross between "duck" and "duke." He tells funny stories about ducks, dogs and people. His pronunciation is almost like the French "duc."

I don't believe that it came from the French. "Duc" when referring to birds, is an American "hooty-owl." The great horned owl. An owl doesn't look much like a duck and he can't swim or dive worth a hoot. Ducks on the other hand can't hoot worth a quack.

When you talk about ducks in Canada you almost automatically include "fish ducks" or mergansers and loons, which aren't ducks at all. Mergansers dive for small fish. They catch enough to make their flesh taste like foul fish. This is a part of an evolutionary protective system. Not many people would want to waste expensive shotgun shells on some bloomin' duck that wasn't fit to eat nor pretty enough to hang on the wall.

Loons dive for fish, too. They catch them by the bunch. They aren't fit to eat either, but their plumage is a beautiful blend of black and white; polka dots and a white ring around the neck. A loon can't walk or run worth a quack on dry land, but when he gets in the water, he can outrun a "hokey-pokeyed" cat.

Some people shoot loons so that they can have them mounted. They keep the stuffed loon on the mantel in the game room or some other place of such honor.

The Canadian government liked the loon so much that they put it on the backside of Queen Elizabeth, on a gold-colored dollar that is worth even less than the one we put Susan B. Anthony on. The Queen is on the side they call the obverse. She is a great lady and deserves something better than a loon on the reverse. The Canadians call them "loony dollars," and they go by so fast that they hardly get to look at them. They go faster than a loon under water.

131

The loon makes a noise like nothing in this world and probably like nothing in the next. It is impossible to acurately describe. It is a high-pitched scream that turns into a tremolo just about the time that you think that it should have stopped. Before your ears stop ringing, the loon starts again. But when you are on a remote lake and haven't seen another person for eight days, the loon makes the sweetest music this side of Guy Lombardo.

Loons are sometimes pretty sociable people. When you are on a small lake in a small boat and sitting quietly, a man and wife will come near the boat and entertain you with a show. They will rear and spread their wings and flutter. They may run a few yards on top of the water. They will dive and play hide-and-seek with you, only they want you to do all the seeking. They can swim underwater for incredible distances. They could probably swim farther if they didn't stop to grab a bite to eat now and then.

If you see a loon nest in the reeds or brush at the edge of the water, try not to make a wake. The eggs are laid near the water's edge and a cold bath is just what they don't need. The loon has a hard way to go with his friend, man. Be kind to him.

One story that should be related in this section is about a fishing trip that I made with my father-in-law to Grafton Dam. It is called Tygart Reservoir now. I haven't finished it for more years than I can recall, but it used to be a good crappie hole.

We were fishing from a high cliff that was normally under water when the reservoir was full. The cliff had been undercut by the water about fifteen or twenty feet from the top, and the water beneath the cliff was in deep shade. The crappies were biting like crazy.

I dropped my bait down the side, and it had just hit the water when something grabbed the bait and yanked so hard that I thought I would lose the rod. Uh, oh! A big bass. I set the hook and had the fight of my life on my hands, upside down. I had hooked a duck, and he took off for the wild blue and I was trying to fight him in with the rod and reel. It was a struggle getting him down and even more trying to get him calmed down so that I could remove the hook. More animal intelligence. As soon as he realized that I really meant him no harm and was only trying to help, he settled down and let me remove the hook from the hard rim at the edge of his beak. He

132

wasn't hurt, just embarrassed. And they say that animals aren't smart.

The only other bird that I ever caught on a fish line was off the big bridge across the Indian River in Fort Pierce, Florida. I was casting live shrimp and fishing for anything with fins that would be fun to catch.

I pitched a shrimp as far as I could cast, and before it hit the water, a brown pelican swooped out of nowhere and grabbed the bait in his flour sack apron of a beak.

Boy, what a fight that was! We finally subdued him by working the rod around the light poles and leading the bird to the sand beach a good stretch below the fish walk. My son-in-law went down to the water's edge and tried to quiet the pelican. That pelican tried to beat him to death. I finally recovered enough slack to hold the bird's head with his beak pointing skyward while Bill came in from behind and furled his wings. He fought every inch of the way, and as soon as the hook was removed, he took off for the south end of Hutchinson Island and didn't look back. I'll bet that he took a long hard look at any shrimp served a la carte in the future.

Fortunately, neither of these birds were injured physically. The hook lodged in the very edge of the beak in both cases and did not penetrate beyond the barb. But I'll bet that there was some damage to the psyches. Their dignity may have suffered somewhat, but if birds can think, they both learned a valuable lesson. Not all humans are bent on doing them harm.

The duck seemed to sense this the minute he felt my hands on his back and wings. He sat perfectly still while I released the hook. The pelican fought it all the way. They were both glad to be freed.

We have come a long way with our relationship with birds in the last few centuries. A short time back, relatively speaking, we were killing songbirds because they ate a few berries or a little grain. Now we welcome them as our allies who eat the bugs that do us harm. Evolution is teaching us a few things, little by little, but sometimes it is a slow process.

Birds are somewhat like their bigger cousins, humans, when it comes to building houses. Some build good solid houses in the better locations. Some don't.

When we lived in Bluefield, West Virginia, my wife watched a pair of English Sparrows build a nest in a peach tree which

133

stood just outside the window of our apartment. They must have been newlyweds.

They chose a small fork (bifurcation, if you would prefer a forty-dollar word to a forty-cent one) that was obviously unstable. There were many better sites in the tree where the limbs were larger and more sturdy. That observation is made from the benefit of twenty-twenty hindsight, by the way.

They worked hard at carrying dry grass, bits of string, plastic, straw and what-have-you to the building site. They wove it all together, but they did some shoddy work. They left several spaces where there should have been material. I haven't spent a lot of time sitting on bird nests trying to raise a family, so I suppose that I should not set myself up as an expert on the construction methods, but it just didn't look good to me.

The spot they chose and the amount of work they did on what surely would prove to be temporary quarters reminded me of the way some humans build houses, particularly those who build astraddle of the San Andreas fault or on unstable fill on the seashore. We do the same thing here in West Virginia, when we build on known floodplains along a riverbank or on the side of a hill where there is a huge mud slide, so I'm not picking on Californians or Carolinians.

The birds completed the mating process, and the clutch of eggs was laid. But before the eggs could hatch, we had a windstorm that wasn't really out of the ordinary for these parts. The slender twigs holding the flimsy nest moved easily under the pressure from the wind. And down came rock-a-bye nestie, eggies and all.

I hope that the pair learned a valuable lesson before they started building their next home.

Sometimes some humans are a bit hard on birds, particularly those that are big enough to eat. The flock of geese that I wrote about earlier had lived in that area for several summers. One of the villagers fed them regularly. They would walk up to anyone who held his hand out with a chunk of bread in it. They walked the street of the village occasionally. Most of the time they were unmolested.

We were up there one year on the opening day of goose season. So help me if some shooter didn't kill three of those pets right there on the street. You notice that I used the term "shooter" instead of "hunter." There is a big difference between the two.

Several years ago, the Department of Natural Resources attempted to start a flock of turkeys near our farm in Upshur County. There was no open season on wild turkeys there at that time, but locals and outsiders saw an opportunity to kill a turkey and kept on until they wiped them out. There were three hens that hung around the farm for three or four years, but nature is sort of funny. Most animals won't dream up artificial insemination by themselves, so the hens eventually disappeared for want of a proper love life.

My wife and I spend a lot of time outdoors for a couple of city slickers. Of course our town, Princeton, isn't what most people would consider a hardcore urban area. What with a population that represents just about the smallest large city in southern West Virginia, where large cities have as many as twenty or thirty thousand, we wouldn't be considered exactly overcrowded by someone from New York or Los Angeles. The population of either of those small towns is five times the population of our whole state. Most of those people probably think of us as wood-hicks.

While we are rambling around in the hills, we come across a number of birds that are somewhat unusual for our area. One of these was a mature bald eagle which we watched for a couple of seasons. He seemed to know that we were friendly and would put on displays for us. We have had him fly for a mile or two alongside the car, just slightly above and ahead of us. He seemed to enjoy the game.

A couple of years back, we missed our old friend when we made several trips to the area for the flowers that my wife uses in her bookmarks. We learned later that a group of poachers from North Carolina had been apprehended with several deer in their possession. Among the deer was an eagle.

The crooks were caught within a few miles of where we had enjoyed his friendship. They were probably some of those who were hungry and had driven more than a hundred and fifty miles just to get something to eat. I don't know how a bald eagle would taste when southern fried, but I'll bet it would be as tough as shoe leather.

Maybe evolution will take care of some of those people in due time. They sure helped it take care of some of our wildlife.

135

The courts and the legislatures, both state and federal, do not seem to be interested in taking care of those people who are bent on destroying. And they don't do much to help those who are genuinely bent on conservation.

Conservation is the wise use of natural resources which results in preservation of species while furnishing employment and recreation for humans who are a part of the natural environment. A conservationist is not one who believes in nonuse. Neither does he ignore nor underestimate the importance of man in the natural order.

BEAVERS

Beavers are funny-looking animals with wide flat tails and buck teeth. To me, the females look just like the males. Evolution has played a dirty trick on the beaver. His teeth grow so fast that if he gets a toothache and has to stop gnawing for a few days, his teeth will grow outside the mouth and past each other so that he can't eat. And they always live a long way from an orthodontist, and transportation is usually pretty slow.

Beavers apparently know this because they will cut trees that are far too big for them to carry home. It may be that they are just sharpening their teeth. If you examine a beaver house or lodge, it is unlikely that you will find any large logs or trees that were used in the construction. It is built mostly of small limbs and twigs that rarely exceed six inches or so in diameter. You may find a larger log in one of their dams once in a while, but I believe that a twelve-inch or larger log was not intended by the beavers. It probably was already there or just floated in either during or after construction.

Beavers are related to honeybees. They work all the time to build their houses and gather food for the winter when the weather permits. They eat the bark from branches and twigs and from the larger pieces of trees which they fell. They seem to prefer aspen (also called poplar in Canada), where it is available, but they will eat bark from other trees, too. Humans use expressions like "as busy as a beaver" or "as busy as a bee" when they want to indicate that another person is industrious. You don't hear the expressions much anymore for some reason.

You also hear the expression, "eager beaver" used in referring to other humans. It also used to mean someone who was anxious to do his job, but today the meaning is different—at least the job isn't the same. That is another kind of beaver that doesn't build dams. It has only half as many legs and doesn't have a tail behind with which to slap the water. The expression doesn't mean anything close to what it once did. You hear it on the CB radio, usually around truck stops and places like that. Those beavers don't call their house a lodge, either.

There is one truck stop that you will have to find for yourself if you want to conduct your own scientific research that is called "the Beaver Farm." Probably because they have so many beavers. I have heard it said that they have more used beavers than most dealers have used cars. Only about ninety-five percent of the truck drivers who run the east coast know where it is, but I couldn't guarantee that one of them would share the secret with you.

These beavers usually have high-pitched, squeaky voices and speak a shoddy sort of English which truck drivers seem to understand. They are bilingual in Canada. That is so that they can work both sides of the street.

I have overheard them talking on the CB. I have yet to hear them talk about how many trees they can cut or how big of a dam they can build. They use some words in both French and English that I have no idea what they mean. Their conversations must be interesting, because I have heard them talking to truck drivers and nondrivers, both who apparently were anxious to continue the conversation face-to-face.

I heard one driver say that at least one of these dry-land beavers had long red hair. I have seen literally dozens of the water-dwelling beavers, and I have never seen one of them with red hair, so they must be a different species.

I have no idea what this strange variety of beaver eats, but I think that they must drink a lot of coffee. I have heard them invite a driver up for a cup of coffee, and you know how truck drivers are. They usually drink at least three or four cups when they eat breakfast. If that beaver drinks cup for cup with every truck driver she asks in, she must have a ba pretty close-by.

They may have buck teeth, too. At least one truck driver told another that one of them did. I have no idea what they could

138

gnaw on around truck stops and "grease pits" to keep their teeth sharp unless it would be pork chop bones. But you can only eat so many pork chops. You know that old saying, "Man (or woman, as the case may be) cannot live on pork chops alone."

The wide flat tail on a water-dwelling beaver is used as a rudder and as a swim fin while the beaver is swimming. It is also used to pat mud in place when the beaver is working on his house or a dam. That may be the reason that there is usually very little hair on the beaver's tail. He keeps it worn off by using it in his work.

Those aren't the real reasons for the wide tail, however. Evolution plans far ahead and can anticipate things that an ordinary mortal could not possibly foresee. It wouldn't do anything that was so obvious as those uses mentioned above. You really have to study long and hard to determine the real reasons for evolution doing some of the things that it does.

The beaver has a flat tail for one reason, and one reason only. The beaver preceded humans by I don't know how many years. If you were to ask a real expert, he would probably give you an accurate figure within two or three millennia. But evolution knew that humans were coming along a while later, and it knew what funny things humans would be doing, especially in the same water holes where the beavers lived. So it provided the beaver with that big flat tail for its future contact with fishermen.

A beaver spots a fisherman sitting quietly in a boat. Every nerve and muscle is as tight as a fiddle string, as he concentrates on catching a nice walleye that he has just spotted sticking his nose from under a "deadhead." The fisherman can see the walleye inching toward his minnow, licking his lips in expectation of a free lunch. The walleye nudges the minnow to be sure it is alive and well, since he doesn't want any old spoiled meat for lunch. This makes the rod tip jiggle ever so slightly. The beaver sees the rod tip move, and sneaks up beside the boat so quietly that the fisherman has no idea that there is anyone else within a hundred miles.

That is the precise moment when evolution proves what it has been doing all those many centuries. The beaver slaps the water with his tail. The resounding whack is louder than someone hitting the water with a flat board. This scares the bejabers out of the fisherman, and he jumps all over like a spring that has been stretched too tight and is suddenly released. He jerks the rod sharply upward and pulls the minnow from under the very nose of the biggest walleye that he has seen in the last four seasons. This startles the walleye, and he takes off for a sanctuary that he had already chosen, and he swears to himself that he will be harder to fool the next time.

The loud whack on the water alerts all the other fish in the area that something is afoot—afloat might be a better word—and they take off as fast as their legs will carry them to their hideouts.

I have read that fish cannot hear you talk. I don't know for sure, since I don't have fish ears. It has something or other to do with the way sound waves travel through air and water being different. It is probably a good thing, if that is true, that they can't hear the fisherman. The language he uses immediately following such an occurrence contains a lot of four-letter words and some brand-new variations mixed in with all the old ones that he knows, and they wouldn't be fit for a fish to hear.

The beaver is an old hand at this sort of thing, and he knows that the fisherman is going to explode verbally and physically. He ducks under at the instant he whacks the water and swims about fifty yards or so away so that he will be just out of reach of anything the fisherman can throw. He seems to know that the fisherman is not allowed to carry a gun for his own protection. If the fisherman doesn't have anything handy to throw, the beaver will always pop up just out of reach of the paddle or the boathook. Then he just sits there and grins, showing a full set of big buck teeth. If he were a little closer you could hear him chuckle.

My wife and I were sitting in our boat, in a small lake in Northern Ontario, watching the purple martins and the dragonflies racing to see who could get to the black flies and mosquitoes first. There weren't any second or third place awards. We were watching a bald eagle soaring far overhead and somewhere to our rear, a cock-of-the-north was yodelling his territorial serenade as he bobbed up and down in his erratic flight. We were enjoying the scenery while we waited for some itinerant walleye to come along to interrupt our peace and quiet. We had both stretched out across the boat with our feet

140

resting on the gunwales and our heads resting on the seat cushions. There was so little noise that you could easily hear the dragonflies nail the black flies that made up their midafternoon snack. Our friends had taken over the job of protecting us from the nibbling rascals.

We could hear, faintly at first, an odd sound that we couldn't place. We thought that it was coming from the shore to our left, which was more than a quarter of a mile away.

The lake in which we were fishing is just a wide place in the river that spreads out to form two good-sized bays. Hardly anyone knows about it except for one Indian guide and 4,837 of his clients and their buddies, and the whole town of Gowganda. The river flows fairly fast through the narrows between the bays, and that spot gets a lot of traffic from fishermen, but not much from fish. That is where we were anchored.

The sound gradually increased in volume but we still could not determine what it was, nor where it was coming from. We were both pushing seventy, and our ears had not become any better with the passing years, but we didn't wear hearing aids yet. It sounded for all the world like a rat gnawing on a board. I even looked at the transom to see if we might have some extra passenger aboard.

We decided to weigh anchor and drift a little closer to that shore. Aha! The noise became a little louder. We still could see no activity except one beaver towing a branch over in a tiny bay, but that could not have made that kind of noise.

We drifted to within about fifty or sixty yards of the shore before we could tell what was going on. A whole family of beavers had invited some relatives in to have a woodchopping party and a house-raising. There must have been at least fifteen beavers in the bush, busily cutting their winter firewood. They were gnawing on big aspens that they couldn't possibly drag home. If they could have floated them to the house, there was no way that they could have placed them on the house, which was around a curve of land at the edge of the small bay. It was built of the usual small limbs and branches.

The beavers paid no attention to us and kept on gnawing and hauling even though they were aware of our presence. They were paying us absolutely no never-mind.

A big old grandpa beaver had been scouting the opposite shore of the larger bay to see if the working conditions were any better on that side which was about a half a mile away. He decided to come back to the lodge for a cup of coffee or maybe to make sure that everyone was meeting his quota. We saw him make two or three false starts from the shore and then didn't pay any attention to him.

He sneaked up to within about eight or ten feet of the boat, unnoticed by us, and decided that something wasn't quite to his liking. When his tail hit the water, we both jumped.

I don't know whether it was our reaction or the sound that startled the other beavers, but everything came to a screeching halt. All sound stopped immediately. There was not a single beaver cutting, and none had taken to the water, but there was not a beaver to be seen. Even grandpa beaver had disappeared.

It must have been nearly ten minutes later that they started up their chain saws and started cutting at full tilt. We were still sitting quietly in the same spot. We paddled a couple hundred yards before firing up the Evinrude.

We moved back to the same area that we had left and sat there and waited some more. We didn't do a whole lot of good fishing that afternoon, but we made up for it later in the evening. But we were having a peck of fun just being.

We returned the next day, but we had company. In another boat was a man and his wife from Gowganda. They were anchored not more than fifty or sixty feet from our boat. They fired up a gasoline stove and cooked their fish and their supper on the rear seat of the boat, not three feet from the gas can. We didn't hear the beavers that day at all. But it may have been that I was straining my ears for the explosion that I knew was going to happen sooner or later. Thank heavens it didn't.

But I was so nervous that I couldn't fish.

I am sure that you must have heard that otters like to play. It isn't so widely known, perhaps, but beavers like to play, too. Sometimes they pick some odd playmates.

We were fishing on Lake Michewakenda one evening and were joined by our friend, Ben Nadeau. The same one in the moose story. He was accompanied by one of his crew and by his regular fishing companion, his dog, Rocky. Rocky is a golden retriever and he likes to fish. He likes to swim, too.

We were in a small bay south of Rhonda Camp and had caught a few walleyes and pike. We were making very little noise and not moving around much. Rocky was watching the fish coming into the boat and inspecting the catch to see if they were big enough to keep. He was busy watching both boats. He may have been counting our fish to be sure that we weren't exceeding our limit. He was telling Ben which lure to use, baiting hooks, helping to net the fish coming into Ben's boat, pointing out fish on the bottom, and generally doing all the things that any good fishing buddy would do. He would even nudge Ben when he was busy talking to us and was getting a bite at the same time. He was also watching a beaver that kept edging nearer the boat and making faces at the dog.

When the beaver got to within about fifteen feet of the boat, he thumbed his nose at Rocky and yelled, "Yah, Yah, Yah, you can't catch me." Rocky bailed out of the boat before anyone could stop him and took after the beaver which had submerged. He surfaced a short distance away, and the chase was on. The beaver would swim just a little ahead of Rocky until he just about caught up. Then he would splash water in Rocky's face and dive again. He would come up just a little way behind Rocky and make a noise to get Rocky's attention and take off again. He led that dog on a merry chase that took them all the way across the lake, up the opposite shore, back across the lake and down the near shore toward the boats. The chase must have covered at least two miles, and the beaver and the dog were having a ball.

Ben finally got the dog near shore and into the boat where he paid them off with a doggy shower, and he stunk. He broke up the fishing party.

I have seen mother birds carry out the same kind of performance to protect their brood from supposed or real predators. But there wasn't a beaver house near enough for us to pose any threat to any young. There was no reason for the behavior except that the beaver wanted to play.

I have observed the tail-slapping and the diving around a boat on a number of occasions. The beaver will stay fairly close to the boat when this happens. I have considered the possibility that the walleyes and the beavers are "in cahoots." "In cahoots" is an old-timey way to say "having a symbiotic relationship."

Both American and Canadian trappers go after beaver. They catch a beaver, kill it, skin it, and stretch the hide on a

143

frame to. dry. The dried pelt is called a blanket. I have never really understood why. They certainly don't resemble a blanket that goes on your bed.

One fur trading company from the earliest days of the fur trade capitalized on this difference. That company sold some fine quality wool blankets that could be acquired in sizes to fit almost any bed. The blankets had short black stripes woven into the edge which indicated the number of beaver pelts that it required in exchange for the blanket. The black stripes were called "points." Beaver pelts were also called "points" at one time, but I haven't heard the term used recently. It may still be in use in some areas.

You can still find copies of the Hudson Bay blankets complete with the black stripes. It might be a bit difficult to swap beaver pelts for them, but the dealers will take "frogskins." "Frogskins" is a colloquiallism for dollar bills that I haven't heard for a coon's age, either. It takes a pretty good stack of frogskins to buy a king-size blanket.

I ran into a West Virginian on one of my trips to Canada a few years back. He was wearing a coat that had been made from a couple of such blankets. It was as red as red can get, and the points were in a prominent location. It made a dandy coat for early spring on the arctic watershed where the temperature can get "down and dirty" when you are sleeping in a tent.

I had never met him, although he lived less than sixty miles from here, but I had driven some of the mountain roads that he had bulldozed through the hills, near Rupert.

Canadian beaver trappers are assigned territories where they are required to take a quota of beavers in order to maintain a stable population which the Ministry of Natural Resources has determined suitable for that area. Failure to meet the quota can eventually result in loss of the permit if the trapper continues to fall short. I am not aware of a similar system in West Virginia, but we don't have the proliferation of beavers that they have in Ontario.

Canadian trappers often save the carcasses of the beavers to use as bear bait during the spring bear season. The carcass is frozen, and when it is needed for bait, it is removed from the freezer, taken to the bear stand, and suspended in a mesh sack from a tree limb that hopefully a bear cannot quite reach. It

144

gets "ripe" after a couple of days in the sun. Ripe means the same thing as rotten.

The beaver usually gets ripe a long time before the peaches and the plums even set on. I have watched this baiting procedure only on the arctic watershed, and peaches and plums don't do well up there. It gets so cold that it freezes their little stones off. They don't make felt-lined boots to fit peach seeds.

A hunter takes a stand where he can observe the bait and waits for a bear to come by to investigate. If he can shoot somewhere near straight, he gets a bear. Sometimes.

Beavers are funny-looking animals, but one of the oddest looking animals that I ever saw that thought it was a beaver wasn't a beaver at all. It was a groundhog.

My wife and I were fishing in a deep narrow cleft on a lake up there on the arctic watershed (there ain't no need for you to ask for better directions, 'cause I ain't tellin' about that fishin' hole), where a narrow creek flows through between two almost vertical, high banks of nearly solid stone to connect a large lake with one that is considerably smaller. It is the only way for walleyes to get from one to the other, and it was full of fish when we were there last. The water is so swift that it is difficult to hold a small boat in position, even with a fluke-type anchor, which my wife says is the easiest for her to handle. (You surely didn't expect me to run the motor and handle the anchor at the same time. I'm doing all the hard part now.)

We could see the locator going crazy. There were thousands of fish so thick that the sonar couldn't distinguish between the layers, let alone individual fish. We had found paradise. Again.

We were drifting slowly on a tight anchor line. The anchor couldn't hold that twelve-footer in one position. It kept slipping and grabbing by fits and jerks, allowing us to fish in one spot for only a few seconds before dropping us to another to repeat the process. But it made no difference where we drifted, the fish were everywhere.

Some movement on the shore to starboard, which was only about ten feet away, caught my eye. So help me, there sat a female groundhog watching us intently. She didn't act the least bit afraid. She may have had very little prior association with humans and didn't know that there were those who would eat her under the proper set of circumstances.

Before you ask how I could be sure that it was a female at that distance, I want to remind you that I have pretty good eyes for a septuagenarian, especially when I am wearing my bifocals so that I can see to bait my hook. And besides that, I have never seen a male groundhog that was so obviously pregnant.

She watched us for a few minutes and must have decided that we were of the friendly type. She started working her way down the steep bank toward the water.

I glanced her way occasionally to be sure that she was still doing alright. I was busy with other things, like yelling at my wife to set the hook and other silly stuff like that and forgot to watch the groundhog. The next time I saw her, she had both front paws on the gunwale which had only about three inches of freeboard because of the 225-pound hulk, plus all his gear sitting on that corner of the boat. She was peering up at me in an obvious plea for help. The water was swifter than she had reckoned. I grabbed a paddle for her to climb, but she couldn't hold on.

I had experienced the long, sharp incisors of groundhogs when I was a kid, and I hadn't forgotten how they can rip a hound's ear or a man's finger. I had also read of rabid animals back in West Virginia, and about the big needles they use for injections when they think you have been exposed. I decided not to tempt fate by using my hands.

I still can't figure why she wanted in the boat. She may have thought that I resembled her obstetrician, since I was wearing my sunglasses. Or she may have simply been looking for a handout and thought we looked like easy marks. Or she may have just wanted to drop by for a chat.

Whatever her reason, she couldn't make it up the paddle, even after three or four tries. She gave up and swam back to shore. When she got settled on dry land, she turned and stared at us with an expression (so help me), that looked for all the world as though she thought that her friends had let her down. I was glad that she didn't speak English. Or French. I can understand a little French, and she might have used some of the words that I understand.

She finally made her way to the top of the cliff, pausing every few feet to look back at us and glare. She looked at us as if we were the two most stupid people in the entire world.

146

I can't explain that behavior. I wish that I hadn't been such a coward. She might have been a nice person to know.

Beavers were hit pretty hard back in the early history of Canada, and the United States. They were trapped in areas where there wasn't a United States yet in the west. There was a huge demand for the fur to make beaver hats for the gentry of Europe. The pelts became almost as valuable as gold and were even used as a medium of exchange instead of money.

The beavers started making a comeback when the style changed, and the demand for the pelts came to a screeching halt.

We have beaver in West Virginia today where there were none in the thirties and forties. Those terrible hunters again. It was their dollars that were responsible for public acquisition of habitat and protection.

The beaver is one more living example of the harshness of evolution. If he stops gnawing, his teeth can grow through his skull. That has got to smart. If he gnaws too much (because of too many beavers), he can literally eat himself out of house and home. But he is still around for us to enjoy.

Bees

I really don't care a whole lot for some of these people who try to mislead you by telling you or by writing that honeybees, wasps, hornets, yellow jackets and the like bite you. They don't bite you—not much, anyway. They sting you when they want to make you smart.

Ask any person who has been running around in his bare feet out in the yard and has stepped on a honeybee. He will tell you that it stings. If you look at his foot, you will more than likely see the stinger still sticking there. It doesn't look like the canine tooth of a bear or a wolf.

Oh, and by the way, don't grab it and try to pull it out. The honeybee leaves a chemical that causes those two little white blobs at the base of the stinger to keep on pumping long after he has left the premises—maybe as much as twenty minutes. The two little pulsing blobs look like a pair of tiny white hearts beating almost as one. When you squeeze them, you are just helping the bee to get even with you for stepping on him. You just shoot more venom into the hole.

Gently scrape the stinger off with the sharp edge of a knife. If you don't have a knife, scrape with a sliver of wood or a key. You should do all you can to help nature, as you are expected, but there isn't much sense in going to the extreme of helping a bee get even. You don't have to overdo it.

There are many varieties of stinging insects. Some of the more commonly encountered in the eastern United States and Canada are the honeybees (both wild and domestic), paper wasps, hornets, bumblebees, sand wasps, yellow jackets, sweat bees, tomato worms (the bristly kind), corn worms and others.

148

Most bees will respond when they are disturbed, some more than others. Most have the same superficial effect, a sharp stinging sensation accompanied by immediate local swelling. If you are allergic to bee venom, the swelling can become serious. The sting can result in death.

I have read that more people die of bee stings each year in the United States than die of snakebites. They probably didn't count the people who died of heart attacks brought on by stepping on a snake before seeing it. That would tip the scales, so to speak. When you do that, the snake doesn't have to do anything but just lie there looking stupid. He doesn't have to be poisonous to scare you to death.

Bee venom is treacherous in a way. You can go for years without severe reaction and believe that you are not allergic, and then seemingly overnight, you develop severe allergy problems. Maybe people should be even more afraid of bees than they are of snakes, but most people never have the well-known genetically transmitted reaction to bees that they have to close encounters of the moose, rattlesnake and big bear kinds.

There is a funny-looking little critter known by a number of names such as paper hornet, bald-faced hornet, white-faced hornet, and a whole string of others that are not fit to print in this book. I prefer to call them bald-faced hornets because that takes the place of a lot of other names that I might feel like calling them.

The bald-faced hornet is a half-brother to a bull moose. You may never know what made him mad, but he will put his head down, paw the ground a couple of times, and charge right into you, no matter how big you are.

When he starts his charge, it looks like he isn't moving more than about ninety miles an hour, but when he gets to within fifteen or twenty yards, he lines up his laser sight and lights all his afterburners.

When he hits you in the forehead, he can knock you flatter than one of Grandma's pancakes. He sights in on your forehead about nine times out of every eight, and if you think the air force was accurate when they mauled Hussein, you ain't seen nothin'.

It probably stuns the hornet, too, when he slams into you at breakneck speed, but he has already triggered all his weapons systems, and they will function on automatic like you wouldn't

149

believe. He gives you a sharp jab with that fiery little thing that he carries around in his trunk and gives it a couple of extra squeezes just to add injury to insult. He may be lying on his back on the ground, kicking his feet, and yelling for help from some of his playmates, but don't count him out.

If the impact of the collision doesn't kill the hornet, he can hurry back to his base and rearm his rocket launchers and ready his systems for another go in a matter of minutes. I have heard some folks say that such an attack kills the hornet. I have not personally seen one that was killed from slamming into a person head-to-head, but if it doesn't kill him, his head must be pretty blamed hard.

When he bangs you in the forehead with all his rockets and bombs, you're going to believe that he must carry a lot heavier armament than it seems possible. It will probably make your eyes swell shut and possibly turn as black as if you had run into a doorknob. Your nostrils may swell. Maybe even that big hole right there below your nostrils—there where you store your teeth.

If you like to sit around doing things with your fingers like playing piano, guitar or ukelele, don't go poking your finger into that little hole in the bottom of a hornet's nest. It will make your finger sore. And swollen. Sometimes it will swell all the way to your elbow. I'll tell you right now that a finger that is swollen until it is as long as your arm is a funny sight. But it doesn't feel funny. It hurts. And if you are allergic to the venom, it can send you on your way to the happy hunting ground.

Don't try to get even by throwing rocks or your empty beer cans at his windows, either. He doesn't have a bunch of stupid laws that won't allow him to protect and defend his property. He would probably yell, "Hey, Rube!" so that the whole family could join in the fun. He can follow the trajectory of your missile right back to your pitching arm by sensing the disturbance in the air. Sometimes I wish I could do that—especially when the neighbors get mad at me and start throwing sticks and clods and stuff like that at my house.

Running is often a losing tactic. He can fly faster than you can run and a lot straighter. He can easily follow you for a hundred yards or more when he is really steamed.

Most domestic honeybees will follow for only about fifteen or twenty yards. Wild bees may follow a bit farther if you happen to catch them in a bad mood on a rainy day when they can't get outdoors without getting their shoes muddy. The so-called "killer bees" will follow as far as a hundred yards and more. They will also boil out of the hive in fantastic numbers. It isn't the venom from one bee that causes the problem. It is the fact that there are so dad-blamed many of them stinging the victim in a single attack.

Beekeepers can generally handle tame bees without getting stung if they treat them gently and kindly, and if the handler doesn't smell like he is afraid. Tame bees do not react to robbing them of their honey as strongly as wild bees—usually. Most tame bees are quite docile.

Bee venom isn't all bad. It has been known for years that some bee stings have relieved arthritic and rheumatic pain and swelling. But woe unto him who is allergic to the venom. I would not advise getting stung forty or fifty times just to get some relief from arthritis.

Some yellow jackets, honeybees and sweat bees will bite. If you sit around where they are working on a clear warm day and don't try to be a sidewalk superintendent and tell them how to do their jobs, one might come over on his coffee break and sit on your arm and talk about the job, marital problems, and the like, just to pass the time of day.

If he does sit down for a friendly chat, don't make any sudden moves, not even to zip up anything that you might have left open. This is the worst possible time that you could choose to start shaking your fist at him or threatening him with a lawsuit. All bees are akin to Irishmen, and they can get their dander up pretty fast and over what seems like the most trivial aggravation. Sometimes they act like Irishmen, too, and would rather fight than eat.

If you can hold still long enough for him to make himself at home, you might feel him nibbling with his little mandibles. It doesn't hurt—it tickles. Mandibles is another word for bee teeth. That may be oversimplifying a wee bit, but who wants to split hairs over a few bug teeth.

After he finishes getting all the salt or oil or whatever else he was after on your arm, it might be a good idea to move to another spot as soon as he leaves. Bees are terrible about keep-

151

ing a secret. When they find something they like and if they don't gobble it all up, they will run home and tell all the hired hands. Bees aren't greedy. They share.

While he was sitting there eating or just nibbling, he was also putting down a scent marker to let the rest of the family know that you are an OK guy and an easy mark. He follows that scent marker if he wants to come back for seconds with a bunch of his relatives so they can get acquainted with you.

The old-timey hoboes did the same thing back during the lean years of the terrible thirties, only they left a chalk mark on a tree or a pole, so that the brothers coming along a little later would know what to expect.

You could possibly get covered with bees if you happen to step into a family feud that you hadn't heard about. That doesn't happen often, just when one part of the family decides that they have had enough of the old queen's high-handed ways, and sneak in a new queen, and then follow her to a new home.

There isn't really anything wrong with getting covered with bees, as long as they continue to be friendly. A coating of bees about three or four inches thick can be rather uncomfortable on a hot day. And you might have to get back to work before they do. Bees don't punch time clocks.

If a queen does happen to land on your chin, you can bet that within a few minutes you are going to have a bee necktie, maybe all the way to your belt. Don't get nervous. And keep your mouth shut. I just saw a picture of a beekeeper who had placed a queen on his chin just to show what would happen. He had bees on his face and chest so thick that you couldn't tell him from a fence post. It didn't mention that he also had bees in his bonnet.

If a bee does come to visit with you for a while, don't get too friendly and decide to pet him. He doesn't like people touching him, and he may let you know in no uncertain terms to keep your fingers to yourself. He doesn't do a whole lot with his front parts, but what he does with his back parts makes up for it.

If it is a wasp or a hornet that lets you know, he will run away and live to fight another day. If it is a honeybee, it is a different story. Honeybees have little barbs on their stingers, and once he pushes it into you, he can't pull it back out. When
152

he flies away, he leaves some of his vital parts hanging on the end of the stinger, and he will die in a few minutes. Then you won't have a little pet bee anymore. He probably knows that he is on a suicide mission, but that is part of his job. Just like the Japanese kamikaze pilots, in World War II.

A lot of people like to call the insect world "the insect kingdom." If you like that term better, go ahead. Maybe "queendom" would be better. Honeybees do have queens, as do most other colonizing insects, one to a colony, except when one part of the colony decides to move out. Then the workers nurture a new queen and start a new colony.

They have kings, too, if you want to be liberal in your terminology and don't dig too deep to find out what a king really is. They are called "drones" and they are the lazy bees. They won't work out in the fields with the common laborers, and they can't fight. Probably because they have laid around on the couch watching television and have become too fat to enjoy life. They just sit around the house all day playing games like solitaire and gin rummy, watching TV, and doing all the little chores that the queen wants done while the slaves are all out in the fields picking cotton and digging peanuts. They do things like sweeping floors, dusting, drying dishes, making the beds, and seeing that the kids stay out of mischief.

The queen doesn't do much of anything except boss everybody else around and nag. She is nearly always pregnant. And barefooted. She is the only female in the house, and all those husbands hanging around all the time must be pretty monotonous.

Evolution hasn't been too awfully kind to most bees.

The insect kingdom has had its share of manmade messes with his fooling around with evolution. Man is always sticking his nose into everybody else's business and piddling around with a lot of stuff that he doesn't know enough about like DDT, cane toads, walking catfish and killer bees. When he gets things fouled up beyond any chance of recovery, he finds some excuse like "They escaped" and thinks that makes it alright. What did he think would happen when he opened the gate? He thinks that he is smarter than God, and the less he knows about God, the smarter he thinks he is. Who does man think

153

got us into the mess we're in today with polluted water, polluted air and polluted earth?

Some even deny that there is a god. Those few just don't know what God is. They probably still are protesting against some old man with a white beard. They must have seen some of the works of Michaelangelo Buonarroti.

Take "killer bees," for example.

If God had wanted killer bees in Brazil, he would have put them there in the first place. He didn't forget army ants and fire ants.

Killer bees aren't really killer bees. Their venom is about the same in composition and quantity as any other honeybee. The big difference is in attitude and application.

I told you earlier that a tame bee was most likely a docile little fellow who worked hard at his job and usually fought only to defend his house, his family and himself. He will fight when sufficiently riled, but he rarely pursues very far, even in self-defense.

"Killer bees" are different in that they will chase an intruder for as much as one or two hundred yards to catch him, and then follow as long as they can still sting or until the victim is defeated.

Killer bees were over there in Africa in their own little village where they had plenty of room to move around without bumping into someone they didn't like and without a bunch of others bumping into them. They were pretty much minding their own business, but every now and again, they just had to get into some kind of a big brawl. Their nature, I guess.

Some old miser down in Brazil who was working his little tame bees nearly to death so that he could sell honey by the barrelful couldn't stand a little prosperity. He got greedy and dreamed up a get-rich-quick scheme. Such schemes rarely work without someone winding up with the dirty end of the stick.

He kept pushing his little hired hands for more production when they were already working their little fool heads off for him, starting just after dawn and staying on the job until after dark. That made a long day. He didn't pay union scale and no time-and-a-half. No paid holidays. No vacations. Not even Saturday and Sunday off so that they could go to a synagogue or church. He sure must have been a mean old rascal.

154

He told his outside men that they were to make more sales calls each day, and they were to bring in a little more nectar each trip. He upped their quotas and cut their commissions, and cut out their expense accounts. No more free lunches and cocktails on his company.

He jumped all over his factory hands and set up tighter production schedules; cut out the coffee breaks and shortened the lunch hour to thirty minutes; made them fan faster to speed up the process; and he cut out the pay for piecework. No bonuses. He still wasn't satisfied.

He decided to interbreed his little helpers with some other bees and didn't tell them about it beforehand. He sneaked forty-six queens from some African villages into the community and settled them right alongside his little tame bees. The African bees were mean little blackhearted rascals. You have to be pretty doggoned mean to sell your own mother into slavery, but that is exactly what those mean little devils did.

The African bees worked like mad, but they didn't have much education and even less self-restraint. They made lots of honey, but they drank up everything they made, and then went out to pick fights and stir up a lot of trouble with the neighbors, painting graffiti on their houses, throwing rocks at their windows, and a bunch of other kid stuff like that. One of them would go out and bait a stranger into a fight, and when the fight started, the whole gang would come boiling out of the bushes where they had been hiding and join in for a huge free-for-all. They had clubs, razors, and knives, and everything they could lay their hands on, just to tear up that one guy.

If they couldn't find a stranger to fight, they would fight among themselves. Kicking, scratching, pulling hair, biting and calling each other dirty names you wouldn't want your mother to hear. That's the kind of people that old so-and-so brought in to mix with his little workers.

I had a lot of relatives like that. You probably did, too, if you just knew where to look.

He got what he was after—and then some. The little illegitimate (I don't like to use that other word in front of the kids, that is spelled with seven letters and means the same thing), workers did work harder. They worked harder, lived harder, and fought harder. They made more honey. But when

155

he tried to steal it from them (he had to, you know, just to keep body and soul together), they got mad. Real mad. That's when he realized that he had made a big mistake.

When he cut their pay so that they couldn't buy cheap wine and lay around drunk all night and come to work the next morning with a big headache, they rebelled. They didn't care that much for the taste of the booze, to hear them tell it, but they really enjoyed the hangovers with the red eyes and sore skull that felt like it would burst. It always felt so good when it quit hurting.

When they rebelled, they made Fidel, Daniel and Manuel look like Santa Claus and a couple of his elves.

The official cover-up for the fiasco was (what else?), that they escaped. I wouldn't be surprised to learn that the real truth was that he turned them loose. The gobbledygook and doublespeak said that some of the queens went to live in trees. They then gave birth(?) to a pure strain of African bees.

You can take your pick between their version and mine, but remember one thing, even a queen must get pregnant before she can reproduce. Even if some of the chosen methods don't make a lot of sense.

Whatever happened, they sneaked out of the bee quarters and went to fend for themselves. They probably did sleep in trees. Back in 1957, there were still a lot of trees in Brazil. Evolution is rapidly taking care of that by destroying the rain forests and turning them into wastelands and eventually into deserts. The correct name for evolution in this case is spelled "man." The bees would have a lot harder time today finding a good place to roost.

Wherever the little illegitimate black bees came from, they started raising Cain everywhere they went. Anytime anyone or anything did something to irritate the irritable little illegitimate rascals, they would all jump on the offender with both feet. Stingers by the thousands. And they were much more persistent than their "tame" half-brothers.

If a hapless cow bumped a porch post on their house, the whole family would come charging out of all the doors and windows and chase the poor old cow and sting her to death. Dogs had to learn to be mighty careful about which trees they tried to kick.

The little illegitimate rascals thought next to nothing of chasing a man two or three hundred yards and literally covering him with stings. It is a wonder that there haven't been more people killed by the stings of these vicious little bees.

They took over the northern part of South America in less time than it takes to fully understand evolution. They overran Central America while the Contras and the Sandinistas (and even some Americans), were fighting local battles and not paying attention to what was going on in the rest of the world around them. They might have been better off fighting a common enemy.

They finished with the small countries, and then jumped onto Mexico.

Mexico is a poor little country that just doesn't bother much of anybody anymore. They are sort of peaceful. And they don't have enough money to stage a real shooting match, let alone a war. They didn't have enough of an army to withstand an attack. The bees took Mexico almost without firing a shot. For those of you not well-versed in geography, Mexico is the long, skinny country, just south of Texas. It looks a little fat around the area just north of the middle, but that is mostly bloat from being too hungry all the time.

The last I heard, the bees had invaded Texas. They sneaked across the Rio Grande one cloudy night and slipped by the border patrols. Some of them may even have swum the river just to get into the United States, where the standard of living is so much higher.

Texas, for those of you who are not familiar with it, is sort of a country within a country. Texans have been pretty badly mixed up ever since the Spanish Conquistadores made good friends of the Aztecs and other Indian tribes in Old Mexico. (I used "Old Mexico" so that you wouldn't get it confused with another place called "New Mexico," which was once a part of Old Mexico. The Mexicans didn't have any use for it any longer, so they offered it to us if we would take Texas off their hands. They even threw in California to sort of sweeten the pot, so to speak. The United States has had to put up with the cantankerous New Mexico and California pot dealers ever since. The New Mexico dealers use clay to make their pots. Californians use weeds.)

157

The people who lived in Texas, when it was still a part of Old Mexico, got mad at some guy called "Santa Anna" (don't ask me why a guy had a name like "Anna"). He wasn't related to that other old guy from up north somewhere whose last name is Claus. The Texans started saying some mean things to old Santa and made him mad. Things like "Go jump over a saguaro—spraddle legged," and "Go take a dive in the Rio Grande—in shallow water," and other such nonsense. He didn't speak good English, but he knew what they meant.

He got a bunch of his boys together, and they jumped onto the Texans every chance they got. They picked on women and children a lot more than on men, unless old Santa was pretty sure that he had the odds, with a lot of extra help handy.

Some of the Texicans (they called them that back there in the old days so they could tell them from Mexicans—it was spelled the same except for the first letter), got their heads together and decided to yell for help. They hollered at a bunch of good old boys from up in Tennessee to come on down there and lend them a hand.

There are two things that you ought to know about how evolution has affected them good old boys from Tennessee. First, most of them could shoot a squirrel's eye out at nigh on-to a hundred yards. They always shot out the eyes so they wouldn't spoil any of the meat, and they didn't care too much for the eyes anyway, no matter how they were cooked. Second, some of them good old boys would rather get into a good fight than drink sour mash whiskey which they dearly loved.

They have gotten over the fighting a bit because a bunch of flatlanders migrated into the hills and integrated with the mountain people. They still drink sour mash whiskey and have even gotten some of those flatland foreigners drinking it, but they haven't been able to teach them to kick and gouge worth a hoot. But evolution takes time—they may make it yet.

Them good old boys used to make their own sour mash, but the Treasury Department sort of frowned on anybody drinking good liquor without enjoying the taxes, and they broke up three or four stills. I know where there is a fellow who has a whopper of a big one, right out in the open. He just thumbs his nose at the revenuers, I suppose, because they haven't been able to find it, and it is in plain sight. I ain't telling where it is for fear they might break it up some night when he ain't to home. He even puts black labels on his and sells it all over the place.

Well, a bunch of them good old boys got up a party and lit out for Texas at a fast trot. They wound up at a little old church called "The Alamo," stuck out there in some place called "San Antonio," which is pronounced only about halfway like it is spelled. They holed up there, and fit (that is the past past tense of fight) the Mexicans to a standstill, even though the Mexicans had them slightly outnumbered something like seventy to one.

It wound up with the Mexicans killing all them good old boys but one.

Texas then hollered at another good old boy from up in Virginia that folks called "Old Rough and Ready." His right name was Zachary Taylor, and he had a whole passel of men, a lot more than that party from Tennessee. They were dressed better, too, so that they could tell which fellows they were supposed to shoot at.

Well, sir, Old Rough and Ready went down there, and he whupped the pants off Old Santa Anna. The Texans have been sort of hanging onto our coattails ever since. Texas has been claiming for several years now that they are part of the United States, but you just don't hear too many people from the United States bragging about owning Texas.

I have heard that some fellows by the names of Lyndon Johnson, George Bush, and Lloyd Bentsen have gone around telling people that they were from Texas, but I just can't seem to remember anyone else who has done that. My father lived in Lubbock, which is way up yonder in northern Texas, but he always kept pretty quiet about it.

Texans might get a lot more government handouts if they would split Texas into four parts. They could call them West Texas, East Texas, North Texas and South Texas, and each would still be bigger than some of the other states. West Virginia did that back there during the War Between the States, and now a lot of the people who live there don't have to depend on anything as unstable as gas and oil for their livelihood. A lot of them don't do much of anything except run up and down the mountain roads in pick-up trucks, shoot deer out of season, eat ramps, drink white lightning (that's hillbilly moonshine), throw out their empty beer cans, bottles, and old junk along the roadsides, and get into fights with police officers and DNR game wardens. If the warden catches them shooting deer, they just tell him that they don't have enough money to buy food. I suppose they stick their thousand-dollar rifle with the scope on it under the seat before they tell him that. They can do all those fun things because Texans have a bunch of oil and gas, and the government takes a bunch of their money and gives it to the boys in West Virginia who drink up their booze and wear out their trucks so quickly.

I got sidetracked again.

The bees have gained a beachhead in Texas, so the United States will probably have to send in the army, navy, marines, air force, national guard and the coast guard to help out again. We had better keep a sharp eye on them though. They might start helping the wrong bunch.

Someone wrote an article that said there wasn't much chance of the bees moving much farther north. They don't like cold feet. But if history is any reliable indicator, there will more than likely be some greedy idiot out there trying to get a government subsidy so that he can start selling them wool socks and insulated boots at bargain prices.

And if history is any reliable indicator, congress will probably see to it that he gets the grant—as long as it is your money.

If that isn't evolution, then I don't know beans from apple-butter or anything else.

PORCUPINES

I have no idea how the porcupine got its common name from the Latin, which means almost literally "pig with quills." I probably have a pretty good idea how it got its nickname, "Porky," which has been commonly used by outdoor people for as long as I can remember and then some.

Years ago, most outdoorsmen and backwoodsmen had not attended Yale or Harvard as most of them today. Most of them, in fact, had not gone beyond the front door of the one-roomer where the McGuffey primers were eventually the most popular reading material of the time.

They couldn't spell "porcupine," so they started calling him "Porky," which they couldn't spell either. I'm surprised that they didn't just call him "it," but that was almost as hard to spell as "porcupine" and every bit as hard to read.

Porcupines are fair to middlin' to eat, if you are hungry and can't find a good T-bone or a couple of lamb chops. When it comes to my eating one just to be different, they rank right up there with moose nose jelly and fricasseed buzzard. They are only one or two notches above curried possum on the delicacies listed on my menus.

I hope that you don't laugh too hard at those gourmet delights. Moose nose jelly is a favorite food of some Eskimo tribes. The gravy from fricasseed buzzard is strong and tough and puts muscles on you in places where you didn't even know you had meat. Curried possum doesn't taste too nasty. (These statements are all from hearsay. I haven't had the intestinal fortitude necessary to sampling them for myself.) I am going to include a recipe for a couple of them, just so that you will know that I am not kidding you. These are legitimate recipes, used by cooks in some of the areas where they eat that sort of thing.

Moose Nose Jelly

The hardest part about making moose nose jelly, if you live south of the Mason-Dixon line, is finding a moose that is willing to have his nose stuck in a pot of boiling water for forty-five minutes. Most of the moose that I have met didn't give one the impression that they would care for that at all.

After you find a moose that is willing to stand still long enough for you to get in a telling shot, make certain that he has four legs. A two-legged Moose doesn't have a near big enough nose to make a good batch of jelly, and he doesn't like to have his nose in hot water for such a long period unless he puts it there himself.

Make sure that you shoot the four-legged moose enough times to kill him thoroughly. Perfectly dead moose sometimes jump up and gouge you in the front or back with those big antlers. That is just a plain nuisance. The sharp little points on those tines will penetrate the seat of a pair of breeches like you wouldn't believe. They can nail a little fat at the same time. That has a tendency to make you leap before you look.

Many people who do kill a big bull moose, especially one that has antlers about six feet or so from tip to tip get a little upset when you ask them for the little piece of moose that is required for a good mess of jelly. You would think that they wouldn't mind sharing with a less fortunate hunter.

A hunter like that is rarely interested in making jelly for himself, either. The process wipes the artificial smile from the face of the moose, and the hunter likes to have the moose look as though he is saying "whiskey" while the hunter drinks a toast to the part of the moose that is hanging on the wall of his den or game room.

I suppose anyhow that a cow moose would have a nose that is just a mite more tender. The females of the species with which I am most familiar do tend to be a little softer in certain spots than their male counterparts. It might be the same with moose. And cow moose don't engage in weight lifting.

First, to make matters as uncomplicated as possible and to avoid future embarrassment at the hands of some overzealous conservation officer, get a license that says that you are now a moose hunter and which entitles you to kill one of the same. Be sure the license states which gender, especially when the issuer has spelled it "licence."

Second, kill one. That may prove to be the hardest part, even up north where they run around in the woods almost as thick as dairy cows in Times Square. Make certain that you kill it near a roadway. If you have to carry a three-quarter ton moose out through thick brush for about three or four miles, it can make your legs tired.

Some people use moose calls to get the moose nearer the road. One way is to call over and over in a loud voice so all the moose can hear, "Here, moosey, moosey." When a big one walks up beside the car, drop him in his tracks. It will never happen twice.

Third, skin the moose. If you can wait a few minutes, do this step after you get him home and hung in the shed. Be careful during this step that you don't accidentally skin anything else when the knife slips.

Fourth, cut the jawbone of the moose just below the eyes. This is one of the most important steps. If you don't get the jaw separated, you have to find a whopper of a big pot. And the other parts attached to the jaw might give the finished product an off-flavor.

Fifth, place the severed front end of the jaw in a large kettle and boil it for forty-five minutes. You have to go through this step just to get to the next one. Otherwise it isn't that important.

Sixth, remove and chill in cold water. This is so you won't burn your fingers during step number seven. If you have ever been burned by a hot moose nose, you won't have to ask why this step is necessary.

Seventh, pull out all the hairs. Be sure to get every one. A moose hair lodged between your upper plate and your palate is almost as uncomfortable as one stuck between your teeth. It takes a lot of embarrassing sucking and digging to get one of those out.

Any hunter who has ever plucked a duck will find this seventh step rather easy to accomplish.

Eighth, wash thoroughly until no loose hairs remain. During this step, you can repeat step number seven in those places where you didn't exercise sufficient care or where your bifocals slipped down your nose.

Ninth, place the nose in a kettle and cover with fresh water. That may be hard to find in many areas, these days.

This may seem like an odd place to put a list of ingredients, but since the balance of the recipe requires a few things other than moose, I decided to stick it right here where you couldn't miss it. And that follows the pattern of the rest of the book, which sticks things in here and there where there is a little extra space.

Ingredients

1. You already have the moose jaw. The upper one, of course. I hope you didn't waste all that time cleaning the lower jaw. I have never seen a lower moose jaw with a nose on it. You have to use your own head once in a while. I can't be there all the time to tell you every little move to make.

2. One onion, sliced. Be sure that it is a big onion. That, along with the next ingredient, helps kill the other flavors.

3. One clove of garlic. If I were making it, I would want more than one clove. A moose nose is pretty big, and it would surely take more than one clove to overcome something that size.

4. One tablespoon mixed pickling spice. No comment.

5. One teaspoon salt. If you like your food as salty as I like mine, you'll want more salt than that. If so, sprinkle in a little more.

6. One-half teaspoon black pepper, ground. Ditto from item five.

7. One-fourth cup vinegar. To sour it up a little.

And now, on with the preparation.

Tenth step, add onion, spices and vinegar. Everybody needs a little spice in his jelly.

Eleventh, bring to a boil, then reduce heat and simmer until the meat is tender. The actual length of time probably would depend on the moose you have chosen and how active his nose was when it was in use. (Also refer to the paragraphs preceding the recipe if you have forgotten my suggestions on choosing a proper moose.)

164

Twelfth, when cool, remove meat from broth, remove bone and cartilage and discard. They are hard to chew. Don't discard the broth, and don't get excited and drink it by mistake for some other beverage which might be sitting nearby. That broth contains all the vitamins and minerals, not to mention all that stuff from the sinus cavities.

You will notice that there are two kinds of meat, white and dark. Just like a wild turkey, but from different places. The white meat is from the big blob that is the nose bulb, the dark is from the jaw and jowls. A wild turkey has very little meat in those places and even less if you get your wild turkey from a fancy bottle.

Thirteenth, slice the meat as thinly as you can with the sharpest knife which you can borrow. Always borrow one from a fellow who never uses his knife for other distasteful purposes. And yours will never be sharp enough to slice the meat without cutting your fingers. After the meat is sliced, place alternate layers of light and dark meat in a loaf pan. The size of the pan will depend on the size of the moose nose.

Fourteenth, reheat the broth to boiling, then pour the broth over the meat in the loaf pan. I always like to boil the broth just a little longer. Boiling has a tendency to provide an unfriendly environment for all those little squiggly rascals swimming around in there that you can't see with your naked eye.

Fifteenth, and final step. Let cool and set; slice and serve cold, but don't save any back for me. I'm going to stuff a few pork chops and then let them stuff me.

If I were making the moose nose jelly, I would add a sixteenth step. I would carry it as far from camp as I could comfortably walk and pitch it to the wolves. Or better yet, I would just skip the whole process and use the time more profitably by going fishing for walleye, which must be better to eat.

If you decide to make some jelly, be sure to follow all the directions carefully. I will not accept responsibility for any ruined moose noses.

I will give you another recipe in case you are out in the bush and can't find anything else to eat. I hope that you take your matches with you when you travel in the backcountry. This recipe isn't worth a hoot if you have to boil the water cold.

The best way to start this recipe is to go north. That is where most of the porcupines live. You don't need to take a

165

gun. A good-sized l-o-n-g club will do to finish off a porcupine. But stand back and away from his tail. He can't throw his quills, and I wouldn't want to mislead you like some of the other outdoor writers whose articles I have read. He can swing his tail, and if it hits you across the shins, you will have more bristles sticking out of it than you can find on a hairbrush. And they smart and burn. Make sure that if he does connect with you that you get every little piece when you pull them out with the pliers. The quills are barbed and just don't know when to give up. They continue to burrow deeper and can wind up in some place that might make you very uncomfortable.

After you commit homicide on the porcupine, skin him. I will tell you of another method in a couple of minutes, but it is sort of iffy. Use a l-o-n-g knife. For the same reasons that you used the long club. Quills in fingers are almost as bad as quills in shins. The quills on a porcupine have absolutely no relationship to jon-quils and shouldn't be compared, just in case you are thinking about it.

After you get all the hair and hide off and the entrails out, wash him thoroughly in cold water inside and out. Porcupine hair, especially the stiff kind, is worse than moose hair in the preceding recipe. Throw the beheaded carcass into a pot of cold water, and set it over the fire. Now you know the reason for the matches. It is a good idea to carry a lighter as well, in case the matches get wet. Boil the —— out of him. When he is done to tender, cut him up and serve him. Preferably with a lot of other food that might be fit to eat.

Now for the little tip that I promised. You can shortcut the system by building a good fire and throwing the porcupine in, hair and all. This singes the quills off him, and at the same time removes the guard hairs which make him look so shaggy and serve as a wool coat in winter. If you choose this method, be careful not to leave him in too long, or you will wind up with roast porcupine. That isn't as tasty as boiled porcupine, especially when you overcook him with all that spoiled food inside.

When you boil him, throw in all the spices and condiments and anything else you can find. After he is done, give anything you can't eat to the dogs.

I don't know exactly how those two recipes have or will affect the evolutionary process. I can only assure you that they have or will. In one way or another.

The porcupine which we have in the United States and Canada is one of eight species found in the Western Hemisphere. The other seven live farther south. Ours had a wide range originally, with only a few of the southeastern states enjoying the lack of some porcupine population.

He is the second largest rodent native to North America. His fuzzy cousin, the beaver, is the only one that outclasses him in size. A porky can go to about twenty pounds and thirty inches in length, plus the hairy tail. I have seen one that I believe exceeded those dimensions.

I was coming out of Restoule, Ontario, several years ago, driving a full-size Ford vehicle and pulling a small utility trailer. The road was dirt and gravel back then. I was tearing along at about thirty-five to forty miles an hour, when I unintentionally hit a porcupine. A huge one. When he rolled back under the driver's side of the vehicle, the wheels left the ground momentarily. I stopped to give him CPR, but he didn't need it.

I didn't pick him up for two or three good reasons. One, I didn't have a good recipe for road-killed porcupine. Two, I didn't relish porcupine soup. Three, he had something like thirty thousand of those five-inch long, hollow one-way needles to which I have a strong aversion. Estimating his size was good enough for me, and I didn't realize that I would one day be writing his obituary and struggling for the truth.

I did steal a few of his quills for the neighborhood kids for show-and-tell at school. I'm not sure if the boys used them to torment the girls, but I would not be surprised. Boys haven't changed all that much since I was one.

Porcupines climb trees to get at the tender inner bark of the upper branches. They will take up residence in a suitable tree and stay there until they have ruined the tree.

I observed one that had invaded a white birch tree in Northern Ontario. I saw him there on a number of occasions and at different times of the day and night over a four-day period. He was still there when it was time for me to head back to West Virginia. The upper parts of that tree were devastated.

As I mentioned earlier, porcupines do not throw their quills. When one is threatened by some predator, he will turn his back, stomp his feet, lash his tail back and forth, and hide his face. Not because he is ashamed of his profile, but because his face is not protected by the quills. Neither is his underbelly.

The porcupine does have a predator that is somewhat more successful than others. Lynx, wolves, and other animals will take a porcupine once in a while, but they pay dearly for their folly. The fisher is a bit smarter. He attacks the porcupine from the front rather than from the underside. He stabs and feints like a professional boxer and then nails the nose or the throat. He is too fast on his feet for the porcupine to retaliate. The fisher is declared the winner in nearly every encounter. His reputation for winning is so good that lumber interests join forces with natural resource departments to stock the fisher in areas that are threatened by overpopulation and the subsequent destruction of the timber resources.

That may be news for those of you who have always heard that the predators of porcupines go for the belly, which does appear to be the logical target. But any predator that wants to bite his belly has to turn him over first. And that can be tricky.

If a predator gets a quill in a paw or in its face, the quill may be broken near the surface. The remaining barbed shaft can penetrate to a vital organ, if it does not become so badly infected that it is ejected when the infection ruptures.

I have heard and read that the quills can be softened prior to removal by soaking them with vinegar. I have never had the fun of being stuck with one, and I have never used a dog in known porcupine territory, so I can't vouch for the effectiveness. It would be worth a try.

Porcupines mate late in the fall. I'll bet that is a sticky wicket. The female gives birth to a single baby in the spring. Even though the quills are soft at birth, two little thistles at one time may be a bit too much for the little mother. It would for me.

The little shaver can expect to live to a ripe old age of ten or twelve years. If he doesn't run head-on into a fisher or start playing with cars.

Porcupines love salt. They will eat some of the craziest menus just to satisfy their lust for it. They irritate humans most because of this craving.

I have seen one eating the rubber tires on a vehicle—maybe because it had been used on a road that had been treated with salt. They will ruin a canoe paddle beyond further use to get the sweat from your hands. They will eat a gun stock that is left where they can get at it. The worst offense of this kind is brought on by their fondness for toilet seats. If one moves into your favorite outhouse, you have limited options. You can kill the animal and repair the damage. You can abandon the necessary facility. Or, you can put up with rough seats. This might be okay for men, but women are a little more finicky. That may have something to do with affected area. You do have one other choice. You can move to Florida like all the rest of the intelligent people on the eastern side of the continent. They don't have porcupines in Florida. The only thing they have there is sneaky snakes. On the other hand, practically all of their outhouses are inhouses.

Porcupines can swim, and their hollow quills help keep them afloat. I am inclined to believe that they are not enthusiastic about bathing for fun and frolic like their first cousin, Buddy Beaver.

My wife and I watched one trying to cross a stream on a fallen log. The log was as slick as that other stuff that CBer's talk about in every spot where the water had splashed over the top. He kept one eye cocked toward us only a few yards away and the other on the log. He should have paid more attention to his footing. He waddled along, slipping and sliding on every damp spot until he reached the middle. He lost traction and tumbled into the water. He scrambled back atop the log after three or four tries and made his way across without looking at us again.

I tried to tell him before he started that the log was treacherous, but he must have spoken only French. I was only about "halfluent" in that language at the time. I have studied hard and have now learned three more words in the last thirty years. But when I try them on people, they just look at me with a blank stare.

He must not have seen me when I stepped on the end of the log or while I was pouring water out of my hip boots a second or so later. That was just after a prominent part of my anatomy bumped twice on the log before it went into the water.

I have had years of experience pouring water out of my boots and chest waders and I have developed a foolproof sys-

169

tem. You may want to share in the benefit of my knowledge.

I lie down flat on my back and stick my legs straight up in the air. Gravity then takes over, and the water runs out the top, which has then become the bottom. My legs are about as fat as broomsticks and are just as long, so each boot holds about four or five gallons. I always remove my hat and hang it on a bush so that it won't get wet when the water runs down my belly and up my back and gets everything else wet.

We were in Northern Ontario a couple of years ago in red raspberry and blueberry season. When we hit those, we spend our un-fishing time in the patches picking. And eating. Then we bake pies. And eat. Then we can a few. And eat. We make the bears jealous. If God made any berries better than wild blueberries, He hid them someplace else and is keeping them for Himself.

We spotted a patch of red raspberries that stretched for at least a half mile in any direction we looked. I parked the truck, and we hopped out of the truck and headed for the fruit. There were more berries than you could shake a stick at. Acres and acres of red berries. Up there, the land is measured in metric, so it was really ares and ares, but it just doesn't sound like it does when you put in the ''c's'' and wind up with less land and bigger numbers.

As we entered the edge of the patch where there was considerable brush, we met a porcupine on his way out.

I needed a picture or two, so I raced back to the truck as fast as my almost seventy-year-old legs would carry me. I grabbed the camera and raced back. The porcupine had raced almost five yards while my wife kept him in sight.

I took several pictures while the camera-shy porky ducked and dodged to get away from the rube with the funny box. He made for the truck and wound up hiding underneath. One more reason for me to practice my *oneupmanship* on Murphy. If nothing can possibly go wrong, it will anyway. The porcupine would not budge although we pitched pebbles at him and pelted him with small sticks, trying to force him to move. I did not want to move the truck for fear of what I might do to him, and I didn't want to leave him under it for fear of what he might do to me. Maybe as much as four times, and I only had the one spare.

I don't know how long we pitched and pelted before a bright light suddenly flashed up there behind my eyes. He didn't like to have his picture taken. That was obvious from his earlier flight to avoid the camera.

I grabbed the camera and squatted down beside the truck. I pointed it at him, ready to snap and he quit stomping his feet and swishing his tail and shifted into low gear. Porcupines are geared low, and they don't have a high side. I did get another picture before he hit the brush, but it was of the wrong end.

Porcupines have a place in the environment and in evolution. I'm still trying to figure out what that place is, but it must be there somewhere. I might be more successful if I could think like one, but I've tried that, too. It hasn't worked yet.

I had a reputation in my earlier years for being a good cook. "Earlier" in this case means when I was about twelve to fifteen years of age, and my mother developed polio, and it fell to me to do the cooking.

I think that my reputation may have been based on quantity rather than on quality. A baking of ten or twelve big loaves of homemade bread would last upwards of four days, depending on the amount of hungry company we had. These were not man-sized loaves, they were big. Each one would have been at least twice as big as a loaf of the stuff that is being foisted off onto us as bread today. And the slices were at least twice to three times as thick as the bakery version. No problem. We never took time to make toast except for special occasions and special people. That was before electricity hit our area with a big jolt, and toast was made over an open flame or on the top of the wood stove.

I cooked old-fashioned buckwheat cakes, the sour kind that has the delicate flavor, by the short stack. That was a stack of about thirty or so pancakes. The nine-inch variety, just so there would be room for some homemade syrup and a big glob of homemade butter on the edge and a ball or two of homemade sausage in the middle. I'm going to have to get off this subject—my mouth is watering and I'm drooling down my chin.

We cooked "graham cereal" in a big pot and served it in a two-gallon crock that was full to the brim. It didn't stay that way long. We didn't know that it did anything for us except to fill our hollow spots.

171

There must be two or three people in the United States who don't know what graham cereal is. Or was, I suppose. I haven't seen any for years. It was just like a coarse-ground Cream of Wheat with all the good stuff left in. The whole wheat was ground and nothing removed except what chaff blew away in the breeze. We cooked and ate everything else.

We didn't know it at the time, but it was good for us. With all the bran and our twice-a-week dose of epsom salts, we didn't accumulate lots of HDL's and cholesterols, even though we ate every part of the hog after the hair was scraped off except the part that made the squeal and the little curly part that went through the fence last. We always gave the tails to a neighbor who roasted them six or eight at a time and had a feast fit for a king.

Our sausage was loaded with sage and buried in grease. That was pure hog fat or lard, sometimes called "renderin's." The strips of hog skins left after most of the lard had been removed by rendering them were called "cracklin's." They were good to eat. You could bake pies by the dozen with enough lard, flour and water to wrap around the apples, blackberries, black raspberries, rhubarb or anything else that we could get our picky little fingers on to help fill our bellies.

The strips of skin were also called "meat skins." I had an uncle who could eat them, but he couldn't say them. He called them "meat nins," but they tasted just as good. He carried a few around in the front pocket of his breeches when they were in season so that he could have them handy for nibbling now and then. This was before the advent of sealable plastic bags. and he carried them bare-headed in his pocket. The residual grease soaked through and his pocket became waterproof before the week was out. You dassn't wash a pair of pants before that, or you wouldn't have anything to cover your shame the following week.

You may be wondering how all that got into a chapter that is supposed to be about porcupines. I'm old and my mind wanders. I get two or three things on my mind at the same time that I want to tell you about, and I have to write them down immediately or the thought is gone. Maybe forever. But there is a train, if you don't try to jump on the caboose while the locomotive is still puffing steam in your face as it chugs past.

172

We stayed in a cottage owned by Leonard and Mae Grawbarger during the long-ago time when we were still fishing around Restoule, Ontario. That country used to be pretty much wild, although it was not exactly backcountry at that time. It has changed. I'm not sure that it was for the better. It became overcrowded.

We stopped by to visit with them several times when we were on our way farther north and once drove the seven hundred miles just to visit with them on a long weekend. They were two of the many fine people that we have claimed as friends down through the years in Canada.

Mae did baking on her woodburning stove and sold the product to supplement their income. She turned out bread and pies that were so good that they would make you want to kick your Grandma. While we were there, she kept us in bread, cakes, pies, and other baked goods. That allowed my wife to spend a few more hours fishing, and she claims that fishing beats doing kitchen chores any day of the week.

Mae's piece de resistance was sugar tarts. I have tasted a lot of good sugar tarts before and since, but Mae's were outstanding.

She always had it figured almost to the minute the time that we should arrive at the cottage. Fortunately, she was always right on target. She always had a couple dozen of tarts waiting on the table for us when we walked in. The life expectancy of the warm tarts was about two minutes after we got our hugs.

The people who bragged about my baking had never tasted Mae's baked goods, and I was smart enough to keep them separated by at least five hundred miles. She made me ashamed that I had ever stuck my fingers into a dough tray.

That, too, has something to do with porcupines, but the preliminaries may be longer than the main bout.

Mae had trouble with the shaggy rascals. Porcupines may be as ugly as homemade sin, but they aren't stupid. And they could smell Mae's bread and pies for miles downwind. They came by the numbers.

They raided the garbage pails, chewed the seats in the country cabanas, gnawed the boards around the bottoms of the house and the cottages, ate the shrubbery and nibbled the bark off the white birch trees. And Mae fought back.

173

She had one of those tiny, old, Stevens rolling-block, single shot, twenty-two caliber rimfires that served as her six-gun in her one-woman war on the pesky invaders. I do not think that she was supposed to use the modern (1950 vintage) cartridges in that gun, but she did anyway. She didn't know about excessive breech pressures that could blow the gun to smithereens and maybe do some superficial damage to her physique. That was unimportant.

But she knew how and where to hit a porcupine to give him a bad case of indigestion that was nearly always terminal. I don't know how many she must have killed over the years, but she must have cut the crime rate considerably. If she had kept score with notches like some of the other gun-slingers, she would have been shooting with just the bare barrel. The stock would have been in notch-chips.

While we were there for the two to three weeks that we spent with them every summer, she averaged about four a day. She must have saved a whole forest or two single-handedly. Big ones, considering how much damage the sharp-toothed porkies can accomplish.

I never knew of her cooking one. I know that she never offered us any southern-fried porcupine breast or porcupine stew. She was a smart woman, too.

If you stick pretty close to the theory of evolution as it is being taught, you must believe that porcupines came from something else. That sounds a little farfetched to me. If a female rabbit ever gave birth to a porcupine, I'll bet that she wouldn't go through the process again for all the carrots in New Jersey. And if it turned out to be either male or female (most everything else does), no other rabbit would want to have an extramarital affair with it, even as crazy as rabbits are about such things. I just can't figure how one porcupine became so many.

Maybe some member of the intelligentsia can explain it to me sometime.

When I have enough time while I am *un-fishing*.

CiGARETTES and Whiskey and...

If you decide to apply the theory of evolution to bears, beavers, bees, birds, bison, bitches, blennies and boys, you have to apply it to everything else as well. You can't just pick and choose.

Cigars, cigarettes, cut plug, pipe tobacco, snuff, Picnic Twist and Mail Pouch are all the result of an evolutionary process that is almost as complicated as the real thing. But the tobacco products have compressed the evolutionary cycle into a relatively brief period.

They may be contributing more to the overall evolutionary process as it pertains to humans than any of us inadequately equipped humans can imagine. They are certainly in a continuing process of exerting an excessive amount of influence on the outcome. This influence is out of all proportion to the actual importance of these products to our physical and mental well-being or to our survival.

Tobacco products did not start back there at the water hole with the old boy who kicked off the agrarian economy by stopping long enough to plant a few taters and a little corn, and then hanging around to harvest his crops. He may have enjoyed a corn silk cigarette now and again or maybe took a couple of good-sized chews of rabbit tobacco, but those bore little resemblance to the later use of that other plant which we call "tobacco."

Tobacco was known at one time in my memory as that noxious weed, but several people that I knew just called it simply "the weed." Even the definition of weed has changed in recent years. If you were to say "the weed" to just anyone you happened to meet, regardless of his age, he would think that you were referring to cannabis, or marijuana. Times change. Often the change isn't for the better. Words change. Meanings change. Sometimes you can even detect slight changes in people.

This new weed (What am I saying? That weed has been around forever but its primary use was for fiber), may have even more far-reaching and more detrimental effects upon the human subspecies than tobacco has had. Especially if its use becomes any more widespread.

And that isn't funny, either. I doubt that it ever will be.

Tobacco products are a "Johnny-come-lately" on the scene of human evolution. They did not put in an appearance for most of the world until after Columbus landed on that little patch of sand and gravel, and then fell in love with the Indians and especially with their bad habits. So as far as most of us are concerned, the use of tobacco is a recent evolutionary development. If you reckon time as the geologists and biological evolutionists do, that is. It seems to me that tobacco has been around forever and then some.

Tobacco is a plant with large leaves that start out pale green, then turn to a darker green, then change to a paler green before they start turning yellow and then light brown. It just can't seem to make up its mind how it wants to look.

That big argument that has been going on for centuries about which came first, the chicken or the egg, can be applied to the tobacco plant, but about a million-fold. The tobacco plant forms tiny little black seeds that you wouldn't believe could develop into such a large plant. Tobacco seeds have even more faith than mustard seeds.

You were once able to buy tobacco seeds from the people who harvested them from the ripe plants, and then counted them out to you when you wanted to buy them. It takes about an hour or two to count the seeds in a teaspoonful, and you run out of a lot of fingers and toes trying to keep a tally. Most people who sold them by the teaspoon or tablespoon just said, "Oh, to heck with it," or something to that effect and then threw as many as a whole heaping teaspoonful into a little brown bag and charged you a little extra for any possible miscalculation. I never heard of anyone charging a little less in case the count was short.

176

The government has even jumped into the act on tobacco seeds. You can't sell them by the spoonful anymore. Vendors now have to sell them by weight. If you decide to buy a few, make sure the merchant keeps his thumb off the scale. Even the little brown bag they used to put them in would weigh as much as three or four hundred seeds, maybe more. Most seeds are now sold in small packets that are preweighed and sealed so that you will be sure to get as many as you bargained for.

The tiny seeds are planted in a bed that would put Mom's lettuce bed to shame for the care that it takes. The seedbed is first prepared, and the dirt and fertilizer are mulched into a fine mixture. Then before you can plant any seeds, the bed is covered with a sheet of plastic and sealed tightly. The bed is then "gassed" to kill any weeds that might interfere with the baby plants or take nourishment from them.

The seeds are then planted in this bed which may be about ten feet wide and about fifty feet long, depending on the number of plants you want to produce. A cloth cover called a "canvas" is stretched over the bed to protect the tender plants from sun and excess rain. A "gullywasher" on a tobacco seedbed would wash the little rascals all the way to New Orleans if you are on the west side of the watershed, or to Savannah if you are to the east. That, of course, is if you are in this part of the country.

If the planter has received a few extra seeds, and they come up in good shape, he might just as well eat the little plants for salad or feed them to his mule.

The government (they just can't seem to keep their nose out of anybody's business) grants the grower a tobacco allotment. This allotment is based upon a formula which considers the total acreage which the farmer has, the arable or tillable acreage and other factors. The term "tobacco allotment" is a misleading term which is a part of what is known in the inner circles of government as "doublespeak" or "gobbledygook." The Indians had a saying for it. "White man speak with forked tongue." What it really means is that some government agency is telling the farmer that he may think that he owns the land just because he bought it and pays taxes on it, but "by Jove," the agency is going to tell him what he can do with it, especially what and how much he can plant on it. He can grow the extra plants if he wants, but he can't sell them if he exceeds his weight allotment. If he tries to peddle them "under-the-counter" he can be in more trouble than if he shot his neighbor's cow. And in today's fouled-up system of jurisprudence, that could be worse than shooting all the neighbor's kids.

When the baby plants get to be about toddler-size, he pulls them out by the roots and transplants them to another patch where they have a little more elbow room. They grow there through teenage, adulthood and middleage. When they get to middleage, the planter or grower gives them a haircut. The plants develop "suckers" that extend above the top of the main plant and steal food from the leaves. These should be removed in order to improve the quality of the tobacco. Then when the plants get to be senior citizens, he pulls all their clothes up around their hips. Just about the time that they get accustomed to this indignity, he cuts their legs off down close to the ground and makes them stand out in the open field, leaning precariously on a couple of poles called "sticks." This treatment is followed by his coming into the field one morning and tossing them onto a wagon and hauling them to a barn. There he hangs them upside down. The barn has big cracks between the boards so that any passerby can see this spectacle. He even has a name for this, since he does it on a regular basis. It is called "air drying."

There is another system for curing which is quicker but more brutal. It is called "flue-curing." In this system, he builds a little fire in a small stove which is attached to the outside of the building and blows smoke and hot air in their faces all day long and for days on end. They nearly suffocate. There is almost as much hot air and smoke as at one of those Democratic National Conventions that I have seen on television, where you can see just about anything if you wait around for an hour or so.

After the tobacco has cured sufficiently, the grower watches for a good shower of rain or two to soften up the brittle leaves. This is called "case." When the leaves are pliable, he goes in and strips all the clothes off the old plants. He also takes out the large veins or stems that are a part of the leaves.

After the tobacco has gone through all this, he compresses the leaves into bales and hauls them to a tobacco warehouse to be sold.

178

In the old days, the grower separated the leaves into bunches, and then tied them together at the base, making a flat bunch of tobacco called a "hand" because that was what it resembled, if you have a good imagination.

There are several different varieties of tobacco. The variety that is grown in the area around Abbington, Virginia, is called burley. There are subvarieties known by a state name and a number, such as Tennessee 76. Don't take that number as an actual variety, it is only an example.

These varieties are also a product of evolution. The evolution in this case might be more properly described as "selective breeding," or "genetic engineering." This is the same system that dog breeders use on the bitches and their sons.

It is a little more difficult to tell one tobacco plant from another than to distinguish one breed of dog from another, except to the trained eye. Your eye doesn't have to be too well-trained to distinguish a dog from a tobacco plant, especially when they are standing close together. The dog is always the one with three legs pointing toward the ground and one pointing toward the plant. I suppose that is because he always wants to be sure that you know which is which.

After about three or four dozen dogs visit the patch to point out the plants to you, the leaves may develop a "pee-culiar" taste. Several years ago, one well-known cigarette company capitalized on this affinity of dogs for tobacco plants and asked smokers, "Does your cigarette taste different lately?." The catchphrase made smokers think that dogs only irrigated the competitors' brands. That may have been subliminal advertising.

Each plant has a number of designations for the leaves, depending upon their location on the plant. The bottom leaves are called "trash," the next ones up the stem are called "bright" (these are the higher quality leaves), the ones nearer the top are called "red" and the top ones are called "tips."

Tobacco plants are different from each other, just as dogs are different from each other. The varieties and breed, that is. Some varieties like shade and some like sunlight. The burley that I have seen in Virginia, Kentucky, and North Carolina was all growing in the sun. Other varieties have names like Cavendish and Latakia. Don't ask me why. I don't know either.

After the tobacco is taken to the tobacco warehouse, it is arranged in rows and held for auction. The sale is conducted by an auctioneer who walks around through the rows of bales and makes loud, funny noises through his mouth while a bunch of guys follow him around and just stand and watch. The noise sounds a little like some kind of a song, but he must not know the words very well. He makes the same kind of a noise over and over until one of the bystanders makes some little motion with his hand or says "Harrumph," or something like that to get him to quit. He then makes two or three more sounds and then yells "Sold," at the top of his lungs. What I would like to know is how he knows that he sold it, and, if he really did, how the guy who bought it knows how much he paid or if he even is sure that he did.

Just as soon as he yells out like that, it is obvious that the guy who tried to get him to quit wasn't entirely successful, because he starts into humming that same tune again. It isn't exactly a humming. It may be a little nearer a chant, but it doesn't sound much like the Indian chants that I have heard at the tribal dances.

And he doesn't do a whole lot of dancing, either.

If you do decide to visit one of these affairs, be careful not to sneeze. If you wipe your nose on your coat sleeve, you may have already bought more of that bloomin' tobacco than you could haul home in a good-sized truck.

It is hard to make any good use of the tobacco when it is in that condition. You have to have some expensive and sophisticated equipment just to get it so that you can chew it or put it in your pipe. It is even worse if you want to make cigarettes.

The Revenuers have hit the tobacco industry pretty hard. They sell the same kinds of little stamps to the manufacturers of tobacco products as they sell to the bootleggers and moonshiners. They are more expensive in the long run, though, because it takes so many more of them, and they make them in prettier colors. They don't make the tobacco taste so much worse, though, like they do the sour mash and the moonshine.

But that isn't all. They also make the cigarette manufacturers buy a little rubber stamp that says something like, "Warning. The Surgeon General reports that use of this product may be hazardous to your health." The little stamp puts that on every package. I'll bet that would make your arm tired after about two million stamps in a day. That girl must have big muscles.

I don't know what one of those costs, but they must be pretty expensive. One of them will do several cartons. I have heard that it is even more expensive not to use them, though.

They have the same kind of a stamp on a snuff can except that it says, "Warning. This product can cause cancer or gum disease." I have a sort of sneaking suspicion that if you had a mouthful of malignant ulcers that you wouldn't spend a whole lot of time worrying about chronic gingivitis. I would like to know how they get that little stamp to print in a circle around that little can.

I don't know who the surgeon general is, but he must have a good-sized army. But I have never heard of any other officers, such as surgeon colonel or surgeon lieutenant, but I did hear somebody talk sort of hush-hush one time about a surgeon major. I don't know if he was in the same army or not. On the other hand, I have never even heard of a surgeon private. Maybe they do most of their work undercover, and the rest of us don't find out about it until they put up one of those little signs. I hope that they are on our side. We need all the help we can get just to protect us from our "friends" in congress.

After the product is finished and has all the proper stamps on it, it is sold to the general public. As far as I have been able to determine, the general public has absolutely no relationship to the surgeon general. They might be from different countries for all I know. The product is sold in a lot of different forms and in a lot of different fancy packages, so that they can get you coming or going. I saw one package the other day that had a pretty pick-up truck on it. The picture was taken before the driver used any of the contents of the pouch. It was easy to tell that. There weren't any brown streaks along the driver's side.

When I was a boy, a lot of men and women used a powdery form of tobacco called "snuff." The snuff came in a little tin can about an inch and a quarter in diameter, and about two or two and a half inches high. It had a lift-off lid that fit pretty snug. Those little cans made the best little containers for all sorts of aftermarket products, such as fishing worms (not very many), buttons (a few more), and small nails (several more), etc. Most of the cans were used for "etc."

One lady up in our neck of the woods made a concoction out of hog grease, chemicals, and a few secret herbs that would heal anything from gonnorhea (which was, as I recall, somewhat prevalent), to cold sores and gum boils. Usually the people who treated those ailments simultaneously used two different cans.

I think it was what was called a "panacea." We called it "Cindy Cook Salve." It was the best stuff I ever saw for what ailed you on the outside. It sure kept a lot of us from running to the doctor's office every whipstitch. The doctor's office was about eight or ten miles by shank's mare, and that was a fur piece off, just for an ingrown toenail. I would liked to have known what was in that ointment, but the secret died with her. The world lost a real remedy with that little bit of evolution.

I looked on the shelf in Kroger's the other day, and wouldn't you know, they still had some of those very same little cans on the shelf, but they looked a lot flimsier than the old ones. They also had some larger cans that must have been two or three times a big as the little ones. The big ones wouldn't have fit in your shirt pocket without making an unsightly bulge and would have banged into your armpit when you were chopping wood with a double-bitted axe. They may have been for refills.

They even had some of the same brands. The one that was obvious by its absence was the one that was the most popular back home, "Three Thistle." Nearly every can said "Scotch Snuff." I don't know if that means that it originated in Scotland (like Scotch Whiskey, which I have heard some people say who use that kind of stuff, tastes like they got their cook fire too hot). It may be that it means that the people who use the snuff may be too tight or too poor to buy better tobacco. In our place and time, it could have been either. Or both.

The people who used this snuff back there invariably tilted the opened can and dumped a big bit of the powder between the lower lip and the gum. Once in a while, you would see someone who was trying to make an impression dip his forefinger into the can and get as much powder as the flat side of his finger (the print side), would hold and transfer it to his mouth where he would place it somewhere between his cheek and lower gum. That was called "rubbing" or "dipping snuff." It was done mostly by women and sissies.

Whichever method a person used for getting the snuff in the mouth, the gob of snuff always left a telltale bulge on the lower cheek area. These bulges varied in size, depending on whether you were using your own snuff or someone else's. The bulges were always noticeably larger when it was the other fellow's can you were tilting.

Bumming snuff was a separate bad habit. It was contagious. The same people who bummed snuff rarely had a can in their pocket, and if they did, they kept it well-hidden until they thought nobody was looking. It was an all-day job to try to bum some of the snuff you had "loaned" to these "snuff sharks."

Some self-sufficient people who were too proud to go around bumming snuff from others carried two cans. One was up front in the right shirt pocket where the bulge could be plainly seen. This was for the bummers who could spot the bulge from a good half mile on a crooked road. The other was hidden in a back pocket or inside a shirttail where it was less obvious. The bummer's can held only a pinch, the other held the reserve. When the guy who met the one who only rubbed "O.P.'s", he let him have the shirt pocket can. It was always emptied. They didn't care if it was the last bit. The bummers weren't particular about brand or flavor, just economy.

The old hoboes who roamed the country back then made marks on trees, bridges, poles, barns, or houses to let the ones who followed them know what to expect at the next house. They had one mark that appeared regularly in our neck of the woods that meant "easy mark." There was another that was almost as popular on poplars which meant "chop wood." I believe that the snuff bummers must have had a similar system to identify suppliers.

I knew of one man, one of my uncles, who could ill afford to supply his own endless needs who was the object of every bummer in the country. He got fed up one day with one particular bummer who never bought any snuff of his own and spiked his "bummer can" with cayenne pepper.

No bummer ever took a small pinch. This one was no exception. He tilted the can and emptied it into his mouth and started coughing and spitting and saying some things that would burn holes in the paper if you tried to print them. But it broke at least one of his bad habits, bumming from my uncle.

Others were still easy marks, though. That cayenne proved to be one of the best investments my uncle ever made. Maybe the only good one, if you don't count his foxhound that could run the legs off any of the competition.

I could never quite stomach snuff, although I had to try. It looked to me like the stuff that might have been swept off the floor after everything else was taken out.

One of my numerous cousins and I decided that we were men enough to start using it. We were about seven or eight years old at the time. We didn't have the dime that it took to buy a can, but we were filled with desire. We decided on the only logical course available to us, since dimes were pretty hard to come by in those days when a full-grown man was lucky to get a dollar for a long day's work.

We made it up between us that we would each snitch or snatch a can when Uncle Frank (not our real uncle), was busy with something else. I am sure when I think back, that he knew exactly what was up and decided to pull his own little trick and teach us a lesson. He was a former teacher and had my uncles in his school, eight grades in one room, and he had the experience necessary to read ornery kids like a McGuffey Primer. We only fooled ourselves.

My cousin took a can of Three Thistle, and I filched a can of Sweet Cherry. We high-tailed it home, skedaddled across the creek that flowed behind our house, and worked our way up the hill to a tree that we had long ago discovered. The hill wasn't quite straight up, but it didn't lack but a few degrees to become a vertical cliff. The tree grew straight out from the side of the hill and then took off toward the sky. That made a nice level bench where you could sit and let your feet dangle in space. There was room enough for both of us to stretch out.

We started using up our booty. We knew enough to spit. What we didn't know enough to do was quit. We got sick. He first turned pale, then he started looking a little peaked. Then his face started turning yellow. Then he turned green around the gills. All those are old sayings that we had learned when we were kids and before we got big enough to rub snuff. I was feeling as fit as a fiddle—and elephants can really fly. We yorked. Then we vomited. Then we threw up. Everything that we had eaten for at least the past week that hadn't already been removed by our physic. We even threw up some stuff that we couldn't have possibly eaten that resembled toenails.

We stumbled back to the house to get some help in our last few minutes on earth, because where we were headed might not have remedies for snuff bite. My mother met us, and she knew immediately that something was wrong. She was the most intelligent woman that I have ever seen. And I am not prejudiced. It must have taken her all of ten to fifteen seconds to realize that we weren't really going to die, even if we were afraid that we couldn't. She also determined the reason for our condition simultaneously. She knew what had happened from the very beginning to the very unhappy end—which was exactly what mine was when she got through brushing the dust off of my overalls with a nice limber willow switch. She was a good-sized woman, and her muscles had been conditioned by lots of hard work. I could plainly tell. I can't remember if Roger got "whupped," but I'll bet she landed all over him, too. She didn't play favorites.

I also had to earn a dime and pay the storekeeper for the snuff I stole and apologize for being such a rotten little kid. My suspicions should have leaped on me with both feet when Uncle Frank gave me a candy bar following my admission of guilt.

The farther I am removed in time from that episode, the funnier it gets. But it wasn't exactly what you would call hilarious then. It completely ruined my desire for snuff.

Back there in that place and time, snuff was more popular than cigarettes. Cigarettes, particularly the tailor-mades, were just too dad-blamed expensive for most people who thought that ten cents an hour was good pay. It was.

Most people who smoked also rubbed snuff. Their cigarettes were rolled by hand from Bull Durham, RJR, Bugler, and Target. The long, slender strands of the crimp cut were more popular than the rough cut. You didn't have a tendency to spill as much tobacco when your hands were shaking uncontrollably.

Most of the hand-rolled cigarettes looked like camels. Not the cigarettes of that name, but camels. Some of them had more than two humps. Every one had a little twisted tail. They might not have tasted like "Lucky's," but they were cheaper. Especially when the papers were included on the sack of tobacco, nestled in a little slot on one side or behind the band on the cloth bag with the drawstring top.

When WPA, DPA and NRA came along, almost everybody could afford tailor-mades, except those few who were still foolish enough to think that it was better to work for their living. The NRA wasn't the National Rifle Association. It was the "Blue Eagle," and the initials stood for the National Recovery Administration, and the little signs were stuck around everywhere and on everything. It is a good thing that the eagle couldn't do anything but fly.

Those programs were the remaking of the cigarette industry which had fallen on hard times like everybody else. As soon as everyone got their first government relief check, they started buying tailor-mades instead of bread. They could get something to eat when they picked up their commodities. They could also afford the new kind of booze which appeared in "state stores" all over the country and had those little stamps on top of every bottle. The beer was only three-two, but who cared as long as the government would make sure that what it lacked in strength was made up in quantity. Twenty-four bottles of the new stuff might make you a little bloated, but it made you feel the same as one or two of the homemade variety which became scarcer and scarcer as time went by.

The signs were there as to where we were heading with the handouts, but everybody was too busy getting his share to worry too much about where it was all coming from. We forgot that when you dance, somebody has to pay the fiddler.

And free lunches don't come cheap. They may, in fact, be the most expensive kind. Especially if they cost you your self-respect and your self-reliance. One or two people won't make much of a dent on the economy of a town or of a nation, but when it gets easier to run in idle than in gear, everybody wants to idle. Then the government (that's you and me), gets into deep trouble. If you go into debt over your head; you go broke. That is as inevitable as evolution.

The signs were there, but it was like waving a red flag in front of a bull that was stone blind. We still can't see them even though the signs are becoming more and more apparent. We had better stop to look.

Today, cigarettes have become a black-market commodity, almost like they were back there in World War II, the other big one. During that period, Uncle Sammy guessed that there might be a few too many people left over after all the bombs and bullets were used up, so he started shipping cigarettes by the ton to our sailors, soldiers and marines. GI's who had never used them started puffing merrily away.

This process of eliminating extra people may have been a little slower than flying metal, but it was just as effective in the long run. It was a lot longer-lived than the war. We are still doing it and denying it with every labored breath. It will be a toss-up between pollution and pollution.

The people who were left at home who wanted to go up in a cloud of smoke had to take the leftovers. They were hard to come by and would fetch a much higher price if the dealer took them from under the counter, rather than from the shelf.

Some merchants would only sell to their regular customers even if Uncle said you had to give everybody equal opportunity. If you were in a strange town and needed a pack, you could easily wind up with an extended nicotine fit.

There were those who sold only cigarettes, often taxed at a little more than normal prices, who lined their pockets with green cabbage instead of tobacco flakes.

The black market today is mostly between states with no or little state tax and those with high state taxes on the cigarettes. The total tax is far more than the actual value of the tobacco, when you take into account the stamps, both federal and state, corporation taxes, income taxes, real estate taxes, transportation taxes, and who only knows what else is hidden under that little flap. Guess who pays all of those. If you said something like American Tobacco Company, R.J. Reynolds, Liggett and Myers, or Phillip Morris, go to the foot of the class, and don't interrupt while the rest of us are trying to get an education. If you said "Me," go to the other end to get your A+.

This difference in price can amount to a right smart piece of change when you stop to think that many smokers go through as many as a thousand packs a year and more. That can come to fifteen hundred to two thousand of those little green pieces of paper that buy fishing lures or pay green fees.

When the black market thrives on trade between the United States and Canada, the trade is all one-sided. The figures skyrocket in Canada where a pack can run as much as seven or eight dollars, depending on where you lay your money down. That is for Canadian cigarettes. People who smoke them tell me that the American brands are cheaper, and they taste better. You couldn't prove it by me. The profits don't get registered against the trade deficit. I'm not sure how that will affect evolution, but it will.

People who do smoke cigarettes are, for the most part, inconsiderate asses. I don't know why I made a stupid statement like that. Asses don't smoke cigarettes, even if they do relish a chew of tobacco once in a while. And they aren't inconsiderate either, unless you happen to stand too close to one's heels. They sometimes kick.

Not all smokers are inconsiderate, either. Many will consider the company and refrain or head for an area where smoking is acceptable and won't aggravate anyone but other smokers.

Those who are insensitive will light up, take one puff and blow the smoke into a nonsmoker's face. They then lay the burning cigarette in an ashtray and push it to one side so that the smoke will be blown toward the nearest nonsmoker. If the smoker can get two or three with the same whiff, he has had his jollies for the day. I have never seen a smoker pick up the cigarette after he gets it into the proper position. He never places it so that the smoke will be wafted toward him. He probably doesn't want to ruin his lungs.

This activity is most apparent in restaurants at about the same time that most people are eating breakfast, lunch or dinner. The smoke usually gives the nonsmoker a queasy stomach. It always ruins his forty dollar meal. The smoker may not realize it at the time, but it seriously affects his ability to interact with others.

One fellow who was thus accosted by the smelly smoke from a smouldering cigarette must have the most control of his alimentary peristalsis in this world. He also deserves a medal for prompt response. There may have been some prior verbal exchange between the two, but I wasn't paying that much attention. When the smoke became too obnoxious, he arose, turned to the offending smoker and vomited gobs all over him. I don't know if the smoker got the message, but he got the mess.

For the nonsmoker, there is a little defense unless he, too, wants to be obnoxious. Sometimes he feels that he must. For his own preservation, if nothing else.

188

Another form of tobacco that has become quite popular is chewing tobacco. It used to be called "scrap" if it was in a pouch. It was also sold in the form of plug, cut plug, dry twist, cut leaf (with a few stems), or one form that falls somewhere between chewing tobacco and snuff. It leans just a little more toward snuff.

Chewing tobacco activates the salivary glands so that a good deal of "juice" is formed during the chewing. Something has to happen to all that liquid that accumulates in the mouth. Real he-men chewers swallow it. They claim that it is a good parasiticide. That means that it kills worms in the digestive tract. I believe it. They hardly ever mention that it is also a carcinogen. That means that it causes cancer. It also means that it not only kills worms but that it can kill you. I believe that, too.

My father-in-law chewed tobacco almost constantly for as long as I knew him. He was already far into his habit when I first stepped through his door in pursuit of some female to walk beside me down the road of life. He went through about a carton of Beech-Nut every week. But he spit. Everywhere. If he ran out of Beech-Nut, he would do without until someone came along who had a chew to spare—if it was that brand. He lived to be past eighty-six, and it wasn't the Beech-Nut that did him in.

My grandfather started chewing before he was twelve. He started on the big plugs that used to be available way back there before 1900. He drove a team of horses for his foster father who owned and operated a country store, and it was his job to make the weekly trip to the depot to pick up merchandise that had come in on the train and dropped there. The depot was about fifteen miles away, and the roads were wagon trails, so it was an all-day trip. He chewed tobacco to keep from getting so hungry and thirsty. The freight consisted of groceries, tobacco, candy, hardware, animal feed and all the other what-have-you that was sold in the country stores of that time. He went alone, loaded the goods, and hauled them back. Imagine doing that today. You would be stopped at least twelve times by people who wanted your wares without paying.

He bit into one of those plugs and tugged and pulled, and finally took out his knife to cut the tough stem. He whittled at

189

it until he could see what was keeping him from getting his chew. It wasn't a stem. It had a fingernail on the end, two knuckles and bone. Some guy had lost his finger and couldn't find it. Granddad did. He quit chewing plug and started chewing Mail Pouch. He would never use any other kind.

Most people had a telltale bulge in their cheek when they chewed tobacco. Not Granddad. It was a rare occasion when you could see a bulge on his cheek. He later owned a five and dime store and ran it for many years. His customers couldn't tell he had in a chew by looking at him. It was there.

Cigarette smokers and chewers had their bouts with bummers, too. It seems that some people only use tobacco, they don't like to buy it.

We had a fellow at a place where I worked (I'm not telling where for fear of reprisals) who quit smoking. He had that Russian fellow and Mark Twain beat by a country mile for number of times.

He would approach his fellow workers on a regular schedule to bum one or two cigarettes to help him taper off. He approached one fellow who had been the object of his bumming at least two hundred times in about four months. The "bumm-ee" said to the "bumm-er," "I thought you were trying to quit." To which the bumm-er replied simply, "I am." The bumm-ee told the bumm-er, "Good. Then I'm going to help you" and stuck the pack back in his shirt pocket. Intact.

We had in my neighborhood a fellow who was illiterate, but he certainly wasn't stupid. He knew everyone felt sorry for him, so his bumming produced cigarettes by the pack and by the carton. He would come right up front and tell you that he liked "Winkstons." That isn't a misprint. He received "pokes" of chewing tobacco from the chewers.

He hit my father-in-law up for a chew one day just after Dad had bought a new carton and had just opened a pouch and taken one chew. Dad handed him the nearly full pack, and he began to load his jaw. This sounds like I might be stretching the truth a mite, but so help me, Hannah, that guy put the rest of that whole pouch in his mouth. He couldn't chew. He couldn't spit. He nearly choked. But he finally got the huge cud moved around in his mouth so that he could handle it. It should have done him for two days. He would not discard even one scrap. Both cheeks bulged, but he chewed it.

190

Tobacco comes in yet another form that has been somewhat popular among male smokers, but I have heard that females have been moving into that area, too. That form is called a cigar, and it breaks down into I don't know how many sub-forms which are named for size, shape or flavor. Among these are blunts, cadets, cheroots, coronas, coronellas, crooks, kings, longs, magnums, panatelas, perfectos, presidents, shorts, stogies, slims, and a whole host of others. It is a wonder that a cigar smoker has any idea at all about what he is smoking.

Cigar smoke in moderate amounts can be more pleasant than cigarette smoke. It usually isn't quite so harsh, but it smells different. Some cigars literally reek. There is one little black Italian cigar whose terrible odor belies its flavor—when you can keep the bloomin' thing lit. You can smoke two boxes of matches to one cigar until you learn the secret.

Cigar smokers sometimes have what is known as a dry smoke. That means that the cigar is smoked without lighting it. When that happens, the cigar gets shorter on the wrong end, and the "smoker" spits a lot. The spittle contains a lot of little pieces of leaves and stems and maybe some other stuff that reminds you of a poor grade of chewing tobacco. I have done that too, but it was because I was busy with something else and didn't have time to strike a match or flip my lighter.

Cigars can sometimes be unhandy. I remember one time when I was trout fishing on a little brook trout stream in West Virginia, and doing rather well on the ordinary-size brookies that were native to that stream. I was smoking stogies, which are long, thin cigars, to keep the gnats and flies away from my face. I had just fired up a brand new one, and it stuck out in front of my face the full length of about seven or eight inches.

I crawled up to the little stream bank behind some willows and peered over the side. That was mistake number one. I flipped my line gently into the pool where I had seen a trout of about ten inches, which is a pretty good native brookie for these parts, and it was immediately snatched by a small brook trout of about five or six inches. I pulled him out and gently returned him to the water. I dropped my bait in again, expecting to see the ten-incher grab it. Out from under the bank charged a brook trout that was about sixteen inches long, and I made my second mistake. I got buck fever and started shaking so hard that I couldn't hold the line in the water. I set the hook before he got within three feet of the lure. I settled down for a few seconds and then made my third mistake. I reached up to a piece of sheepskin that I wore around my hat which held several dry flies. I stuck my wrist on that hot cigar that was still glowing and started a ritualistic dance on all fours that would have put a Hottentot to shame. I didn't get the trout. That time. I caught that trout I don't know how many times, until one summer I sneaked up on the hole, and my old friend didn't answer his doorbell. I was a Sunday School teacher back then, teaching a class of children about my own age, which was about thirty five or so, and we got a new member in our class. I found out where my old buddy went. To the new man's house for dinner. He didn't return.

The form of tobacco which is a little more than halfway between chewing tobacco and snuff consists of finely chopped or ground tobacco. That little something can be salt, wintergreen flavor, peppermint or menthol, and I don't have any idea what else.

This product is used like snuff only more so. It is already damp when you pull it out of the can. Some cans are filled with tiny little pouches of tobacco which resemble miniature tea bags. You don't use them like tea bags, though. But I'll lay you even odds that somebody will try it after they read this. The tiny pouch gives you a premeasured amount that is just a little too small and a little more than half enough so that two makes too much. They may be designed so that the owner can pass out one pouch to a bummer. Or they may be so that you won't get your fingers dirty when you pop one in your mouth.

The last form of tobacco that I want to talk about is pipe tobacco. Some companies grind up tobacco into thin slivers and call it "crimp cut" or into flakes and call it "rough cut." I think that what they grind up for pipe tobacco depends entirely on what they have left after they take out what they want for everything else. Chewing tobacco is called "scrap." Pipe tobacco should then be called "scrap scrap," but it has to share the honors with snuff which should be called "scrap, scrap, scrap."

Most pipe smoke is aromatic and is not so offensive to others as cigar or cigarette smoke, unless the happy puffer happens to be puffing a dirty pipe or using strong tobacco. And pipe smoking isn't too expensive until you start buying pipes and paying for their upkeep.

There are companies that make pipes in which this tobacco is supposed to be smoked. That is the only purpose of these objects, but some irresponsible people have started using them for other things, like blowing soap bubbles and filling them with what is known as "controlled substances." This bunch has just about made the tobacco pipe a thing of the past. Especially if pipes are outlawed because of this illegal use. Just think what a blow that would be to the already shaky economy.

Making pipes is about the only practical use we have for corncobs now, since the catalogue ran them out of that other business. If they can't use them for pipes, how are the poor dirt farmers going to exist? They can't live by corn alone. The first thing you know, Congress will have to enact a "corncob allotment."

Most pipes are made from brier root. Not just any old blackberry root. It is a special root that used to be imported from Italy, and it will shine glossier than the extended face on a baldheaded man. I suppose that it still comes from over there, but don't breathe a word of that to that guy up there in the Federal Reserve Board, or he might shut down the plants just to balance the trade deficit.

If the crazies do get the pipes completely outlawed (don't laugh, look what the other bunch of crazies has done to guns), it won't have much effect on the diggers in this country, but it will surely play havoc with all those people who spit and polish to get them so shiny. It may put some plants out of business where they make those rubber and plastic stems. Those people will be forced to go on welfare and to start smoking expensive cigars.

Pipe smoking is probably the most enjoyable of all the bad habits associated with tobacco. Except for two or three slight drawbacks.

A veteran pipe smoker will usually have several pipes. Several can be as many as three or four dozen or more. Some pipes run into the thousands of dollars. People who work for a living usually pay less than forty dollars for a pipe, and most of them run about ten to fifteen dollars or less. But pipes are fragile and are easily mislaid. If one of them happens to get into the wrong drawer, the smoker just has to run out and buy a new one.

The biggest drawback to pipe smoking is the design of the pipe. Practically every pipe that you see is designed so that it will fall over just after you set it down. I have a theory that the carpet manufacturers, the furniture builders and the tailors have formed a conspiracy with the pipe makers to perpetuate this faulty design.

When the pipe cants to about forty degrees off plumb, the burning tobacco falls out. It never falls on any nonflammable material. It lands on carpets, easy chairs, sofas, and clothing where it immediately makes numerous neat little round holes which are trimmed with a narrow black ring. The pipe may be an inexpensive model whose initial cost was quite moderate, but the maintenance costs which are transferred to the next immediate flammable material are sometimes extremely high.

A brand new suit with a gaping burned hole about the size of a quarter just to the left of the fly is a sorry sight. And it won't bring a good price at a yard sale. The nasty burn on the birthday suit just under the hole in the new suit is also a sorry sight. It smarts. And it has absolutely no trade-in value.

I used to smoke a pipe. I liked to smoke a pipe while travelling in a car. I used to bear hunt. I liked to ride in a car when I went bear hunting. I used to fall asleep while I was in a car on my way to bear hunting. Sometimes I would fall asleep even when someone else was driving.

My father-in-law and I had bounced out of bed one wintry morning shortly after midnight, all bright-eyed and bushy-tailed, ready to go in pursuit of another favorite sport, bear hunting. With dogs. I don't care at all for shooting bears at garbage dumps or under bait.

Dad wanted to drive. He didn't need to have someone around just to hit him over the head with a big stick to teach him a thing or two. He had ridden with me before on some of our early-morning safaris for trout and game. He figured that he had a better chance with him driving with his eyes open than with me driving with mine closed, even if that old crate had run the road so many times that it knew the way.

I had just bought a new Woolrich shirt. All wool and buffalo plaid. And eighteen ounce material. I haven't seen another like it in years. It is forty years old and I still wear it every spring for fishing and every fall and winter for outdoor activities. I allowed my wife to wash it. Once.

It has a big hole in the right pocket. The hole is on the *me* side of the pocket. That is where I stuck my pipe that wasn't quite out. Just before I dozed off.

The burn marks are gone now from the brown part of my otherwise white chest, but let me tell you one thing about wool. When it burns, it gets hot. And when it gets real hot and it happens to be directly over one of those little brown things that are called mammary glands on a woman, it makes your eyelids fly open. Men don't need those little nubby things on their chest anyway. He men, that is.

There are reactions when that happens. You start beating your chest with both fists and letting out one bloodcurdling Tarzan yell after another. Even Carol would have had to take a back seat. Then you pick off the little pieces of crisp flesh that the shirt missed when you yanked it away from the tender spot. Then you search frantically for the first aid kit that you left setting on the railing of the back porch while you were stumbling around in the dark so bright-eyed. Then you start getting angry and disgusted with your father-in-law who is laughing so hard that his heavy wool pants are getting wet. Down both legs. It is enough to make a sane person want to take up golf.

Then you realize that the whole episode didn't last for an hour at all, but only a couple of minutes, except for the sore teat and being mad.

The third drawback to pipe smoking is also in the pipe. The stem or bit is usually made of hard rubber or plastic, or, in the case of old corncob pipes, of bone. I used to smoke corncob pipes and bought extra pipes just to have a few extra bits, which I bit to pieces. When you lose your temper as frequently as I did, you bite the bits and nibble off a number of various-sized pieces. Those little pieces are mighty uncomfortable when you inhale them.

I liked the corncob pipes with bone bits for work pipes. I smoked Five Brothers and Cutty Pipe in my pipe so that I could keep my tobacco to myself. You would be surprised how many people regain their memory and remember where they left their pouch when you offer them one of those two tobaccos. It weaned a lot of people from O.P.'s. That stands for "other peoples" and it isn't a brand name. Some people will smoke anything if it is free.

195

If you decide to smoke a pipe, cigar or cigarette, don't do it in bed. If you just have to have some tobacco before you go to sleep, chew tobacco or rub snuff. That may make some ugly brown stains on your sheets which are hard to tell from the real thing, but you will at least have some bedclothes left. Smoking in bed may take all your sheets, pillowcases, bed, carpet and wallpaper and let it all float gently upward as smoke. Heat rises, you know.

Sometimes evolution plays some pretty dirty tricks on human beings and other people. Tobacco is one of those dirty tricks. But then humans who didn't have the good sense or the willpower to use it in moderation may have been the real culprits.

Whatever happened, tobacco has left an indelible imprint on the evolution of humans.

Whiskey and...

This portion of the book should probably be called "alcoholic beverages," because the first of these must surely have been wine. It certainly was neither whiskey nor beer. These must have evolved at a much later date, since wine must have been an accidental discovery. Beer and whiskey require a more complicated process that surely could not have evolved by accident, unless the rudimentary beer from potatoes and pumpkins got itself out of order in the process of evolution. The accidental discovery of wine and it's effects must have happened very early in the period of human existence. It's use happened tomorrow. Again.

One fine day, many millennia ago, some old codger went out to pick elderberries. He got a piggin full of nice ripe berries, still clinging to the stems, and took them home for his wife to clean and make into elderberry jelly. That was woman's work, and he wasn't about to stoop so low as to do any work that might cause his buddies to call him funny names.

For those of you who don't know what a "piggin" is, it is a wooden bucket with no bail. It has one of the staves extended about eight inches or so above the others, and that stave usually has a hole near the top so that you can insert your fingers or hand through the hole. That makes it easier to carry—in a pig's eye. It might be better than nothing, but not by much.

A bail has it beat forty ways from Sunday, but bails didn't evolve until the old guy tried to climb a kudzu vine, and it broke. When he picked himself up from the dirt, he was still clutching a short piece of the vine. It looked exactly like a bail, so he fastened it to his piggin and called it a "bucket."

197

See how simple it is to understand evolution when you know the facts.

He took off for a couple of days to go trout fishing with a buddy or two. He "fingered" some nice trout and had a few for supper. He took the rest of the trout home the next afternoon for his wife to cook for breakfast the next morning.

When he asked about the elderberry jelly, she made some excuse or another about not being able to get around to it because she had to look after the younguns. He jumped up in a veritable rage and ran out to take a look at his berries. There they were, the stems floating on the top, the piggin full of elderberry juice, and not a berry in sight. He grabbed a shillelagh and tore into the house and lit into beating his wife until she was black and blue. The colors were a little hard to discern under the brownish gray layer that had accumulated over the last two months since she had time to go swimming.

Okay, so they just called it a club way back then. The shillelagh didn't evolve until later when a pretty little green island popped out of the ocean just this side of England. It was filled with a bunch of delightful people who discovered the process for making what is known today as "Irish Whiskey" (sometimes pronounced "whuskey"), which the whole population drank like their ancestors.

After he gave her "her comeuppance," he went back out to pitch the juice to the hogs. After it had set around in the sun a couple of days, it had begun to ferment. When he picked up the piggin, he noticed a strange odor coming from the juice. He sniffed. Then he sniffed again. He was what you might call "a little on the frugal side," and the juice didn't smell that bad, so he decided to try one little sip. He picked the floating stems off the top and discarded the "pummies" that had settled to the bottom.

Then he turned the piggin up and poured the liquid into a crock. Then he took one little sip from the crock. He swished it around in his mouth for a couple of seconds, swallowed and smacked his lips. Then he tried another little sip. Then he took a couple of bigger sips. He sipped another little try. Then he tippled one more little nip. Then, he was crocked.

He sat down against the big oak tree and burped a few times. He closed his eyes for a short nap that had sneaked up on him. He dreamed of a field of elderberries that had turned to nothing but purple juice. He could see trout swimming around in the juice picking flies from the surface. He could even hear the flies buzzing around his ears as they headed over to feed the trout.

When he decided to stand, he pulled himself up the side of the tree, holding on with both arms so that the tree wouldn't fall over. He tried to open his eyes, but every time he cracked his lids, his head throbbed, and bright colored light bulbs exploded behind his eyeballs.

When he finally managed to get them open, the whole world had gone crazy. The tree that he was holding in place with his arms was standing still, but all the rest were dancing around him in circles. He decided that he needed another short nap. He slept the same kind of sleep that those who overindulge sleep today. We haven't changed that much.

When he awoke, he was as dry as popcorn. He grabbed the crock and downed every bit of the remaining juice. This has come to be known as "the hair of the dog that bit you." I don't know why, nor what it means, but I have a hard time trying to tie dogs to tying one on. When he hit the crock the second time, he was off to the races again. By the time he had recovered his senses this time, he had formed what is called in some circles, a bad habit.

When the elderberries dried up as they do every summer, he started experimenting with other fruits and berries and even with a few weeds and vegetables.

He tried apples, apricots, blackberries, grapes, peaches, and two or three others.

One old geezer even picked a bushel or two of dandelion blossoms at a much later time and made them into dandelion wine. He may have gotten the recipe from someone who preceded him by a few millennia, but I knew that guy. He insisted that I taste it. I was still a teetotaler at that time, and the stuff tasted absolutely terrible to me. It has lots of vitamins and minerals, so he claimed, and was supposed to be good for your stomach. Thank heavens, I had absolutely nothing wrong with my innards, and I was getting my necessaries from some other source.

The old boy back on the farm wound up making most of his fruit juice from grapes. He didn't call it wine yet. He still had to think up a name for it, and thinking made his head sore. The

199

grapes were plentiful and easy to harvest. The vines didn't break so readily when he tried to climb them. No sharp thorns on the vines to jab you in some tender susceptible part when you backed into one trying to get away from a snake. Blackberries were bad for both thorns and snakes.

He hit his peak of perfection when he made some delicious plum wine. Plum wine doesn't have such wide acceptance as grape wine, but that is because most people have never tasted good plum wine, and they have been misled by false advertising by the grape industry.

The grape wine industry has evolved into a highly specialized system of growing, harvesting, processing and marketing that the old boy, back there about a few millennia ago, could not have foreseen. The vineyards even have certain varieties of grapes that they produce, and they won't so much as look at another variety of grape. You wouldn't believe the names of some of those varieties if I listed them for you. They put some of them on the bottles.

It got started when some old nomad turned his herd of goats onto a small hillside, and they ate themselves out of house and home. His nannies had just about dried up as a source of milk, and his sales were way down, so he decided to branch out. He was just too tired to move on to new pastures, so he gathered up his goats and took them to the flea market. Nobody else would buy them, but he did find a guy there who was trying unsuccessfully to peddle some wild grape vines that he had dug up from a little patch back east. They worked up a swap.

He wanted to try to sell another kind of "milk." One that was a little tastier, a little more potent, and didn't depend on the whimsy of a nanny goat. He anticipated a much broader market base since there were considerably more wine-bibbers than milk-bibbers.

He took the vines home and planted them against the side of the hill that the goats had picked bare. They turned out to be full of a dark red juice that reminded him of something or another that he had seen somewhere, so he decided to call it "Burgundy." That might not be quite the way it happened, but it makes a good place for a story to start.

For many years, even centuries, the French dominated the wine market. They did and still do produce a number of varieties. Each variety has its own distinctive aroma and flavor, some of them more distinctive than others.

The French grow their grapes on plots of land which also house the winery. Some of these are called "chateaus." That is a secret code word to let you know that the wine inside a bottle which says "Chateau" on the label has been approved by the French government and an association of producers who say that you can bet your bottom dollar that it is better than the run-of-the-vat wine. Since my rare wine drinking has been limited to the more expensive table wines, some of which may run as much as six or seven dollars a gallon, my classification as wine taster may be somewhat nearer to wino than to connoisseur. But I can't tell the difference.

I read somewhere, or maybe saw it on television (where you can see just about anything if you are willing to spend a little time on the couch), that the American domestic wines are every bit as good as the French. That guy sure saved me a bundle by getting me off those expensive French wines. That stuff can cost as much as four or five dollars a bottle.

I'm going to be real serious for a moment and divulge some very private information. This is just between you and me, so don't go blabbing it all over the place. If you can't keep a secret that involves a friend, just skip this next paragraph. That friend is me.

I used to suffer from flatulence. Both kinds. The Germans had a word for the kind that caused me the most embarrassment, although it was the other kind that caused me the most trouble. The German word is "blahung," and if you say it quickly enough and with sufficient force, it even sounds a little like my problem. Sometimes.

I was in a service station one day talking to a very good friend of mine who was, fortunately, a forgiving person. As I turned to leave, there was an uncontrollable explosion. I apologized and tried to explain as best I could.

There was an old fellow sitting over in the corner who looked a little like an old hill farmer who had come to town to get a little rest. He overheard the whole thing. Some of it would have been pretty hard to miss.

He waited until I had finished my apology and then joined in the conversation. He said, "I can tell you how to cure that."

Once in a great while, I listen when someone tries to help me without my being hit over the head with a two-by-four to get my attention. My ears popped up like a jack rabbit's listening for a coyote. I had spent hundreds of scarce dollars and worn out four or five doctors trying to effect a cure. I was all set for some home remedy like we used when I was a kid.

He told me to go over to the liquor store (also known in this area back then as "state store") and buy a bottle or two of decent table wine with as low an alcohol content as I could find. I was to drink three ounces of it a half hour before supper (that is the same thing as "dinner" to you city slickers), and take fifteen minutes to drink it. Repeat the dose and method before going to bed. If you have ever tried to stretch three ounces of wine into a fifteen minute drinking spree, you know how hard it is to make the wine and the time come out even. I had already told him that I had taken only one little taste of whiskey and less than a bottle of beer and a tiny sip of dandelion wine during my lifetime, which at that time had spanned fifty years. The score on the whiskey and the beer is still the same, but the game has gone into extra innings.

I walked outside, and the guy who was, amazingly, still my friend followed me to my vehicle. He told me that the old fellow was the local doctor who came to the station and sat around just to get a little free time from his patients. He was trying to take early retirement, but couldn't get away from the people who depended on him for health care. He was a little less than two years away from ninety, and he just wanted to rest and enjoy life and maybe get in a little hunting and fishing between trips from coast to coast and maybe do a little surf casting for bluefish in his spare time.

I made a three-hundred-yard dash for the liquor store. The manager recognized an amateur drunk when he saw one and was very helpful. He steered me to some French wine which was low-alcohol and inexpensive. I suppose that he recognized a poor old hillbilly when he saw one, too. I bought two bottles of the most expensive wine that I could afford, since I didn't get food stamps. If I remember correctly, my bill came to a bit over six dollars.

I took it as he directed, and I haven't been to a doctor for that problem since. I do have one big problem with the remedy. I have to keep buying wine, most of which turns sour before I can use it up. I can't seem to remember to take my medication more than about once a month. My wife has become a wino, though. She takes a small glass every time I do. She forgets about it, too.

Some people buy wine with a high alcohol content. That stuff will make your head sore and your stomach sour. It gives you a peculiar form of halitosis and it will make your ears jingle. I only know that from observation and hearsay, but I have had a lot of close encounters of various kinds during those observations. Sometimes it may be difficult for me to add two and two and come up with something close to five, but one and one I can handle. One bottle plus one human who turns the bottle up and empties it in one long drink equals problems. For him and for everyone else concerned.

Although I am pretty certain that wine came first, knowing how nature and evolution work hand in glove, I am not at all sure of the order in which beer and whiskey evolved. It could have been either or both, but it was likely beer. You can make a crude beer that will knock your hat askew by putting the proper ingredients inside a hollowed-out pumpkin and letting it ripen on the vine, so to speak. Be sure that you put it in a sunny corner of the garden. And don't tell the missus. It will drive her up the wall trying to figure why you come in from diggin' the taters with such a big grin on your face and a big stench on your breath.

It may have happened when the old coot (same thing as an old codger) let a bunch of his potatoes spoil and he sampled the juice. It is only a small evolutionary step from spuds to suds.

He began experimenting with a few grains which his wife had beaten into meal with a couple of rocks. Believe me. That was the system used by the Indians until late in the last century. Other people still use two stones, but they finally got smart enough to get out of most of the work. That is one nice thing about being a human. You can always shove the dirty work onto some other animal, or maybe figure some way to get nature to work with you once in a while instead of against you all the time.

If you are lucky enough to be able to walk around in the backwoods areas once in a while, you may also be lucky enough to stumble upon a "grinding rock" or "meal stone" that the Amerinds or the early settlers used. Such a stone is characterized by a bowl-shaped depression that is round or nearly round and with a smooth bottom and sides. There may also be somewhere in the vicinity the pestle that was used with this mortar.

If the stone is not near a stream or waterflow, you may have found a relic. Don't try to steal it.

Some of these stones weigh tons and may have several such cavities or grinding pits. Just picture the Indian girls sitting on the rock grinding corn, and let their spirits rest in peace. We have given them too much trouble already...when we took their homelands.

The early beer must have tasted terrible, but everyone was too chicken to say they didn't like it. They drank it anyway. The concoction that eventually evolved from that first beer put the city of Milwaukee on the map.

There are a few places here and there in that city or within about two or three thousand miles of it that brew the liquid that we now call "beer."

They charge a little extra for the little brown bottles and for the shiny cans. They then take the little extra and spend it on advertising in magazines, newspapers and on television to tell you how good it is. A few people believe the ads. The objective is to get the people who drink it to drink just a little more so that the brewers can get a little more extra to spend on additional advertising in the hope that they will get a few other people started, and then they will drink a little more. They need to advertise.

Anyone who has so much as taken any time to taste it as it goes down his gullet knows that it tastes nearly as bad as that first batch of accidental beer back there in the bush. But they drink it anyway. Just to keep up with the others who are drinking it just to keep up with them. If it were really as good as they claim in the ads, they wouldn't need the ads.

Beer gives most people a change of shape. The area just below the ribs and sort of toward the front develops a big pouch that is sometimes held off the ground by a leather strap called a "belt." The belt may contain the pouch for a short time, but after a few sessions with the brew, gravity overcomes this restraint and it almost invariably begins to escape over the top of the belt and flows down toward the feet in a large rolling tide. When this happens, the belt cannot be seen. It is only evidenced by the narrow groove between the main part of the pouch and the overflow. This huge pouch is sometimes called a "beer belly" by more knowledgeable people. Too much beer can also cause a slight pouchlike swelling below the eyes. I don't know what they call those.

There are at present several different names for the variations in beer. These include bock, lager, pilsener and for a similar brew, stout, brown, October, pale and others. The list isn't intended to be anywhere near complete. It is just to let you know what to expect.

When I was still a boy, a lot of people made their own home brew. This was before the days of food stamps and welfare checks. They might not have enough money to buy flour, but there was always a hop vine in the corner of the yard fence and two or three cans of malt in the cupboard. That leads me to believe that drinking beer must be more of a habit than any real desire for the taste.

The bottles back then were mostly quarts, and they had a wire gadget around the neck that had a rubber stopper attached to the bail that went over the top. The wire bail held the rubber stopper in place when the pressure accumulated in the bottles during the aging process. This, if I remember correctly, took upwards of three weeks. It was pretty hard to fix a definite period of time, because I can't remember seeing any beer that had fully aged.

This arrangement of stopper and wire served another purpose. It sorted out the weaker bottles. If the bottle was a little thin in spots, it would explode like a homemade bomb and throw suds and glass all over everything, and it made a loud bang that was considerably louder than a twelve-gauge filled with black powder ammunition. When you opened the bottles that hadn't blown, the smoke would roll out of the neck of the bottle like a miniature Vesuvius.

That was potent stuff. I have seen a grown man drink two bottles and pass out. It may have just made him drowsy, but he was hard to awaken.

The revenuers didn't like for you to make that stuff, either. I suppose that it would have been okay if the little stamp had been affixed to the rubber stopper.

Things change. Now they will let you make your own, but they don't want you to exceed your limit, and they sort of frown on your going into competition against the big breweries who kick in a goodly share of their revenue to support the revenuers. This guarantees them a monopoly.

The beer industry has had a hard time keeping up with the population explosion and all the converts it has made through advertising. They have wasted a powerful lot of good water making beer when there is so little good water anywhere any more. Maybe some agency should conduct an environmental impact study. Fat chance. The revenuers have friends in congress.

If beer was the second step in the evolution of alcoholic beverages, then whiskey must have been a close third. The old geezer used some of the same raw materials for whiskey as he used for beer, but the process was different. The flavor of the finished product is nowhere near the same.

Moonshine could not have been made very easily before the advent of the "metal age." Some people like to separate the era into the iron age, the bronze age, and the atomic age. But to make good corn liquor, they had to have copper. I don't know when that age started.

They probably had some sort of whiskey before the metal age arrived. They had the basics well-learned before some guy found out that copper tubing can be easily coiled and that immersing it in a barrel of cooling liquid to speed condensation will not damage it a whole lot. I can't quite figure how they accomplished that before they could get the tubing.

By the time this country had been "discovered" and the people just couldn't wait to leave Europe, both beer and whiskey-making had long since ceased being secret formulae.

The first people (other than the Spanish) who came over here in the early 1600s were not exactly royalty. They were accustomed to hardships in the "old country" where they had been imprisoned or exiled for indebtedness and other minor crimes. They were tough and self-reliant. Most already knew how to work, and if they didn't before they landed on these shores, they soon learned. Some of the colonies had an amazingly effective rule, "If you don't work, you don't eat." After two or three winters of existing on white oak acorns and pine needles, the work ethic becomes pretty strong in most people. Rock salt in a blunderbuss was a slight deterrent to stealing. Sometimes the owner forgot to make the changeover.

We have changed the rule ever so slightly. Our rule goes, "If you don't work, you only eat slightly better than if you do." The working people have been talking in little huddles about making some changes. They may get into bigger huddles before long and if they do, look out. There are three or four congressmen and a couple of senators who are going to be looking for a job in a car wash.

Those first people brought with them a taste for spirits and some knowledge of how to make them. It seems to me that a lot of those who had that knowledge liked to live in the hills where the farm tractors and semi's wouldn't keep them awake nights. They moved to Appalachia and started producing corn products by the gallon and by the barrel. They also grew rye and barley.

The processed grains had a strong odor and a tangy taste, and hidden underneath was a powerful kick. The proof (that is how you tell how much alcohol is in a jug) was up around one hundred on the watered down stuff. Each percent of alcohol is two degrees of proof. Some of the liquor must have been impossible to grade until they added a little branch water. It had enough alcohol in it that the people back East could start fires, run steamboats, and get on a bender with it. Most of it was used for the latter purpose. There wasn't much sense in wasting good whiskey, even to run a steamboat, when there was so much wood around.

Most Easterners feel the same way today when it comes to cars, but they have substituted petroleum products for wood, which has just about disappeared. Even here in coal mining country where alcohol can be derived from coal, the coal miners don't want to burn it. They might just as well, If you drink that other stuff, it can make you blind.

The mountains were the western edge of civilization up until the middle of the eighteenth century. Just at the edge of the foothills, Indians still roamed and hunted and scuffled. Sometimes they scuffled with the white settlers. They may have been looking for firewater.

The mountain families from New York to Georgia, and probably a bit beyond on both ends, made and drank whiskey. Not every family had its own "still," but they were stuck in just about every place that had a water and wood supply and a place to get the ingredients. Many of these farmers peddled their produce back East. A gallon of moonshine (that was a later name) didn't take up as much space in a wagon as a burlap bag of corn and was a lot easier on the horses or oxen. It only weighed about a tenth as much, counting the jug. And it brought more money. And there was a ready market.

Congress has long been known to keep a sharp eye on the natives so that they can devise ways to get a little more money to throw away on "worthless-while" projects. Someone just told me that congress has funded a study to find out why people pick their nose. That is pretty hard to believe, even of the same bunch that funded a study on the sex life of frogs. They could have saved all of your money on either or both of those projects by just asking me. I am an expert, especially on frog sex. It is simple. They do.

Evolution hasn't had much success in improving congressmen. It has only made them continually and progressively worse. It has shown them how to blame the president for all the stupid things that congress does.

Somebody came up with the bright idea of taxing farm produce; certain kinds. They slapped a tax on the jugs that the farmers were hauling back East that nearly doubled the cost, and the farmers were hurting badly. They got a bunch of those old Pennsylvania ridgerunners together and started a revolution. They called it the "Whiskey Rebellion" and it petered out before it really got off to a good start. The farmers didn't recruit enough help from Virginia and Tennessee. That was way back there in '94. (That is 1794.) That should give you some idea of how long this has been going on.

Communications were pretty poor back there in those days. If they had owned some CB radios, they could have had a big party like some of the truckers' strikes today. We've learned a couple of tricks. If they could have rallied all the whiskey makers from North and South Carolina, Georgia, New York, and the New England states, we might not have a congress. As it was, the revolution was a flop.

Congress is now trying to cut the defense budget and raise taxes. They had better hang onto enough of the military to help them fight off the old people in this country who are just about ready to start their own rebellion. A big one this time. They already have a president of the A.A.R.P. I think those letters mean "Ancient Army of Retired People."

208

The whiskey industry has just about been taken away from the small operator. The revenuers made it so hard on him when he wouldn't pay the exorbitant prices for those little stamps that the revenuers sell that he just gave up. Government is opposed to small business unless the business is so unsuccessful that it has to depend on government handouts to stay in business.

The produce from the small business era of whiskey-making was called by a lot of different names over the years. "Corn squeezin's," "liquor," "white lightnin," "sour mash," "rye," "sippin' whiskey," "moonshine," "shine" and "rotgut" were a few of the names. Some still owner-operators took great pride in the quality of their product. Others had absolutely no evidence of pride or quality. Some of the stuff sold by unscrupulous operators would make you deathly sick. They must not have been interested in after-markets.

The big distilleries today put ads in the various media to convince you of the pride they take in their products. They must be justified, judging by the amount they sell.

The old-timey operators sold four kinds of whiskey. Crying whiskey, laughing whiskey, dancing whiskey and fighting whiskey. Some of the whiskey that was classified as fighting whiskey may simply have been the result of partaking of a bit too much of one or more of the other three.

Up in my neck of the woods, most of it was fighting whiskey. I swear to you that I have seen brothers, fathers, and sons go look for trouble after drinking some of that kind. If they couldn't find anyone else who had also been drinking to fight, they would jump on to each other. They were serious. I knew of one case where two sons knocked their father down and then kicked him and broke his hip. They were just fighting for fun.

They fought with pick or mattock handles. They pulled hair, bit, kicked and gouged.

One fellow I knew hit an opponent on the chin while that guy was chewing on the first one's finger. The blow landed with such force that the finger popped off at the second joint, and the flesh was so badly chewed that it had to be amputated.

Ears were obvious targets for teeth, and lobes and flaps were often mutilated by teeth marks. Fortunately, these deformities were rarely transmitted to the progeny. That generation had to get its own.

Evolution, that's what it is. I don't pretend to know where we are headed. But I hope that the human race lasts long enough to see some positive results. Beer, wine and whiskey have also left their marks on the evolution of humans. The marks might not look so good on paper, especially those little long pieces that police officers call "citations." But it looks to me as if a certain segment of humanity must have enjoyed getting the low grades.

...aNd Words

Evolution affects words, too. Or it may be that our words reflect evolution at work. No matter which is correct, words
change, and the meanings change. This is one area where we
can see evolution at work on a daily basis. This is not exactly
biological evolution, but it will eventually affect us in a
biological manner.

If you don't count the language that has evolved in recent
years within the computer industry that is known as computer
basic or "computerese," most of our language in America has
been imported. We have stolen words from other languages as
far back as Latin and even beyond. These include French, German, Spanish, Swedish, Norwegian, Chinese, Japanese, and
just about any other language currently in use. Most were
derived from the English spoken in the United Kingdom, but
we sure have murdered the King's English, as someone once
said. Some of these have stolen words from us, so I suppose
that you could say that it is borrowing rather than stealing.

Slang words and phrases that are in common usage cause a
change in language and in the general manner of speaking.
Some slang terms, or words, fall by the wayside after a brief
period, but some hang on for extended periods and become a
permanent part of our vocabulary. Take "twenty-three-ski-
doo" for example. I have no idea what it meant sixty or seventy years ago, and I am not interested in knowing. It went out
about the same time as the raccoon coat. "Ain't" on the other
hand, has stuck around long enough to become widely accepted as proper. A few people still object to its use, but those
who use it just keep plugging away and pay the others no

never-mind.

Many of the words in our everyday conversations have come to America from the native countries of those who came to America to find for themselves a better life. They brought with them their customs, their foods, their beliefs, and their languages. We have adopted them as our own.

Many of the citizens today are descended from ancestors who came here before there was a United States. The Scotch-Irish, English, Germans, French, Scots, Irish, Polish, Italians, and others were among the earlier settlers, and we still use some of the language that these ancestors brought with them. Some of it has been "Americanized," but the origin is still apparent.

My own ancestry includes most of those mentioned, and parts of my family were here to help in the French and Indian Wars, Lord Dunmore's War, and the American Revolution. I am so mixed up ethnically that there is a particular term applied to those just like me in lineage. It is "barnyard" Irish.

There is another more colorful term, but you will have to find that one for yourself. It means "a conglomeration." That means something like "made up of everything." That isn't exactly the dictionary definition, but it is close enough.

No chapter on the evolution of words would be complete without a listing of some of the words which were used by some of the early settlers and which persisted until I arrived on the planet. Some of them are still in use. Some have different meanings or spellings. Some are of more recent origin. All are interesting. It was a fun way of getting your message across.

My list is not nearly complete. I have seen a similar list in just about every book which I have read on Appalachia (wherever that is), and even some books that didn't even mention hill people. I have tried to include those words that I have not seen published, but there may be some overlap.

Every isolated locality developed its own set of words and it's own pronunciation of some of the shared words. This resulted in dialects that are even more interesting than individual words. Words and dialects have both affected the evolution of our language.

This list is almost in alphabetical order. I have strayed once in a while in order to put related words close together to make more interesting reading. I told you earlier that I was different.

abide   stand. "I can't abide that person."

addlepated or **addlebrained**   a little off his rocker; a few bricks shy of a load; about a couple of degrees off plumb; he was behind the door when the brains were passed out; confused. He has bats in his belfry; His noggin is screwed on wrong (or—ain't screwed on right).

agin   against. "Put your shootin' airn agin that tree."

aim   intend. "I don't aim to do no more work today."

airn   either a piece of steel or a sadiron, or the act of pressing clothes.

allow   think or reckon. "I allow as to how I'd better git to the chores." "I allow that he is all right."

almanac   usually the "Old Farmer's" or the "Hagerstown" around my home. It was the book of importance second only to the Bible. It told you when to sow and when to reap; when to weed and shear the sheep.

amidst or **amongst**   among. Same as today but now less frequently used.

anneller   (guessed at spelling); a mispronunciation of "another." "Other" was pronounced "eller."

applejack   a hard liquor made from apple cider.

argy sometimes **auger**   to argue.

ary   any. "There ain't ary one of them boys worth the salt that goes in his bread, or worth his salt."

   antonym: **nary.** Used in the same sentence and in the same place as above.

atter   after.

aynt   aunt. Your mother's sister; also a term of respect to an older lady.

213

backbone spunk or spirit. strength or character. "He sure does have a lot of backbone."

backhouse see "privy."

backseat a place of inferior importance. "He don't take a backseat to nobody."

bakin' a batch of bread or baked goods, always homemade, and always at least ten loaves at a baking.

balderdash nonsense.

banjer a banjo.

bar a bear. It was pronounced somewhere between "bar" and "bear." It was never pronounced "bar" except by amateurs or somebody imitating them.

bark to hit the limb of a tree with your bullet just under the squirrel so that you didn't spoil any of the meat; the head went in the gravy.

bee gum a bee hive. The gum was made from a section of hollow tree, usually gum, which was usually hollow when it got big enough to make a gum.

bergoo a kind of stew. (Believe it or not, both of those last two words are also place names in West Virginia. Bergoo is near Webster Springs, and Beegum is a wide place in the road between Mannington and Hundred.)

bloody bucket or **bucket of blood** every community had a beer joint after repeal of that notorious ammendment, and ours was like all the rest. It was a regular port of call for the local constabulary and the state police from as much as thirty or forty miles away. The name was earned, not lightly bestowed. The police earned every penny they got on that call.

bootlegger a private source of moonshine; I suppose it came from carrying a bottle in the boot top. Not many in our area fiddled around with a bottle small enough to fit in the top of a boot, if they could afford a jug. It didn't apply to my Grandma who rarely hid an undersized fish in her hipboot, making my Granddad lose his self-control when he found out about it. She liked to eat fish as well as she liked to catch them.

brute a bovine animal, such as a cow or an ox. I have heard of cowbrutes but I have never heard of a horse-brute.

cabbage money, the green kind. Also, "spondulics."

cain't a mispronunciation of can't.

cathead a large biscuit. This term wasn't from my area, I first heard it after I moved a few miles farther south.

cat's whisker a small distance about twice as big as a frog hair.

chimbley a chimney.

cinch the game of "setback." We played dominoes, checkers, cinch, hearts, old maid, rook, and any other games we could find. We also read everything we could get our fingers on. We even read the catalogues at least seven times before consigning them to their final destination(?), the outhouse. That was before we all evolved into watchers and couch potatoes.

cobble to put together poorly. "He sure cobbled up that job."

corned or **cornt** fed corn. The original meaning was "fed on oats" in Scotland.

cousin not necessarily a relative. A "kissin' cousin" was a cousin who was far enought removed in a family that it was okay to fool around with. This got pretty close in kinship once in a while.

damn a four-letter word. I know that I said that I wasn't going to, but I felt that you ought to know the definition of two. When used by itself or with other four-letter words, it resulted in getting your mouth washed out with lye soap. I don't use it much, because I can still taste the suds.

dew preceded by "mountain." Strong spirits, the liquid kind.

doodle-dasher You're going to have to guess at that one. Think hard.

dornick a small stone.

durst dare. antonym: **dassn't** "You dassn't pick your nose at the table".

elbow grease we used a lot of that on the farm. It means hard work.

et ate. "He et before he came." That is pure fiction. Nobody ever et before they came, and if they did, they wouldn't be stupid enough to pass up another square meal.

far fire. I never did hear anyone pronounce it "far" until I ran into some people who were trying to sound like hill people. It was pronounced about halfway between far and fair. Sounds like bear.

feud what hill people used to do to be sociable with the neighbors, but we never did call it "feudin'."

fiddle there weren't any violins, just fiddles. It was the primary instrument at barn dances, square dances, round dances and taffy pulls.

fiddle around fool around. pass time idly.

fiddle sticks nonsense. tommyrot.

fiddlededee more nonsense.

firewood almost any tree that would burn. We preferred ash or oak for heat. We used apple, sassafras and hickory for smoking meat. We spent a lot of time with axes and cross-cut saws, which ran on elbow grease, getting firewood.

fit past tense of "fight."

five and dime a variety store. "Nickel and dime" was something of little value.

fixin's usually foodstuffs before they were prepared for eating.

floozy a loose woman.

foldin' money a rare commodity, carried only by bootleggers, etc.

fox the red fox. If you meant "gray fox," you said "gray fox."

fox hunting not like the fox hunting done in England and eastern Virginia, where they ride horses to the hounds. We built a bonfire on the highest peak we could find and listened to the dogs bark as they chased the red fox. The fox was never killed unless by accident. If you did kill a red fox, it always brought bad luck. Your barns would burn and maybe your house. It was arson, plain and simple, but I never heard of anyone who was ever apprehended.

frizz past tense of freeze. Sometimes future tense.

gall nerve. effrontery. "He sure has a lot of gall."

gallon a liquid measure used for buying moonshine. I can't remember any of my family buying a smaller quantity before repeal, except when the jug was maybe a half pint or so short, due to evaporation.

gazabo a man. We had a man in our area called "Gazabo Charley." I can't remember his last name. It was not a derogatory term, just a term.

goose grease I have never seen any, but we used the phrase, "Slicker than goose grease." I have no idea how slick it really was.

grayback a body louse.

gypsy one of a nomadic group that used to roam the back roads. They were never trusted, but I can't remember that they ever stole anything from us. We gave them vegetables from the garden once in a while. They probably figured that we were so poor that they should be giving to us. They wouldn't have wanted another hungry kid like us, even if they had thought about it.

harp a harmonica or mouth harp. Also a Jew's harp.

hawkbill a mean-looking folding knife with a down-curve blade.

heared heard.

hell where you were going as sure as if you didn't stop using those four-letter words that required the lye soap mouthwash.

hillbilly formerly a derogatory term. It has evolved into a complimentary one in recent years with hillbillies realizing they are a rare breed.

217

hither here. As in "She gave him a come-hither look." I suppose that he went.

hokey-pokey I've asked everyone who will still talk to me what chemical that was, and they won't tell, even if I am seventy years old and promise not to put it on a cat. When you slipped and got a little on your finger, it felt as though your finger would freeze "clean off."

honest an almost obsolete word used only to describe old-timers. I suppose that most new-timers must not qualify. It was also used in a phrase "Honest to goodness."

hungry as in "hungry as a bear," or "hungry enough to eat the north end of a southbound bear;" looking back, we must have always been, even after a full meal. It wasn't a colloquialism, it was a condition.

infernal an expletive meaning hateful. As in, 'That infernal contraption.'

innards insides.

jackleg as in "jackleg machanic" or "jackleg farmer." About one-eighth trained. An amateur in pro's clothing. Also "shadetree mechanic."

Jew's harp a popular instrument for nonmusical players. Same as today, except that they were better quality then. I never did learn to play one. (Also called "juice harp," a mispronunciation.)

Jew peddler we used to have itinerant peddlers who walked alone through the backcountry with huge packs on their backs. Each peddler carried a pack that must have weighed at least a hundred pounds. He would make his rounds pretty much on a schedule and always had a home he could visit to make the last call of the day where he could stay with the family overnight. The pack contained an unbelievable amount and variety of hard goods such as pins, needles, Jew's harps, etc. You hear of a lot of anti-Semitism today, but we didn't know what a Semite was, so we weren't. They were always delightful people with stories to tell and were always hungry like the rest of us. We "put them up" for the night, and they would always leave a trinket for someone.

218

They always carried a whole five and dime store in that pack, with every little thing in it's proper place. We thought that they were just like us. Honest, hardworking, nice people who never used foul language, never overindulged, and never overstayed their welcome. I didn't find out until I was well past forty that I was supposed to be anti-Semitic, and then I read it in the paper or saw it on television. Old habits are hard to break, so I'll just go on believing as I did when I was a kid that they are just like me until somebody with a much stronger case than I have yet heard comes along and proves me wrong. And besides, some of those Jew peddlers may have been named "O'Reilly" for all I know.

Job's Knob a high point. "Higher than Job's Knob." I found out when I was in my fifties where it is. When I was in my subteens, there was no way that I could have dreamed where it was. Neither could my family.

Job's turkey maybe it came from the knob. "Poorer than Job's turkey" meant that you were sort of bad off. I doubt that Job (biblical) even knew what a turkey was. It is now something entirely different than when I was a boy.

lead poisoning we never used that term, but it meant a frequently fatal condition resulting from ingesting too much lead through some opening other than those normally provided; the lead, in the form of bullets or buckshot, made its own openings in the most unhandy places.

long drink of water tall, as in, "He's a long drink of water." similar, "He's long for this world, even if he dies tomorry."

'low allow, reckon. "I 'low as to how I ort to go to the store."

lucifer a kitchen or farmer match. The "lucifer" was a sulphur match which evolved before the modern kind, but the name hung on. Farmer matches were used before there were pilot lights. Before there were matches (not too long ago, as we reckon time), we used flint and steel, friction and embers from the previous fire. You saved the embers by covering them with ashes at night and then digging them out in the morning. We did it to keep from buying matches which could run as much as a nickel a box.

mind attention. "Don't pay him no mind," and more frequently, "Don't pay him no never-mind."

might-nigh or **mought-nigh** nearly. "I mought nigh got kilt when that car slued toward me."

Model T the Ford that chased the horses off the road and into the barnyard. Also called "tin lizzie." There were other cars somewhere back then, but the only one that I can recall seeing was a "Chevy" coupe that came along after the Model A, which was the successor to the T-Model. I heard of a lady who drove a Stanley Steamer through our country one day. It whooshed and huffed along the roads and scared the cows and pigs, but I didn't get to see it. My foster grandfather had a Durant touring car, but I can't recall it. That was before the big Depression. When it arrived, he was gone.

moleskin the toughest pants we could buy. We needed that kind, but a lot of us wore bib overalls because they were cheaper. We wore them long after the only original parts left were the straps and the bib, which were held off the ground by innumerable patches.

mountain boomer the blue-tailed skink. Also called "fence lizzard."

mountain bump a shift in strata in the coal mines of southern West Virginia, and in southwestern Virginia. I have never heard it anywhere else.

mountain dew moonshine. We never called it that until some song came out, and we figured out what it meant.

mountain fiddler the red or pine squirrel. The "fairy-diddle."

mutton what a lot of people ate instead of groundhog. That is if they didn't get shot while capturing a sheep in a farmer's pasture.

muzzle-loader a kind of gun used before you could afford a breechloader.

night jar ours didn't look anything at all like the bird of that name. It was a combinet. Also called "slop jar," "pee-pot," and by one of my great uncle's, "white owl," but it didn't look nor smell like a cigar, either. It was right handy on cold

220

nights, what with the outhouse so far out. It had several other names which I do not consider to be sufficiently sophisticated for this book.

nip a little (?) drink of moonshine, usually straight from the jug. Sometimes two little nips made a person tipsy. Four nips made a snort.

nubbin a small ear of corn. Also a small boy.

old an adjective which didn't mean "old." Used as in "Good old boys," "Old Charley." Often pronounced without the "d." "Ol' Buck" could mean that Buck was eighteen, or eighty, or somewhere between.

ort ought. "You ort to of seen the fish I caught."

outhouse see "privy."

Par two. As in "a par of shoes." It was pronounced somewhere between "par" and "pair," and sounded like "bear." If you aren't from the hills, don't even try it. It won't sound right anyhow.

persnickety fussy.

peter out to diminish or disappear gradually. "His job petered out."

physic same meaning as today except that we took one regularly to get rid of all that stuff we et that never quite filled us up. Thinking back, it may have been the reason my cholesterols are low. Food never got a good chance to stop long enough to leave any.

piffle a mild expletive. "Oh, piffle." Nonsense.

poaching what we were doing when we didn't really know what we were doing. All we wanted was something to eat. If it had four legs and hair, we figured there must be meat of some kind holding all that hair together.

poor man's pie a slice of homemade bread with applesauce and milk, eaten like pie with milk.

poverty what we were in the middle of but didn't know it, since everyone else was in there with us. Today it is not so

221

much a condition as a state of mind. People in poverty today have about forty times as much as we had then. But we used ours to better advantage. With lye soap.

privy see glossary.

rabbit tobacco field blossom, sweet everlasting. The dry leaves were smoked or chewed like tobacco, but they tasted a lot better than tobacco. You had to strip a lot more plants to get a little.

revenuer see Glossary.

sakes alive a mild expletive. "Land sakes alive," "Land sakes," "Saints alive," "Saints preserve us" and "Land o' Goshen."

Sam Hill used as an expletive. "What in Sam Hill?" Also, Sand Hill.

Sawbuck a ten-dollar bill. I never saw one until after I got married, and my wife showed me one that she had saved for just such an occasion. It was also a sawhorse with x-shaped ends that held a log while it was being sawed for firewood.

setback the game of cinch, which we played after the chores were done and before we found out about that newfangled radio called "television." For me, that was several years after I had slipped into double harness.

shank's mare a method of travel that required you to put one foot firmly on the ground while you brought the other up past it and placed it firmly on the ground about two or three feet in front and then repeated the process enough times that you finally arrived at the target area. If it was more than about thirty miles in one day, it had a tendency to make your feet and legs tired. Most times, it was the only way to go.

shif'less shiftless. lazy. Said of people who were too sorry to earn the salt that went in their bread.

shuck what we did to corn when we pulled the husks off by hand.

shillelagh a club or cudgel (Irish). In our area, it meant a stout switch as well. As in, "If you don't straighten up and right now, I'll take a shillelagh to you." I knew what it meant.

show a movie. Before we fell on hard times (I can't remember that far back) my uncle took my maternal grandfather to see his first show, a silent western. During the inevitable chase, my Granddad leaped to his feet and shouted, "Look out! The S.O.B. is hiding behind that big rock." He didn't use the initials, and he brought the house down.

skeeter a mosquito. And you wouldn't believe some of the ways "mosquito" is pronounced.

skillet a heavy iron pan to fry taters in.

Slim a nickname given to every tall, skinny guy within your range of travel which may have been as much as thirty or forty miles.

smut dirty talk.

spark to court or woo (a girl). One of my daughters came to visit and just about did a flip when a little, short fat guy came to the door and told her that he used to spark her mother. I'm glad that it didn't burst into flame.

spinster an old maid. Any unmarried woman over about eighteen or twenty years of age.

sport a spinster chaser. Sometimes chased nonspinsters.

star to gaze intently. Pronounced the same as bear.

upstars one floor up, sometimes more in tall houses.

stick-in-the-mud a sorry person.

stinker a stick-in-the-mud's older brother. Also expelled intestinal gas.

sugar tit that is how it was spelled, so don't blame me. A pacifier. Made by putting brown sugar in a cloth sack and tying it to the baby's wrist so that he couldn't swallow the whole thing. It was sticky, but it was fun.

swaller a drink of whiskey a little bigger than a sip or a nip. I have seen a fellow take a single swaller that was a pint before taking the bottle away from his mouth. You usually took a swaller when drinking from another person's jug.

switch a long, slender branch, usually willow, used to chastise rotten younguns. I couldn't begin to tell you how many I have worn out with the back of my overalls.

table where you sat when you et, except when you had kinfolk come for a meal.

floor or ground where you sat to eat when you had kinfolk in.

tick what you slept on when you didn't have kinfolk staying overnight.

floor or ground where you slept when you did. The tick was filled with straw, or if you were well-to-do, feathers. Ours had straw.

tart another word for "floozy."

tax an involuntary contribution to the government. Usually collected by revenuers in one way or another, such as confiscation of trade goods.

tea same as mountain dew.

twit not quite a tart.

tomorry tomorrow.

ugly as homemade sin. ugly as a mud fence. ugly as a mud fence with sticks in it (self-explanatory).

ugly tree how you get to be one or more of the above when you fall out of it.

vow another expletive, as "Well, I vow." We had a hundred of them.

wapper-jawed our spelling was "whopper-jawed." Out of kilter. Out of square.

War Between the States *The big one.* Yankees mistakenly call it the "Civil War." That is how evolution and history get all fouled up.

woods colt an illegitimate child. We used to say, "When you run through a blackberry patch, it's pretty hard to tell which brier scratched you." A lot of women ran through a lot of patches. The guys were right close behind and must have caught up with at least three or four.

It is difficult to imagine that our American language has changed so much in only three or four long lifetimes. It is even more difficult to remember that my lifetime began only one long lifetime removed from the days when my ancestors were fighting the "cabin-burners," and the "lid-lifters." Scalps, that is. And some of my ancestors, so I am told, were the ones who were lighting the fires and sharpening their knives on the skulls of the early settlers. Our language has taken on a whole new system of pronunciation and spelling in that time span. It has also evolved into something full of double meanings and hidden intentions. "White man speaks with forked tongue," has taken on a whole new meaning of its own.

One of my pet peeves is people who change the meaning of a good word, just about the time I have become acquainted with the original meaning. It makes you feel as though you don't know what to say or how to say it. Once in a while, this inability to keep abreast of evolution is embarrassing.

One of the best examples that I can think of is the names we call homosexuals. We started with "queer" (in my lifetime and ken, that is). A queer isn't a homosexual, and a homosexual isn't a queer. Why do we do such silly stuff? The same applies to "fairy," "queen," and now "gay" and "good buddy." None of those words ever really meant homosexual. Some of these words may have originally been used by people who couldn't either spell or pronounce "homosexual." It is time to stop this nonsense.

Heterosexuals have a term for what they do. When you say "hornycaboogery" you just know that it couldn't be anything else. That term isn't in very wide use, but there are others even more explicit.

If homosexuals want to call themselves something else, let them think up one of their own words. They can have the one I put in the glossary. But I hope now that they have heard "hornycaboogery," they don't steal it.

Another group that has adopted some names that mean something else is the prostitutes. We used to say "lady" when we talked about someone of good breeding and culture. A refined woman. Now I'm afraid to call someone that for fear of getting my face slapped.

I think that "lady" only applies to those prostitutes who are regularly employed in their chosen profession. There is another term in common usage, "hooker." I always thought that was someone who made rugs. It is really confusing. Now when someone says "hooker," I don't know whether it is someone who hooks rugs or someone who does something else. I am not an expert on the subject, but I think that a "hooker" is a woman who only works part time as a prostitute. Maybe we should call her a "substitute."

I have heard of instances of an ordinary housewife (well, maybe not quite ordinary), who occasionally worked as a "hooker." I suppose that you could say that she is a substitute substitute. It becomes even more confusing when you learn that she only charges on an ability-to-pay basis. And she doesn't take American Express, nor personal checks.

I just read in one of the newspapers (not the *Wall Street Journal*), about a couple of guys who were petitioning the courts to let them get married, since they had been living together as man and wife. Or I may have seen it on television where you can see just about anything if you flip to the right channel. I really don't pay a lot of attention to what I see on television, but you can get the equivalent of a PhD by reading the newspapers. Sometimes you have to read between the lines, though.

As I understood it, the basis of their petition was that they had been living together as man and wife. That surely must have been intended to be a play on words. If they are both built like me, there ain't no way. When you live together as man and wife, there are only two letters between what you're doing and what you're making. "Ni." I'll bet that will make you run for the dictionary. Look under the "O."

But when you are both built the same, you hardly ever add to the population explosion. At least not yet. I hope that we don't all evolve into hyenas.

My wife and I have been married a little over fifty years. I'm glad that our courtship took place when it was easy to tell the difference between boys and girls, and the names meant just what they said. Once in a while, you may have needed to look at the booties to be sure.

I can't imagine what might have happened if we had gone through that period given today's unisex fashions and names that mean something other than what they say. Zippers can be anywhere. Tee shirts don't tell you a whole lot in some cases, but there are some exceptions. A lot of time, the words that tell you which is which aren't fit to read.

You can't make any distinction by looking at the hair. Boys may have ponytails and long hair; girls may have crew cuts. It can be any color of the rainbow and then some.

You can't depend on earrings anymore, either. Some wear only half a pair, but I have never been able to determine which is "some."

If I had discovered after about three or four years that my wife was a boy, we would probably have had a quickie divorce. It is hard to tell what else we might have had.

I am glad that the males and females back in that time understood each other and knew pretty well what we were. All because of the words we used.

All of that above came about because of words. They changed them, I wrote them, and you read them. Isn't evolution great? You can blame it for just about everything. If you are careful.

227

Bits of Wisdom and Unwisdom

Evolution of language has given us words. I have put togeth-er a few words that may help you survive evolution, for a short while. Each of these is an original thought, I hope. You will notice an occasional one that is obviously an old thought with a little different angle.

Sometimes wisdom is simply not allowing your tempera-ment to unhinge your jaw.

Don't let your "want-to's" outrun your "have-to's."

Don't shoot off your mouth while the other person is holding the gun.

Never play poker with anyone who makes his own rules.

Don't kill dragonflies.

Don't spend your lottery winnings before your number is drawn.

When you walk in a den of rattlesnakes, wear high boots.

Do the same thing in manure piles. For another reason.

Don't fool around with anyone who is as foolish as you.

DON'T WORRY. Everything will turn out all right in the end—or it won't.

Don't let the tail wag the head.

Remember who must sit on the blister if you get burnt.

Put a little aside for your old age. It happens a lot sooner than you can imagine.

Don't use drugs. The doctor will see to it that you get plenty of them after you pass sixty.

Every dog wags its own tail.

Every farmer should feed his own chickens and gather his own eggs.

If you throw your money to the wind, it will never land in any place that it might grow.

Don't be anti-anybody. Someone might be anti-you.

Television is a ten-letter word.

"Read" is a four-letter word that you should exercise frequently.

"Just because I want to" is not always a good reason.

"Just because it feels good" is even a worse one.

When you are buying a car or a can of beans, pick and choose.

Don't depend on the neighbors to stack your hay.

Don't watch movies that use worse language than you do.

There are two things that are inevitable. Evolution is both of them.

Beauty is more than skin.

A good man is hard to find. He's probably off somewhere fishing.

Hard work never hurts anyone, but it may make you wish that you were smart enough to have someone else do it.

It is difficult to learn with your mouth open.

God made one big mistake when he made man and woman. He should have reversed them.

Expect the worst. Sooner or later it's going to happen.

Don't be afraid to earn your money. It's better than starving.

Congress is the worst possible example of fiscal responsibility in the United States. Don't emulate it.

The worst trouble with skin is that it can cover so bloomin' much ugly.

Don't fret about becoming bald; remember that many trees are at their most beautiful stage just before they lose their leaves.

Mother Nature sometimes makes mistakes, too. After all, nobody is perfect. Except me. And I have begun to wonder a little about me.

If you have a bullet, bite it.

A hog can appear to be happy, even in swill. He doesn't know that he is heading for that big smokehouse; a lot of us humans could learn something fom a hog.

The soul of man lives forever, but his body takes a terrible beating during the seventy or eighty years that the soul is living inside.

The devil is a sneak thief.

Little rabbits have big ears, but they are not blabbermouths as well.

It is better to trust and be deceived once in a while than never to have trusted at all.

Don't squander your money. That is the stuff that pork chops and cat-head biscuits are made of, not to mention the mashed taters and hog-grease gravy.

The man who rolls his own cigarettes is twice cursed.

Don't just see—look.

A well-recognized reporter with whom I am acquainted, once said that she would like to open up my head and look inside to see what made it work as it does. The hospital reported that the results were "negative."

Laugh and the world laughs with you—all except the one about whom you told the knee-slapper.

He who laughs at himself laughs best—and loudest.

It is better to give than to receive. But it is much harder on the cash flow.

Don't try to drown your sorrows by pouring alcohol on them. It is much better to beat them to death with hearty laughter.

If you want to see history being made and evolution in process, just take a peek out your back door.

That old saying, "Birds of a feather flock together," isn't for the birds.

There are times when "too long" just isn't long enough.

Did you ever stop to think that Edison couldn't have invented the incandescent bulb if Franklin hadn't burnt his fingers on his own kite string.

Man is about the only animal who can always blame his mistakes on someone else—or needs to.

Anyone who offers you nothing for something is probably correct, but be somewhat dubious about the one who offers you something for nothing.

Recycling is accepted as an environmentally sound practice. But knowing that probably won't do much to help when you realize that the glass of beer that you are holding contains a lot of an ingredient that has more than likely been recycled at least eight or ten times.

Did you ever notice that the best salesmen were the ones who led you—not the ones who pushed you into buying their product. They were the ones who cared about you more than about themselves or their product. You should apply the same principle to your family relationships and to your friendships.

Have respect for your elders, even if they are old fogies or old geezers. Maybe within the next year or two, someone will have respect for you.

Before you decide to walk a mile in another man's moccasins, try them on to be sure they are the right size.

Evolution is the living end.

Sex

In the foreword I promised you that I would tell you everything I know about sex in the final chapter. I'm going to keep
that promise now.

I discovered during my intensive study of the subject that
there were one or two things that I didn't know for sure, and I
would not want to mislead you by giving you any more incor-
rect information. You've had enough of that from everybody
else who thought that they were the only persons who had ever
heard the word and knew everything there was to know about
it and that they just had to tell everyone else, whether they
asked or not.

I also told you that I might even offer some conjecture
about sex. I have also done that in this final chapter.

You will no doubt find any number of writers and other absolutely final authorities on the subject who will disagree with
my projections, but that is to be expected. Every person is en-
titled to his or her own opinion. The big problem has been,
historically, for everyone to keep his opinions to himself.

So far, this book has been entirely factual. Every incident
described in the previous chapters actually happened in just
the way that I perceived it at the time. If there were some
question about a story that was not of my own experience, I
told you that at the time. If there are any items in it which you
felt should or could be questioned, you will have to complain to
someone else. They are the ones who told the big lies, not me.

This final section which contains my own predictions about
the future of sex is not presented as fact. It is pure conjecture
and should be considered as such when you read it. No human

can predict the future as accurately as he can recount the past. That is the difference between foresight and twenty-twenty hindsight.

But my foretelling the future should be just as good as anyone else's.

(Maybe not quite as accurate as some, but just as good.)

Everything I Think I Know About Sex(es)

As far as I have been able to determine after years of intensive study and research, there are at present only two sexes in the human subspecies. These are called, for the most part, "male" and "female." I don't know why.

A Tentative Look at the Future

If we continue in the same direction in which we have been headed, within the next millennium or so we may wind up with three or four sexes, at least.